Glimpses
of the Great

*also published by University Press of America, Inc.

Glimpses
of the Great

A. L. Rowse

UNIVERSITY
PRESS OF
AMERICA

Copyright © 1985 by
A. L. Rowse

University Press of America,® Inc.

4720 Boston Way
Lanham, MD 20706

Library of Congress Cataloging in Publication Data

Rowse, A.L. (Alfred Leslie), 1903-
  Glimpses of the great.

  1. Great Britain—Biography.   I. Title.
CT783.R69   1985   920'.041   85-20358
ISBN 0-8191-5008-8 (alk. paper)

To

Kay Halle

in friendship

and with so many memories

we share

Contents

Preface

This book is in some sense a sequel to my *Memories of Men and Women*. With regard to the title, I could not resist the alliteration, though not all my subjects (or victims) can be regarded as 'great'. Winston Churchill (in my previous book) was both a great man and a man of genius. Ernest Bevin was a great man, if not a genius. H. G. Wells was a man of genius, but certainly not a great man. Was Bertrand Russell a man of genius? – I suppose so, in mathematical logic and analytic philosophy – as to that I am no judge. Of my other subjects Keynes, John Buchan and Evelyn Waugh were at least touched by genius, as was Elizabeth Bowen. Lionel Curtis and C. S. Lewis? – indefinable, but both thought themselves prophets.

In writing about these people I have confined myself to personal contacts and personal knowledge.

I am honoured by my friend Kay Halle allowing my dedication: she has had her own fascinating glimpses of the great, through her close relationships with the Churchills, Kennedys and Roosevelts – would that she would write about them! I wish to pay tribute particularly to her good work over a lifetime for Anglo-American relations.

A.L.R.

I

Bertrand Russell

Was Bertrand Russell a great man? – Certainly not. Was he a great intellect? Wittgenstein thought not; he considered that Russell had a clever sharp mind, but did not see into the bottom of things. Who are we to differ from the most revered sage among modern philosophers? – who thought that after all there was not much to be said for or about philosophy, and 'as to that about which nothing can be said, nothing is to be said.'

I had more glimpses of and contacts with Russell, over a good many years, than I had with Keynes; and yet I felt closer to Keynes, more sympathy, more in touch with his mind and intellectual concerns. Nevertheless, Russell was a more present figure to me in my younger years. This was partly due to the influence of my Cambridge friends, particularly J. G. Crowther, who had been at Trinity – and Russell was very much a Trinity man. Russell's troubled relations with Trinity make quite a story, and indeed his fellow mathematician, G. H. Hardy, has told it.

My old friend, G. M. Trevelyan,[1] was a contemporary of Russell there, and a fellow Apostle. He knew all about Bertie over a long life, and would say to me: 'He may be a genius in mathematics – as to that I am no judge; but about politics he is a perfect goose.' I think that that was put not unkindly; I came to think worse of him, his influence deplorable.

I did not think that when I was young and innocent; I was rather dazzled by him and admired what he had and retained all through life, one source of great appeal: intellectual vitality and vivacity. His mind genuinely sparkled, sharp like a

[1] For him cf. my *Memories of Men and Women*.

diamond; he was stylish and crisp, not a word wasted; no sentiment or emotion was expressed. All was ratiocination, argument, with sharp summings-up, epigrammatic, never halting or slow or ruminative. Perhaps this was why he was so liable to be wrong – he concluded swiftly and brushed the matter aside without giving it a further thought at the time. When he thought about it another time, he often thought differently. He constantly changed his mind – abruptly: there were no gradual transitions.

There was paradoxically a marked impersonality about him; for, though a striking personality who stood out in any company, he was such an absorbed egoist, with more than a touch of megalomania, that few could get through to him. One of his mistresses, Constance Malleson, with whom he had his longest affair, wrote, with perhaps unintended irony: 'It seems a dreary end to all our years – I see now that your inability to care for anybody, for longer than a rather short time, must be more painful to you than it is to those who are able to continue caring in spite of everything.' I do not think that this caused him much pain – he was not very human.

My first meeting with Russell was when I was no more than an adolescent undergraduate. I was Secretary, then Chairman of the Oxford Labour Club, and it fell to me to invite the speakers. Russell accepted, in his own prim, small hand. I took him out to dinner at a little restaurant, which was all that we could afford. I don't think that Russell was interested in food (as Eliot was); he had no taste and had been brought up in Spartan Victorian fashion. I remember nothing of the evening, except that before we went off to the meeting he said, not unkindly: 'I wish on such occasions that I could fall down and break my leg, or that the earth would swallow me up.'

This struck me so that I never forgot it: I was so nervous at speaking that I felt oddly consoled. If this is what the great man feels before speaking then I ought not to be so nervous, I thought: so innocent that it never occurred to me that he was just plain bored. In subsequent years I have often thought of his remark, girding myself up to speak; and now that I am of his age and experience I suspect that it was boredom, rather than fear, at having to go through the hoop yet again.

Another meeting with him was more in character, for he

told a bawdy story of his brother Frank, Earl Russell – the last peer to be tried by the House of Lords and sentenced to prison for bigamy. Frank was an admirer of *le beau sexe* (poor Santayana was in love with him, in vain),[2] and an ardent supporter of the suffragettes and Votes for Women. At a public meeting one of these ladies declared that people talked about the difference between men and women, but for her part she couldn't see where it came in.

'Couldn't she?', said Frank, who was Chairman.

Bertrand had moved away from the strict high-mindedness in which he had been brought up, the ascetic Stoicism he declared so rhetorically in 'A Free Man's Worship', which he subsequently disclaimed – as he did so much of what he thought all through his life. This essay was much admired; it appeared in his *Mysticism and Logic*, which had been given me to read by my mentor, Crowther. I couldn't make much of it. It didn't occur to me that there wasn't much to make.

Russell had lived with his first wife, Alys Pearsall Smith, of that distinguished Pennsylvanian Quaker family, under the strain of these principles. It was more than flesh and blood could stand. One day, in the course of a bicycle ride – those blissful early days – Bertie decided that he was no longer in love with his wife and came straight home to tell her so, just like that.

Perhaps his experience in prison helped to broaden his experience as to the facts of life. He was not in principle a pacifist in all circumstances – he was not as foolish as that, when you consider the facts of human nature, what humans really are. But he was almost as foolish, in opposing Britain's resistance to Germany's threat to all Europe in the First German War, 1914–18. When it came to Germany's second attempt in 1939–45, Russell at last saw the light and supported Britain's resistance. Very well, he should have seen that the Second was continuous with the First, and that if right over the Second War he had been wrong over the First.

All that distinguished Cambridge circle were wrong about Germany, and Russell maligned Sir Edward Grey's foreign policy with equal injustice and lack of intellectual responsi-

---

[2] Frank, Earl Russell, is recognisably the hero of Santayana's long and somewhat abortive novel, *The Last Puritan*.

bility. The policy of the Entente had been worked out within the Foreign Office by the able brain of Sir Eyre Crowe, who understood Germany and her intentions perfectly, and had a German wife to help him. So indeed did Queen Victoria's intelligent daughter, the German Empress Frederick, and her husband. Bismarck called her 'die Engländerin', because she believed in the proper constitutional development of Germany into a responsible Parliamentary system: she wrote that Hohenzollern Germany was on a course that could lead only to catastrophe. She was right: it has taken two appalling world-wars to force Germany into the decent course of Western civilisation – and even then it took all the might of the United States to do it.

None of that clever circle of Cambridge and Bloomsbury had the historical sense, or even common sense, to see it. Least of all Russell, a paragon of intellectual arrogance. When the United States entered the war in 1917, all too belatedly but in order to save Britain, all that Bertie could say was that the purpose of bringing American troops to Britain was to break strikes! He wrote an article to that effect publicly, and for it he was sent very properly to prison for six months (and Trinity dismissed him from his Fellowship).

Russell was given preferential treatment in prison, pens and paper, reading and writing, and while there he wrote one of his better books – it enabled him to concentrate better. (Evidently prison was good for him.) When he read Lytton Strachey's *Eminent Victorians* – one of that elect circus's performances – it made him laugh so much that a warder had to remind him that prison was supposed to be a place of punishment. What a lot of clever schoolboys they were!

Garsington just outside Oxford, exquisite Jacobean house of Philip and Ottoline Morrell, with its terraces, parterres and peacocks, had been the haven for these people during the war. There they were regarded as martyrs, while braver men were dying for the civilised values Garsington stood for.

As a promising young Fellow of All Souls, I was introduced there by David Cecil, and Ottoline was always kind to me – she was a genuinely kind-hearted woman, for all the things said about her. But, a young fanatic of the Left, serious-minded and prim, I did not like the malicious tone of the circle, and was rather shocked by the outrageous things they said about each other – not used to it in my working-class ambience. Ottoline would tell me how D. H. Lawrence and the awful Frieda (cousin of the German air-ace, Richthofen) beat each other in bed. Though I wasn't interested in their mixed-up, heterosexual goings-on, I regret that I never met Lawrence; by the time I graduated to Garsington he had left England for good.

However, I did meet Desmond MacCarthy, regarded as the most seductive of conversationists (to which he sacrificed his writing, a weak Irish character, like Connolly), whom I treated to a Marxist diatribe all over the terraces of Garsington. He was not amused; however, I was not amused by what *he* had to say: Russell was another matter.

I did not know what Bertie's relations were with Ottoline, and would not have cared to know that she was Bertie's mistress. One day when Ottoline was saying that I should see more of him – I had already met him in Oxford – I said in all innocence that I could not see what people saw so much in him with his scrawny, gander-like neck, active Adam's apple and all. Ottoline replied in her extraordinary way of speaking as if it were Italian – which Lawrence took off so exactly in *Women in Love*: 'O but, my deah, you've no ideah how *ir-res-istible* he is!'

She herself had put up some resistance to Russell, who was very pressing – having emancipated himself from Alys's cold embraces and then married the warmer Dora Black, whom I heard holding forth at Oxford, on women's rights, in the last stages of pregnancy. I youthfully thought that rather unappealing. One thing – or rather another thing – that Russell and Ottoline had in common was that they were both ducal, family-wise.[3]

Russell behaved badly in this affair; for Philip, though rather *égaré* himself, was in love with his wife, and Russell tried to break up the home. And Julian, Philip's daughter, had to threaten legal action to stop Russell years later from writing the whole affair up for money. As for Russell, he wrote, 'what Philip might think or feel was a matter of indifference to

[3] Russell descended from the dukes of Bedford, Ottoline from the dukes of Portland.

me. . . . I have a perfectly cold intellect, which insists upon its rights and respects nothing.'

This is in flagrant contradiction with what Russell laid down in his *Autobiography* as having been a guiding principle in his life. 'Three passions, simple but overwhelmingly strong, have governed my life: the longing for love, the search for knowledge, and unbearable pity for the suffering of mankind.' I regard that as a piece of humbug, or a preliminary puff to his book, and what he really thought expressed by his unrhetorical, 'I am quite indifferent to the mass of human creatures.'

At this very time of the affair with Ottoline took place the episode of the American Professor's daughter, a young girl whom he seduced, when an eldering famous man visiting at an American university. The girl had fallen for him. Others of us have had the experience of being pursued by girl students over there, but if one has an affair with one – affairs with one's own sex are more superficial – doesn't it involve a certain moral obligation? Russell gave her to understand that, if she came to England, he would take her under his wing.

When the girl, of good family and upbringing, followed him hither, Russell cold-shouldered her and put her off on to poor Ottoline. 'I don't think she realises *quite* what you and I are to each other,' he wrote, 'and now there is no reason why she should.' Ottoline, in the goodness of her heart, found the girl a job: Russell was 'amused and pleased to hear you have provided H.D. with work. Never mind if she is hurt.' And then, 'I feel now an absolute blank indifference to her, except as one little atom of humanity. I feel I shall break her heart – but the whole affair is trivial on my side.' It did break the girl's heart; she eventually committed suicide.

I am not so much concerned with morals here – sex makes fools of us all – as with the intellectual self-contradiction in his protestations. He contradicted himself again and again all through his life. Anyone else would condemn him, setting up for a moralist, as a humbug – as he would be, if he were aware of the contradiction between what he set himself up to be and what he was. Russell's case is more curious: he was not aware. George Santayana, who knew both Russells intimately, put his finger on the explanation with his usual perception. He saw that both Russells – Frank so adept at practical science and engineering, and Bertie at mathematical abstractions – had little or no human understanding. There was the gap. The consequence was, as the historian Trevelyan said, that Bertrand Russell might be a genius at mathematics, but was a perfect goose about politics.

History and politics demand above all human understanding, knowledge of men, what they are like and how to handle affairs. Training in abstract mathematics is in itself a disqualification for history and politics. Russell was almost always wrong in his political judgments and should have confined himself to what he really knew about – mathematics, mathematical logic, and analytical (*not* moral) philosophy.

As a comic addendum, it was remarkable that this great-grandson of a duke, who didn't know how anything practical worked, and could hardly make himself a cup of tea, was always prepared to lay down the law how governments should act and the world be run. People were asses to listen to him on these subjects – responsible men of affairs of course never did; it was chiefly Left Intellectuals who took him seriously, with their infallible gift for getting things wrong, forever snatching defeat out of the jaws of victory. It is appropriate that, for Michael Foot, 'Russell is my Man of the Century.'

Was Russell any better then as a guide to Education and Marriage, Morals and Religion? He set up for a guide and wrote prolifically on all of them, books, brochures, pamphlets for the Rationalist Association.

It is not for me to write about the relations between Russell and my friend T. S. Eliot's first wife, Vivienne, in which Russell may not have been much to blame. For she was a psychotic woman whom Eliot should never have married – he realised that on the day he married her. Eliot had been a student in Russell's philosophy class at Harvard. He married and settled in England without much money, to his father's disapprobation, and his allowance was cut off. Bertie, involved with Vivienne, made over the Armaments shares he had inherited and disapproved, as a loan to Eliot, who sensibly had no compunction in holding them. He was convinced that

Bertie's relations with Vivienne were a factor in disturbing her mental balance, precarious anyhow, and Eliot condemned him in the characteristically scrupulous phrase: 'Bertie has wrought Evil.'

Marriage to Dora Black and begetting children in middle age gave Russell a new interest: the Family and children's psychology, which he observed, if at all usefully, as he went along. They set up a school at Telegraph House, on the latest modern principles of freedom, absence of discipline or religion etc. This was a fad at the time – experiments like early Dartington, which I never regarded seriously. An elementary schoolboy myself, proletarian horse-sense told me that all young animals need discipline (I am fond of cats and dogs and donkeys myself), and that it is unfair to them to bring them up without discipline. Especially so for kids – it makes it more difficult for them to learn in school, which is what schools are for, and it ill prepares them for what the world is like and what they will encounter when they go out into it.

On the basis of his and Dora's experience at their school, Russell wrote his book, *Education and the Social Order*. 'Sentence after sentence that could be written in the teacher's golden treasury of wisdom', said *The Observer* with its usual optimism. The school was a flop, and so was the marriage, leaving the oldest child of it a permanent invalid from its strains and stresses.

This did not prevent gallant old Bertie from a third attempt, this time to an Oxford girl, an undergraduette one-third his age – who, to complicate things a bit, was always known as 'Peter' Spens. I knew her as a beautiful, bouncing red-head, bent on becoming the Countess she eventually became.

Russell was also experimenting with history, and wrote *Freedom and Organisation in the Nineteenth Century*. His Preface expressed thanks to Peter Spens for many 'suggestions' in the course of writing it, which sounded well enough to the innocent. Bertie then inserted an erratum-slip: for 'many suggestions' please read 'many *valuable* suggestions'. How many people appreciated the naughty joke? One of the irresistible things about Bertie was his wit, and the stylish humour that played around everything and everybody, except himself.

At this time Russell was out of a job, having blotted his

copy-book in America and been dropped from a chair by a university there. I ran into him one day outside All Souls. Everything about him was memorable, and I can visualise the scene on the pavement in the High Street now: Russell in the gutter, in his shiny old black suit, practically threadbare. He said that the first £1050 of everything he earned went to the upkeep of three women. I thought to myself, 'Serve you right, you old fool.' At the same time I thought it might be a good idea to recruit this eminent Cambridge luminary, one of that most scintillating pre-1914 world, dropped by his own college of Trinity, for Oxford.

At that time All Souls had among its Fellows some five former Fellows of Trinity. I proceeded to approach our then Warden, W. G. S. Adams, with the idea that we make Russell a Research Fellow – a distinguished capture for Oxford: I felt sure that our philosophers, Stuart Hampshire and Isaiah Berlin, would approve. I had no luck with the Warden (he had recruited Hubert Henderson to All Souls), any more than when I had tried to find Ralph Fox, the Communist, a footing in Oxford. Adams was a wise old Scot: he wasn't one for raising a hornets' nest of controversy; also, though he was too shrewd to say so, as a believing Christian he would have disapproved of Russell. (The Warden, I hasten to add, was also a great dear.)

I did not share many of Russell's views – in any case he changed them often, went round like a weathercock; once, lecturing on an important point, in philosophy, 'I changed my mind in the middle', he said blithely. As for his philosophical work, about which so much fuss is made by the fashionable analytic school (Freddie Ayer and others), Bryan Magee concludes: 'whereas most great philosophers seem to have managed to write one or two masterpieces in which their fully developed views are presented, Russell wrote no such masterpiece; but, instead, umpteen flawed and superseded books.'

Russell admitted that the investigation into the logical basis of mathematics, upon which he and Whitehead spent ten years, was abortive. It eventuated in the large abortion, *Principia Mathematica* (shades of Newton, that other Trinity man!). I well recall yet another Trinity man, D. H. Mac-

Gregor at All Souls, chortling over the mouse the mountain brought forth at the end: after some 900 pages establishing, by no means a certainty, but a distinct probability, that 1 plus 1 = 2.

He thought that a great joke: I thought it a great waste of time. Russell considered that never had his mind achieved such acuteness again (he had colossal vanity: a leading clue to him). An historian has little use for philosophical abstractions, and only a limited respect for abstract theorising. He is apt to remember the famous reply, at the Sorbonne, to the guide in the hall where the theologians and philosophers had disputed for 300 years: 'And, pray, what have they settled?'

My own disapproval of Russell, to whom I had looked up when young, grew with time and related to his public stance and statements, on public issues. After all, his private life and its imbroglios – the third marriage, with Peter Spens, came unstuck too (evidently no good guide to Marriage) – were his own affair. I did not know about this apostle of Truth's private habit of lying – the ultimate sin to an historian, whose rule must be 'the truth at all costs'. The full biography by R. W. Clark, based on an immense documentation, catches Russell out again and again, showing how unreliable his *Autobiography* is. His account of his longest *affaire*, with Constance Malleson, for instance: 'an urbane example of his ability to make the best of his own story. The truth is very different.' Clark goes on to show how different.

It was over public and political issues that I grew to disapprove so strongly. Take the crucial one to us all today, the Nuclear Issue. He actually advocated nuclear war against Soviet Russia – and then denied that he had ever done so. In 1948 he wrote: 'Even at such a price, I think war would be worthwhile. Communism must be wiped out.' (So much for his opposition to the war in 1914–18.)

He continually denied that he had urged this evil course. Clark tells us that in a letter denying it to the *Nation*, he 'conveniently ignored his articles in *Cavalcade* and the *Daghens Nyheter*, his letter to Dr Marseille, his talks to the Royal Empire Society and the Imperial Defence College, and the private letters' he wrote urging it. Even 'three years after being driven into an admission that his earlier denials had been completely unjustified,' he wrote in a private letter, in 1962: 'I should be in your debt if you would contribute towards putting the lie to the fiction that I have advocated war against the Soviet Union.'

It was *not* a fiction: he had done so. When faced with this publicly on a BBC interview, by John Freeman (subsequently British ambassador in Washington), 'Is it true or untrue that in recent years you advocated that a preventive war might be made against Communism, against Soviet Russia?', Russell replied without turning a hair, 'It's entirely true, and I don't repent of it.'

What is one to think of such a man, such a philosopher, such a seeker after truth? – A Man of the Century, indeed! What would be said of an historian, Trevelyan or myself, if we had advocated anything so criminally irresponsible? The least we can say is that he was no guide whatever in the dangers of our appalling time.

In fact a dangerous mentor for people silly enough to listen to him – as was proved by the decisive confrontation over Cuba, when Krushchev began placing nuclear missiles there, within sixty to eighty miles of the American coast. If the United States had allowed that to continue, *then* it would have led to war. President Kennedy had to have a showdown and prevent it. The withdrawal of the Russian missiles produced a better mood on the part of Soviet Russia, was actually the beginning of a period of *détente*.

Russell came out on the wrong side as usual, with maximum publicity: Kennedy and Macmillan who supported him were 'about fifty times as bad as Hitler', he trumpeted. What is one to think of such mad irresponsibility? To have allowed Krushchev to put missiles sixty miles from the American coast was the very way to lead to war; to stop it led to peace, and even better relations with Russia.

This is the perspective in which to see the last phase in his life, the Peace Campaign in which he took the lead – processions, sitting out on pavements, clamouring to be taken to prison again – all tremendous publicity, soothing to vanity. The overriding truth is that for one side to go in for disarmament is an invitation to the other side to gamble on aggression

– as we experienced with Hitler's Germany. The proper way is
to achieve balance, and *on that basis* to secure peace. Absolute
pacifism is, alas, not of this world, and no way to peace.

However, Russell got world-publicity by his campaign,
and with it the Nobel Peace Prize. Well, we are all in favour of
peace – though we do not expect to get a Nobel Prize for it.
Fancy awarding it to so crazy a candidate!

What then is to be said for Russell, what remains of him?

He was an aristocrat, with the moral and intellectual
courage of an artistocrat; he spoke out and never minded what
he said – like Churchill – and that was something in a world
where humbug is common currency, the contemporary
universe of discourse. A great-grandson of a Duke of Bedford,
grandson of Lord John Russell the Prime Minister, as a Russell
he belonged to the most distinguished intellectually of
aristocratic clans. So he thought he had a right to say whatever
occurred to him; and he said it with style. On his mother's side
he belonged to a hardly less remarkable family, the Stanleys of
Alderley. They had a vein of doctrinairism indistinguishable
from fanaticism: one Lord of that ilk sat in the Victorian House
of Lords as a Moslem.

Wasn't there also something slightly dotty about them? I
always thought that there was something significant, perhaps
a pointer, in the story Russell tells in his *Autobiography*, of
setting himself up one day in his youthful Cambridge rooms
for God, and getting his friends to kneel down and worship
him. A joke typical of the Cambridge Apostles, of course; but
wasn't there a streak of megalomania in the later avatar?

Bertrand was certainly no democrat, didn't care what
anybody else thought, and didn't subscribe to the demotic
humbug of the time. He always had some private means,
which help one to independence of mind. 'The Shelleys and
Darwins and so on couldn't have existed at all if they'd had to
work for their living. And surely one Darwin is more important than thirty million working men and women.' Exaggeration as usual, but there I can agree with him in principle. 'Let
us not delude ourselves with the hope that the best is within
the reach of all.' Here Bertie deviates into commonsense. Or
again, 'I believe in several definite measures – for example,

Infanticide – by which society could be improved.' We should not allow ourselves to be shocked by Bertie: we could meet him half-way – say, only for mongols or congenital idiots; otherwise, birth control – a more civilised way.

Of his philosophy, his mathematical logic, I am not qualified to speak, though I have no very high opinion of the value of philosophising, except as intellectual exercise. Russell certainly had a strenuous athletic mind, always engaged in theorising and arguing, for what that is worth – historians do not think much of it: they prefer to watch facts and what they point to. Russell always spoke with absolute certainty – and then changed his mind; he never learned to speak with less certainty, and then wait for thought, observational and empirical, to mature. His fellow Cambridge philosopher, C. D. Broad, pronounced sentence on him: 'Mr Russell produces a different system of philosophy every few years.'

It was, however, great fun to have known him, and I found him stimulating intellectually, as others did, when I was young. I read almost everything he wrote, even a number of his philosophical lucubrations. Did one profit from them? – in the way that some more reliable thinkers left an enduring mark, a permanent deposit: Frazer's *Golden Bough*, for instance; still more Sherrington's *Man on his Nature*, physiologist of genius, *my* Man of the Century, along with Churchill.

Russell wrote with verve and style, an admirable prose style, brisk and spare, springy and stringy (like him), lean and spare, no poetry about it. His ideal of beauty was mathematics – otherwise no aesthete; and I prefer aesthetes – Keynes for instance collected pictures and books, as well as Duncan and Lopokova. Such are the salt of the earth.

An American admirer of Russell, the Leftist philosopher Sidney Hook, provides a fresh angle from which to regard him. He charges Russell with two main failings, vanity and greed for money. I think we may let Russell off both charges rather lightly, without undue seriousness. No doubt he needed to grab all the cash he could to provide for his women, their alimonies, and his family. Even the vanity had its comic side. Hook's observant little daughter said, 'Daddy, Uncle Bertie's wee-wee is larger than yours', at which the old philosopher was highly gratified. No doubt it had been a factor in his success with women – as also an element in his obsessive need for them.

Hook, when young, had been taken in even as I was earlier. Hook was influenced by 'Russell's cool demolition of the myths about Teutonic frightfulness' in Belgium during the First German War; 'his passionate lucidity and dedication to the truth sustained me in the difficult years after the Armistice.' I had been brought up under the myth put about by H. N. Brailsford, E. D. Morel and the pro-Germans that the Germans were no more responsible for the war than we were. When I came to think things out for myself and could judge from the evidence, I soon appreciated that *that* was the myth – especially after I came to know Germany and the Continent. Not many years after the Armistice I was in Louvain, where the Germans in 1914 had set fire to a quarter of the town; an act of 'Teutonic frightfulness' to intimidate the population. Those who remember the sudden evisceration of friendly Rotterdam in 1940 will have no difficulty in recognising the patent and the pattern.

No: I regard Russell's blithe disregard for truth as far more damaging, and its influence more poisonous. When a world-famous guru could say of the United States, 'Anybody who goes so far as to support equal rights for coloured people, or to say a good word for the United Nations, is liable to a visit by officers of the F.B.I. and threatened with blacklisting and consequent inability to earn a living' – what nonsense, what poisonous nonsense!

We have seen that with him the truth was largely at the mercy of his prejudices – and how silly people were to heed such nonsense, let alone take such a type as guide.

2

J. M. Keynes

Lifelong Oxonian as I am, my glimpses of Keynes were at Oxford, never at Cambridge. Oddly enough, Keynes when young was prejudiced against Oxford, and did not want to come up to Balliol from Eton. This was a pity, for Oxford's essentially historical outlook would have done him a power of good, instead of the mathematical and moral abstractions of Cambridge. And ironically Oxford's historicism was more in keeping with Keynes's later thought, as it developed away from the abstractions of economic orthodoxy. A Cambridge historian, G. M. Trevelyan, never had this rather adolescent prejudice – really a form of irrelevant inferiority-complex from the equipollent daughter university.

My first glimpse of Keynes was a public one, as an undergraduate, when he came to give the Sidney Ball Lecture (Sidney Ball was an early Oxford Socialist of the previous generation). This was in 1924, the subject the rather scandalous one, *The End of Laissez-faire*,[1] in which he announced tentatively his widening breach with economic orthodoxy. Since my generation of intellectuals was attracted by the prospects held out by socialism, we all crowded to hear the great man in the Schools. – Or, not yet a great man, rather a notorious one for the world-wide interest his book, *The Economic Consequences of the Peace*, had created, with its attack on the Treaty of Versailles and its malicious, Stracheyesque portraits of its makers – Lloyd George, President Wilson, Clemenceau – on a par with the caricatures of

---

[1] Published by Leonard and Virginia Woolf at the Hogarth Press in 1926, the year of the General Strike.

Eminent Victorians.

Keynes's appearance came up to expectations, though he disappointed our further, Leftist hopes. He did however prefigure the end of the economic orthodoxy under which we were restive and about which I already had my doubts. Deep in history, I was ravaged by scepticism about political theories and economic doctrines being 'true' for all times and places: I considered them both historically conditioned. In my last term I openly challenged the Regius Professor, H. W. C. Davis, on this at a lecture (my fellow-historian, Geoffrey Barraclough, witnessed the embarrassing scene). Davis politely rebuked me with, 'That is a degree of historical scepticism with which I do not agree.'

Keynes's challenge was in keeping, one to which I was sympathetic. He said, 'For more than a hundred years our philosophers ruled us, because, by a miracle, they nearly all agreed, or seemed to agree, on this one thing' – Laissez-faire. Keynes summed this up – 'Suppose that by the working of natural laws individuals pursuing their own interests with enlightenment in conditions of freedom always tend to promote the general interest at the same time!' The doctrine held that 'State Action should be narrowly confined and economic life left, unregulated as far as may be, to the skill and good sense of individual citizens actuated by the admirable motive of trying to get on in the world.'

This was the middle-class orthodoxy of the Cambridge sage and mentor, Alfred Marshall, who dominated the subject with an authority largely moral, under which Keynes had been brought up and from which he was with difficulty now emancipating himself. He no longer believed in it. A recruit from the working-class (a rarity at Oxford in those days), I had read a great deal of Carlyle and Ruskin before coming up, and I didn't believe that Laissez-faire was Revealed Truth either, laid up from on high and true for all circumstances and places.

When I got to All Souls – where H. W. C. Davis was good enough to introduce me to my more admired Trevelyan – Keynes came to visit us occasionally. He would complain of the Spartan conditions under which we lived, our Arctic bedrooms. Quite rightly; for one difference between Oxford and Cambridge in those days was that, over there, the dons did themselves so much better. They had sets of three, some even four, rooms, where we mostly had only two; one or two Cambridge dons (R. V. Laurence of Trinity was one) died simply of over-eating. See A. E. Housman on Cambridge life. All Souls provided a combination of public splendour with private squalor.

Keynes came to see Professor Edgeworth in the course of their editing the *Economic Journal* together. Edgeworth was a rare bird, even at All Souls. Anglo-Irish on one side – his great-aunt, Maria Edgeworth the novelist, had instructed him to say Brighthelmstone, never Brighton, like the people – he was Spanish on the other: Francis Ysidro Edgeworth. He kept people at a distance by his oblique courtesy. A distinguished intellect, he had a fabulous memory. On his one journey to America, laid up in his cabin by sea-sickness, he managed to reconstruct about a half of the *Iliad* in Greek. His lectures were only for the elect; a few Fellows attended them out of loyalty: nobody could understand them. He had once proposed marriage to Beatrice Webb, who has a characteristically disparaging account of him. He was a pure mathematical economist, an outpost of Marshallianism in Oxford; from that point of view, *he* should have been at Cambridge, Keynes at Oxford.

It was a joke at All Souls that one could never get Edgeworth to pronounce a definite judgment about anything – his motto might well have been his dictum, 'I like the duplicity of things.' One exception to this was his disapprobation of Karl Marx: Edgeworth condemned him with a moral distaste that was worthy of the sainted Marshall.

They were all supercilious about Marxism, and obtuse as to its real significance. In his Laissez-faire Lecture Keynes spoke of the 'poor quality of its thinking, of inability to analyse a process and follow it out to its conclusion. How a doctrine so illogical and so *dull* can have exercised so powerful and enduring an influence over the minds of men and, through them, the events of history', he could not understand. There was a great deal in the events of history which Keynes did not understand, but which Marx did.

Let us be clear about this. I no more subscribe to the dogmatism of Marx's economic or political doctrines than

Keynes did. I do not think that Marx was a pure economist or political scientist, or 'pure' anything (except a pure egoist); but he had deeper insights into the processes of history and the forces at work in society than Keynes ever had, with his superficial rationalism and his Bloomsbury superciliousness. That is one reason for Marx's influence upon 'the minds of men and the events of history', altogether greater and more 'enduring' than Keynes's.

Of course Keynes was a more generous man, encouraging to other people's work, especially of young men – where Marx was a nasty man, unwilling to recognise quality in others: an envious, recognisably German type. Both men were justifiably arrogant, but Keynes was occasionally willing to admit where he had been wrong. In the *Treatise on Money* he admitted how much he had underestimated J. A. Hobson, who had emphasised the importance of under-consumption in the shortcomings of the economic system. Hobson had been effectively excluded, as a heretic, by the economic establishment and academic economists all hanging tgether, when this solitary thinker was on to something more important than most of them were.

Keynes was good enough to encourage my reviews in his *Economic Journal* of books on political theory – Tawney, Russell, E. H. Carr, Laski – in spite of my obsession with Marxism. He would send me brisk p.c.s to urge me on, and in fact published my first piece of research, on the Dispute concerning the Elizabethan Plymouth Pilchard Fishery, in the *Journal's Economic History Supplement*. This had some relevance as an illustration of the conflict between state regulation and free economic processes.

I knew Keynes only intellectually, not personally, and nothing at all about his rip-roaring homosexuality. So I was much amused when my stockbroker friend, Nicholas Davenport, who had invited me to Covent Garden, told me that Keynes said, 'You can't do that: he's *my* boy.' Actually I was not his boy (or anybody else's either – more's the pity: such relentless repression, when young and rather sexy, cannot have been good for duodenal ulcer).

Naively enough, I was constantly concerned for Keynes's intellectual well-being. I never ceased to be amazed throughout the appalling Thirties at his inability to see the significance of the Marxist approach and insight into the gaping problems of society, the conflicts of class interests – indeed the crucial rôle of Class in history and politics; and his refusal to come to terms with the Labour Movement, make an alliance with it, which would give his views – about Unemployment, economic expansion, etc – the *fulcrum* they needed, and make both the Labour Party and himself more effective. Why couldn't he see it? After all, the Webbs had seen it and formed the most effective alliance with the Labour Movement – which ultimately proved the foundation of the Welfare State.

I wrote a number of articles urging this line upon him, in the *Nineteenth Century* and elsewhere, some of them reprinted for the historical record in *The End of an Epoch*. Reviewing it, Professor Denis Brogan referred to the continuing dialogue I had engaged in during that wasted decade when all went wrong. But there was no dialogue, for Keynes did not reply. Privately, I considered that no reply was possible. Professor Skidelsky reminds me that Labour was out of government throughout the whole of that decade and couldn't do anything anyway.

True enough; but it need not necessarily have been so but for the fatal events of 1931, the turning-point in history between the two German wars. The year 1931 saw a ganging-up of the upper and middle classes, and of their political parties, both Tory and Liberal, against the Labour Movement to keep it out. The long-term effects were disastrous; in some ways Britain was crippled by them.

In terms of immediate policy at that time Ernest Bevin and the Labour Movement were right. The proper way to correct the deficit on the balance of payments in 1931 was a temporary 10 per cent tariff on imports. Keynes was in favour of this (as I was), along with correcting the exaggerated fixation of the pound at 4.86 to the dollar. Keynes had been against this measure – which precipitated the prolonged Coal-Strike and its train of consequences, General Strike and all: see his *The Economic Consequences of Mr Churchill*. Actually, Churchill's instinct had been against the return to the Gold Standard, but he had been overruled by the combined weight of the Treasury and the Bank of England. – As the Labour Movement was – and was kept out of responsibility and power the whole of that disastrous decade. Until 1940.

Bevin had served on the Macmillan Committee (Lord Macmillan, not Harold), to which Keynes had contributed the most important evidence, clean contrary to the paralytic policy of the National Government, and the Bank of England under Montagu Norman, who admitted that he had never 'considered the effect the Return to the Gold Standard might have on Unemployment'! (It naturally contracted exports and increased unemployment.)

Instead of the obviously sensible policy, a moderate amount of expansion, a measure of controlled inflation at the right time (not, as in the 1960s, at the wrong time), the Old Men of the Sea of 1931–9, of whom the most powerful was Neville Chamberlain, went in for a consistent deflationary policy, worsening the situation. The dominant man in the Labour Movement, Ernest Bevin, and Keynes were of one mind in all this. Why could they not have joined together, and worked together, for the right ends in that miserable time? Keynes could have provided intellectual leadership, the Labour Movement the mass backing and support.

Lenin said, 'Politics begin with the masses.' Keynes needed a mass movement behind him to be effective. He had not that Marxist perception. As Skidelsky replies to me today, Keynes thought that he could be more effective as an individual, with no party affiliations, i.e. no movement behind him. A massive imperception – Marx could have told him; a historic mistake, for of course the government of 1931–9, with its enormous majorities – could have done anything, dealt with Hitler too if they had wanted to – did nothing, and Keynes had no effect whatever. Until the Second German War, which they brought down on Britain in the worst possible circumstances.

Keynes realised his ineffectiveness, a lone voice in the wilderness, and at length chose to link up with the wing of the Liberal Party led by Lloyd George, whom he had so much maligned in the *Economic Consequences of the Peace*. Together, he and Lloyd George produced a Yellow Book of constructive proposals for dealing with Unemployment which was better than anything else produced. But what on earth was the point of urging that on the country *without any leverage behind it*?

Anybody with any political sense could have seen from 1931 that there was no future for the Liberal Party; that there would never be a Liberal government again.

Actually I was in favour of bringing together all the elements opposed to the disastrous course of the 'National' government, Appeasement of Hitler, caving in to Mussolini over Abyssinia and Spain, etc – both the Labour Party and the Liberals, and even including Churchill and the Tories who were anti-Chamberlain. When I urged this to Hugh Dalton, who was sympathetic, he replied, 'But – how many Tory MPs can Churchill count on in the House? Only 20 or 25.' Baldwin and Chamberlain had that unspeakable Assembly with them all through that decade, to the edge of disaster: at first with a majority of 450, even after 1935 a majority of nearly 300! They could have done anything. In the long-term they ruined their country. Britain's great days are now over.

In these years the combination of experience and an original inquiring mind was undermining Keynes's belief in the rigid economic orthodoxy in which he had been brought up and which was inflicted on us all. Not to believe it was not only an intellectual but moral deviation; to challenge it was to be rewarded with exclusion from responsible teaching posts and even from notice and discussion of one's ideas. Keynes himself, in his earlier orthodoxy, had refused to review any more of J. A. Hobson's original books, describing his criticism of the quantity theory of Money as 'Mythology intellectualised, brought up to journalistic date, most subtly larded with temporary concessions to reason.'

Unforgivable superciliousness, which Keynes had reason to regret, for he came to see that Hobson had been largely right. In his classic *General Theory of Employment, Interest and Money* he admitted, 'It is astonishing what foolish things one can temporarily believe if one thinks too long alone, particularly in economics, where it is often impossible to bring one's ideas to a conclusive test either formal or experimental' – i.e. as in either mathematics, or in physics, chemistry, etc. That is why it is absurd to insist on a rigid orthodoxy in economics, which is not a 'pure' science like mathematics, but an impure subject of mingled theory and practical affairs. However, as Skidelsky says, 'Authority in economics had come to demand adherence to certain orthodoxies.'

I had observed this in the unnecessary 'crisis' of 1931, which panicked everybody, when not a single economist, except for Keynes, would subscribe to the commonsense remedy of a temporary tariff on imports, let alone a release from the strain of retaining sterling at 4.86 to the dollar. Not one of the academic economists at Cambridge or Oxford (where D. H. MacGregor stood for Cambridge orthodoxy), still less at the London School of Economics, where Lionel Robbins trumpeted the purest milk-of-the-word Free Trade, would allow a temporary departure from it. Events in the real world framed a showdown: Britain was forced off the Gold Standard, and the world did not come to an end.

As an historian, I had never had much belief in economic or political theories as absolute truths, and ever since the experience of the Thirties I have not had much respect for academic economists. Economists with experience of practical affairs, which is what the subject is about, are another matter.

It is hardly surprising therefore that when Keynes completed his revolution in economics with *The General Theory of Employment, Interest and Money*, he should have been greeted with incomprehension and obstruction by his academic colleagues. Skidelsky points out that not one of his eminent *confrères* at Cambridge agreed with him – not Pigou, who as Professor was head of the Faculty. (Keynes was never a professor: he said stylishly, 'I will not have the indignity of the title without the advantage of the emolument.') Nor did Denis Robertson – there was even a breach between them over it. Nor did Hubert Henderson, who never understood Keynes's argument. But he tied himself in knots over it at All Souls, whither he had removed, and could argue the hind leg of a donkey off, as I found to my irritation.

It always irritates me that supposedly intelligent persons, particularly academics, simply cannot think outside the categories their minds have been formed in. When the greatest of our physiologists, Sir William Hervey, conceived his idea of the circulation of the blood, people would not credit it, and his practice as a doctor fell away almost to nothing. He had to wait for a new generation to grow up accustomed to the new idea. Fortunately Hervey lived long enough to see that happen. Something of the same kind happened to Keynes: though he did not live as long as Hervey, the succeeding generation of economists gradually filled up with his disciples.

I have experienced something of this phenomenon myself. The revolution in our knowledge of Shakespeare effected by, after all, a first-rate authority on the Elizabethan Age, background to his life and work, has been met with blinkered incomprehension. So far from wanting to know, the second-rate put up a wall of obstruction and make no effort to go into the new discoveries and findings: it will need a new generation accustomed to them. What is irritating – I am sure Keynes would have agreed – is that it is properly the business of the second-rate to mediate the discoveries of first-rate minds to the third-rate. A further factor today is the *vis inertiae* of an egalitarian society – naturally low-grade intellectually, no standards.

When Keynes's revolutionary book came out, I set myself to grasp its argument and draw out its implications in economic and social policy as a basis for a wide agreement on the Left, against the paralytic hold of Chamberlainism on the nation. (Right up to 1940 they really thought, and even said, that they were indispensable. See the evidence in the Memoirs of the time, the complacent Sam Hoare and Simon – let alone Chamberlain, who wrote down his conviction that he was superior to Lloyd George, the only political figure of genius to compare with Churchill!)

In 1936 I produced my tract, *Mr Keynes and the Labour Movement*. I do not claim to be an economist, but I certainly put enough effort into the small book – long out of print and unobtainable. What I was anxious to do was to draw out the common ground between Keynes and the Labour Movement's line, dotting the i's and crossing the t's. My Preface affirmed that 'there is little or no divergence between what is implied by Labour policy and by Mr Keynes.' I hoped that the booklet was 'a contribution towards clarifying and building up an agreement between various sections of opinion of the Left, *on a wide front*; a body which, if an understanding had

been reached before, might have given this country progressive government for the past ten years, and to Europe an
effective and progressive lead.'

Keynes wrote to me from Bloomsbury, 12 May 1936, 'I
agree with you that there is, or ought to be, little divergence
between the political implications of my ideas and the policy
of the Labour Party. I should officially join that party, if it did
not seem to be divided between enthusiasts who turn against a
thing if there seems to be a chance that it could possibly
happen, and leaders so conservative that there is more to hope
from Mr Baldwin.' But was this true to fact, or an adequate
excuse? The 'enthusiasts' had no real weight, and there was
nothing to hope from Baldwin – look at his record over the
coal-miners, and his declared indifference to foreign affairs.
'Wake me up when that is over', he would say when they were
being discussed in Cabinet – with the danger already looming
from Hitler and Mussolini!

Keynes continued, 'But perhaps it is better for several
reasons that I should remain aloof and stick, for the present, to
my academic standpoint. . . . My book is not, in truth, well
adapted for carrying the gospel beyond academic circles. But
if you can help to get it read more widely, I shall all the same be
very grateful. Those whose heads are already too full of
preconceived ideas sometimes find it harder than more innocent readers do to understand.' Supercilious as this was, it was
true enough of his fellow economists (as I find today with
fellow Shakespeareans).

I followed this up with a pamphlet urging a Popular Front,
as wide as possible, against the Old Men before it was too late.
Keynes wrote in October, 'Some of it makes me blush a little,
and I hope your eulogies won't irritate people too much. It is a
problem how best to bring ideas into relation with politics. I
am, of course, in favour of a popular front. But I should like to
see some group of like-minded people formed which one
could join, and which then could seek affiliation with the
official Labour Party, in the way that the old I.L.P. and the
Fabians used to, I think. To try and make the official Liberal
Party join with the official Labour Party raises unnecessary,
and perhaps hopeless, difficulties.' Why should they not?
Anyone of sense could have seen that there would never be a

Liberal government again, their day was over. The only way
to be effective was to join together and co-operate before too
late.

He went on, 'I believe the solution may lie in a number of
groups, having ideas of their own not wholly along the party
ticket, but definitely subordinated to the Labour Party and
affiliated to it.' 'A number of groups' – how *ineffective* that
would be! Just like an intellectual liberal, I thought; imagine
what Lenin would think of that. . . . However, I considered
that this, from Keynes, was a step forward, and suggested his
standing for a University seat at Cambridge then occupied by
a Conservative Chamberlainite.

Keynes replied, 'I hope that next time you are in Cambridge
you will let me know. I agree with you that the Next Five
Years' Group would be the most hopeful, if they could be
persuaded to affiliate with the Labour Party. I fancy that
Harold Macmillan would agree, but whether all his Committee would I am not sure. I have, of course, often considered
standing for Cambridge University. But I am convinced that
it is useless to go into politics except as a whole-time job, and I
have so many other avocations that I care about much more.'

No doubt. At this point I gave him up, and turned to
another possibility for the Cambridge seat. What was clearly
necessary was a non-party man who could collect the widest
support against the fraud of a 'National' government. This
was the way Arthur Salter had won a seat at Oxford; and for
Cambridge I raised a candidate willing to stand in Sir Ralph
Wedgwood. I did not let Keynes know when I was next in
Cambridge, though I find a message from him dated from
King's, 24 April 1938: 'A very excellent letter in today's
M.G.', i.e. *Manchester Guardian*. What was the point? I suppose it was advocating an understanding with Russia before
too late. But Neville Chamberlain, as he said, 'preferred to
trust Herr Hitler's word', and we were along the road that led
to Munich, and the Second German War, in the worst possible
circumstances – virtually no allies. After nearly twenty years
of Tory government!

It was heart-breaking to live through the Thirties, if one was
intelligent, seeing quite clearly the way things were going and

what it was leading to. No-one would take the obvious and sensible steps. All over Europe the parties of the Left, who stood for the right objectives – international peace, freedom, social progress – would not pull together. The idiots preferred to fight each other, like the Social Democrats and Communists in Germany, the Communists even collaborating with the Nazis in the Berlin tram-strike just before Hitler came into power. *He* knew all about power. The evil forces were all too effective: those on the side of good causes all too ineffective. I used to find this maddening in my arguments with Ralph Fox, whom the Communist Party sent to Spain, against his will, to be a martyr.

Neither in Britain would the opposition to the paralytic Old Men of the Sea come together to get rid of them – though Churchill too hoped for such a consummation. In consequence they stuck to power, until the country was in fact overwhelmed in 1940. L. S. Amery, a good Tory who was right about all this, one day said to me at All Souls that, in politics, it is a mistake to walk too far ahead of your following. With a sinking feeling I recognised the truth of that.

I will not resume the argument of *Mr Keynes and the Labour Movement* here – merely say that it was dedicated to my particular leader in it, Herbert Morrison, who had effectively set the model of the semi-public corporation with the London Transport Board. This was in line with what Keynes had proposed in *The End of Laissez-faire:* 'I suggest that progress lies in the growth and the recognition of semi-autonomous bodies within the State.' He went further than this: 'It is true that many big undertakings, particularly Public Utility enterprises still need to be semi-socialised.' This was what Herbert Morrison stood for as our leader in London, and what we in the Labour Movement thought. Why could not Keynes combine with us, to make us both more *effective*?

I was then very active in the Labour Movement: a political candidate throughout that decade, whose uphill work for years in Cornwall eventually brought over my constituency, Penryn and Falmouth, to the Labour Party in 1945 (too late for me); speaking, lecturing, writing in Labour papers, having created one for Cornwall, wearing myself out.

Victor Gollancz was in the lead as socialist publisher at the time, so I naturally offered my Keynes booklet to him. He kindly asked me to lunch at the Savoy, into which I had never penetrated, and capped it with an invitation to his country villa, with the added attraction of a swimming-pool. Little did he perceive that his combination of opulence with extreme Leftism did not recommend itself to my austere and rather Puritan outlook; nor did I swim. He turned down the book – insufficiently Leftist for him. He preferred the trash of the Left Book Club he was promoting – Harold Laski, John Strachey, Michael Foot, Tom Driberg and such, some of them Communists or fellow-travellers. (I did not know that he had also turned down George Orwell.) That finished Gollancz for me; I at once took the book to Keynes's publisher, Macmillan, who made no difficulty about publishing it.

I saw Gollancz only once again. After the war he made another name for himself for his more-than-Christian attitude, falling over backward, with much publicity, to forgive the Germans for their appalling crime in massacring six million Jews. This won him much sentimental admiration: 'that Jesus-Christ-like man, Victor Gollancz,' said one of his employees (female of course). Meanwhile, forced to give up politics by illness and despair, I found consolation in the past and was writing history with some success. Gollancz and I happened to be coming back from America on one of the *Queens*, he travelling first-class of course, I second-class, of course. He kindly invited me up to visit him: 'Friend, come up higher.' I did not avail myself of the invitation. I did not wish to know him.

With the Second German War, it was just a question of survival – all earlier possibilities and hopes, discussions and arguments put behind us (though I did not forget or forgive). Keynes moved into his period of greater service to the country – out of my ken, into the stratosphere of high Anglo-American financial relations.

What had accounted for his refusal to line up with us and make an effective Opposition – ranging from Stafford Cripps to Churchill – against disastrous Chamberlainism and Appeasement of the dictators while there was yet time? He certainly didn't see the Marxist point that it is a mass movement that provides the backing and the power to move things in politics. He looked to persuasion, in fact produced a book, *Essays in Persuasion*: just the way to be ineffective – as if people were rational enough to be persuadable.

He was a Liberal, and a Cambridge Rationalist. Fancy thinking that men were reasonable! – you need only take a look round the world today: you do not need to go so far as the Lebanon or Middle East, darkest Africa or Central America; Northern Ireland gives the lie to rationalist assumptions. In the Thirties I was constantly attacking in my writings the Rationalist Fallacy that dominated the Left. The Right had no such illusions, they knew that politics were about power. The ineffective fools of the Left denounced this as 'power politics' – their cliché for the facts of political life: what was their alternative, 'powerless politics'? That was in effect what they achieved: their ineffectiveness, all over Europe, Liberals, Social Democrats, decent people, sold the pass to the malign criminals who had no such illusions and were all too effective. Hitler, Mussolini, Stalin had utter contempt for the political idiots the masses are – and the masses rewarded them with devotion, died in millions for them.

If I have ceased to write about politics and given up girding against the Rationalist Fallacy, it is because I no longer care – as I did when I was young – about what happens to people bent on remaining fools. I write now simply for the record that is history – and we know what Gibbon, greatest of our historians, thought that was: 'the register of the crimes, follies and misfortunes of mankind.' As a modern historian, living alas in democratic times, I add – their idiocy, their sheer silliness. (One has only to look at their newspapers, or listen to their media!)

Keynes was a Liberal, and there was an element of snobbish superciliousness in his refusal to line up with a Labour Movement. I had come across that with other Liberals at the time, to whom I urged the historical conclusion, obvious enough, that there was no future for the Liberal Party and that they should throw in their lot with effectively the only two political parties, either of which could have used their ability. As it was, the country was robbed of the ability of a number of good men ploughing the sands.

But Keynes was a Cambridge-and-Bloomsbury Liberal, the *crème de la crème* – and the superciliousness of that lot, though well enough known, is hardly credible. Here is the young Keynes on his first official visit to America, writing to handsome Duncan Grant with whom he was in love: 'The only sympathetic and original thing in America is the niggers, who are charming.' Fancy writing like that – and he a Liberal! No wonder the poor British Ambassador thought him 'really too offensive for words.' This select group, who thought themselves so superior to the mass of humanity – and were – in fact did not know what humanity was like. They were not historians, and Keynes himself had a very naif view of history: they were addicts (and victims) of G. E. Moore's adolescent ethical views – I find him a faintly ridiculous figure. They were utterly taken by surprise by the war in 1914: dear Duncan, a conscientious objector: 'I never considered the possibility of a great European war. It seemed such an absolutely mad thing for a civilised people to do.' But this is precisely what peoples have done all through history, civilised or not, and still do.

That Cambridge group, as Skidelsky points out, were really pro-German, and supposed the Germans – with their record in philosophy and music – the most civilised nation in Europe. There was another side to the coin, of which they were ignorant. Couldn't they *see* what Germany was heading for? Hadn't they noticed what Germany was up to since Bismarck? The leading German historian of these matters today, Fritz Fischer, recognises that Germany meant war and was responsible for the war in 1914.[2] Actually – an historical point no-one notices – the Germans as a whole were more keen on war, *der Tag*, in 1914 than they were in 1939.

That Cambridge circle was childishly confused about Germany – and Cambridge became the centre of a distinguished anti-war, 'conscientious objector' group whose organ was *The Cambridge Magazine*, run from King's Parade by my eccentric acquaintance, C. K. Ogden. The files of that periodical make fascinating reading for the time, the office once raided by patriotic Cambridge men and its contents thrown

[2] The two fundamental works for the reader to study are Fritz Fischer, *Germany's Aims in the First World War*; and *War of Illusions. German Policies from 1911 to 1914*. Both translated.

into confusion. It has now become known that Keynes himself, though working in the Treasury, was also a 'conscientious objector', under the influence of the Bloomsbury
Weltanschauung. He wrote to dear Duncan, 'I work for a
government I despise, for ends I think criminal.' I find this
shocking. Was it criminal to resist a militaristic Germany's
attempt to subjugate Europe? This was the crest of the first
wave of aggression into which retrograde Germany swept
Europe, ruining the hopes of the twentieth century – and it
would have succeeded, as the second attempt under Hitler
nearly did, had not the United States come to the rescue.

Again and again Keynes's judgment is shown to be wrong.
In January 1915 he told Woolf 'German finance is crumbling'.
He was wrong: in fact Germany managed. Partly through the
genius of Walther Rathenau, the head of the electrical
industry, who successfully re-organised German industry on a
wartime footing. He was a Jew – so, after the war, the Right
murdered him. (Another Jew, Balin, creator of the Hamburg-
Amerika shipping line – when he saw what Germany was bent
on in 1914 – himself in touch with the outside world and more
sensitive to world opinion – committed suicide.)

In April 1915 Keynes was predicting financial collapse for
Britain; or, if not, then October following. Wrong again.
Then he fixed '31 March 1916 for the end of the world, though
this had been postponed for a few months.' In fact, Lloyd
George – whom Keynes as an Asquithian at this time detested
– was usually proved right as against the Treasury experts.
Also Lloyd George was the only man with the leadership to
win the war – not Asquith, drunken, lazy, spending hours of
Cabinet time writing love letters to young Venetia Stanley.

All through 1916–18 Keynes was in favour of a Compromise Peace. That would have meant that Germany's way was
clear for a second attempt. This is no biased opinion – the point
is proved by the peace of Brest-Litovsk next year, 1917, which
Germany inflicted upon Russia, annexing all Eastern Europe
up to the threshold of St Petersburg. Hitler's aim was simply
continuous with Germany's in 1914–18.

The pro-Germans were appallingly mistaken, and the light-
weights of Bloomsbury not to be taken seriously. Those
superior intellects had just not thought things through: would

it have been a good thing for *them* and their view of life if
Germany's aggressive militarism had won? We have more
reason to respect the brave men who gave their lives to resist
it, and save a society for *them* to be so civilised in. (At the
memorials to the fallen all over Britain, particularly at Oxford
and Cambridge, I always remember them.)

At the end of the First German War Keynes told Virginia
Woolf that he was 'disillusioned. No more does he believe –
that is, in the stability of the things he likes: Eton is doomed;
the governing classes; perhaps Cambridge too.' More important matters were at stake than Eton or Cambridge, or even the
English governing class. The future of a decent, civilised
Europe was in the balance (the New World saved us – not only
the United States, but Canada, Australia, South Africa, New
Zealand, as again in 1939–45). Germany's crime in 1914
portended the end of the old civilised nineteenth-century
world, and started the chain-reaction of violence and revolution that has been going on ever since, and ended in the
Nuclear Age, that may end us all.

How petty and narrow the want of historical perspective in
Cambridge-Bloomsbury and their prophet Keynes!

This is the proper historical perspective in which to consider
his *Economic Consequences of the Peace*, of 1919, which brought
him fame and a fortune, first made him an international figure
– and did so much damage. By far his most historically
influential book, it did more than anything to undermine the
Peace of Versailles and to give the Germans an alibi for what
they had done in 1914–18, and thus prepare the ground for
their second attempt. It was of the highest possible value to
German propaganda against the Treaty, which never ceased,
not merely Hitler's. Worse: it confused the minds of British
and Americans over the German question, and helped to fuel
the Revisionists in Britain and the USA, and the Appeasement
which played straight into Hitler's hands.

We should be historically clear about the Versailles Peace.
On the territorial side it was fair enough – and what a contrast
with what the Germans would have imposed is quite clear
from their record at Brest-Litovsk. Poland was re-created as a
nation-state; a great historical injustice rectified. The peoples
of Central Europe – Czechs, Slovaks, Slavs – were given the

independence and self-determination they demanded: inevitable, and historically just.

On the economic side, it was again only right that Germany
should pay some Reparations for the enormous damage she
had inflicted on Belgium and on eleven provinces of North-
Eastern France; let alone on other peoples in Eastern Europe
and elsewhere. Wickham Steed, under whom *The Times* was
well-informed about Europe (as under the arch-Appeaser,
Geoffrey Dawson, it was not), put the issue squarely: 'Germany went to war because she made it pay in 1870–1, and
believed she could make it pay again.'

No difference of opinion on the principle – differences arose
on the question of How much Germany could pay?

Keynes's book was chiefly concerned with the economic
issue – which was never satisfactorily settled, because it
transpired that Germany never intended to pay for what she
had been responsible for – and Keynes's book was a great aid in
helping her to get away with it. French economists never
accepted Keynes's arguments. Etienne Mantoux – killed by
the Germans in their Second War – showed that they spent
twice the amount on Re-Armament for it that they paid in
Reparations. As for these, they borrowed largely from Wall
Street and the City of London; and this had the excellent effect
of re-inforcing the pro-German sentiments prevailing in those
quarters. For the rest, Germany deliberately depreciated its
currency. The French felt themselves cheated – as they were.
(No wonder they were not keen to fight for us again in
1939–40!)

Skidelsky points out that 'the constant revision of the
schedules of German payments in the 1920s paved the way for
Hitler's successful assaults on the territorial clauses in the
1930's.' It set the pattern: the economic, and then the territorial, undermining of the Versailles settlement played
straight into Hitler's hands and made the Second War possible.
What fools his opponents were! – as indeed he thought them.
And Keynes bears a heavy responsibility here: *The Economic
Consequences of the Peace* had a greater historic effect, an
influence on events, than anything else he wrote.

Much of its popular success was due to the brilliant, malicious portraits of the men at Versailles – Lloyd George,

President Wilson, Clemenceau – wrestling with the intractable issues. Keynes's wise mother asked him to tone these caricatures down; Brand, the judicious banker, an All Souls man, warned Keynes of the damage the book would do in America – as it did. (Brand said to me during the Crisis of 1931: 'Only two men understand the Gold Standard, Keynes and I – and we don't agree.' Note that Montagu Norman of the Bank of England was not one of them.)

Keynes subsequently retracted something from his deleterious book, but it was too late – the damage had been done. In later years, with more experience of the world if not of history, he retreated from the Rationalist Fallacy I held against him and liberal intellectuals generally. In 'My Early Beliefs' he wrote, 'As cause and consequence of our general state of mind we completely misunderstood human nature, including our own.' So much for Cambridge-Bloomsbury; there could not be a more complete disclaimer. 'The rationality which we attributed to it led to a superficiality, not only of judgment but also of feeling.'

His view of history, however, continued to be naif and superficial. I noticed that, both in the *Treatise on Money* and in what he wrote about Sir Isaac Newton's papers. He was astonished to find that Newton had spent a great deal of his time on trying to make as much sense of Holy Writ as of the Universe; and that Newton was as much a Magus as he was a scientist, seeking the transmutation of metals as well as their analysis. Historians take that sort of thing for granted: the science of chemistry arose along with, if not out of, alchemy; astronomy along with astrology, etc.

Naiveté goes with optimism: historians are not prone to it. Keynes's idealistic liberal optimism arose from the happy circumstances of his early life – Cambridge – Eton – Cambridge again – in those pre-1914 days when it was bliss to be alive (and the world was never the same again).

When the Second German War was coming to an end – with all the devastation it had wrought this time in Britain and the erosion of her resources, the destruction to replace and make good – Churchill asked his economic experts what the country would be able to afford to devote to Social Services. Keynes, over-optimistic as a liberal would be, put in the maximum estimate; his colleague, Hubert Henderson, cautious Scot, suggested a minimum. Though all my admiration, and indeed affections, were with Keynes, I suspect that Henderson's was the better judgment.

3

Ernest Bevin

'The outstanding Trade Union leader produced by this, or perhaps by any other, country', so Bevin's biographer, Lord Bullock, describes him, with justice. Bevin would have agreed, for he had no middle-class false modesty: he described himself as 'a turn-up in a million', as indeed he was. No nonsense about equality in that quarter: he was indubitably a great man, essentially constructive, a builder-up.

And from what wretched beginnings! He was illegitimate – like several of the early Labour leaders: Keir Hardie, Ramsay MacDonald, J. H. Thomas. No-one knew who was Ernie's father; his mother described herself as a widow and, a fine woman, she worked herself to an early death to bring up her children. Bevin was devoted to the memory of his mother, but would never speak about the appalling struggle of his childhood. In his way he was more reticent and reserved than Attlee, who had nothing to be reserved about: all was very normal with him. Someone who had known young Ernie said, 'I'm sure there's no one in this wide world was ever poorer than he and his mother.'

In spite of this depressing background Mrs Bevin did her best for her boy. He scrabbled what intermittent elementary education he could, just reading, writing and arithmetic. He was always unsure of his grammar, but did not let that stand in his way, was a more effective and commanding speaker than those who were perfect in their English. His real training came from the West Country Nonconformist chapels he attended, in the Somerset and Devon countryside, then in Bristol, where he worked as a boy labourer, eventually graduating to driving his own horse and cart. He joined the Christian

Endeavour Society, attended evening classes at the Y.M.C.A. after the day's work, and became a local preacher. Those solid, old-fashioned Nonconformist principles stood him in good stead all his life.

He was an ardent reader, and had a passion for acquiring knowledge and for argument – in this like his later colleague, Attlee, who in his younger days at school was held to be 'self-opinionated'. Ernest Bevin was always that, never had any qualms about expressing his opinion on anything – and justly so. But he did not move his sights from chapel to politics until he was nearing thirty. He was in his sixtieth year when he became a Minister of the Crown. He was late in developing his remarkable potential, naturally enough; but, by the time he arrived at the front rank in politics, a national figure, he had a world of experience behind him – wider than any, except Churchill's.

A remarkable characteristic of Bevin's was his sheer *intellectual* ability. I have remarked elsewhere that I never heard him speak without being intellectually convinced. Most people were unaware that, behind the rough, clumsy, ungrammatical sentences, he was a match for anybody – lawyers or economists, let alone industrialists or politicians. I am astonished to realise how much he *knew*, the range of information he commanded. Another thing: he had no inferiority complex whatever, not a shadow of one – unlike MacDonald (it went with *his* sensitiveness and romanticism, but was a source of weakness). Bevin was a very masculine character; I do not think he had much sensibility or taste – it was hardly to be expected – but immense horse-sense.

My glimpses of him, though not considerable, were fewer than those of Attlee, with whom, after all, there was Oxford in common. Bevin had not much interest in universities and a great distrust of intellectuals. This was unlike his rival Morrison, who liked coming down to Oxford and several times stayed with me at All Souls; he was generous too with his time, was good to Nuffield College in holding seminars on government there, and (I think) accepted a Fellowship. Magdalen tried to corral Bevin – a very large rogue-elephant – as a Fellow; but he made nothing of it, and never came. Was Bevin a generous man? I doubt it.

It is not my purpose even to sketch his achievement, but I must point out that much that was constructive in the Labour Movement, speaking widely – Trade Unions first, the Party second – was of his doing. First, casual labour at the docks he organised into the Dockers' Union. Then he built up the big and efficient Transport Workers' Union; to which he eventually annexed the rather ineffective General Workers' Union (to which my father as a china-clay worker nominally belonged, though nothing of a Trade Unionist). Bevin was an empire builder; he made the Transport and General Workers' Union the biggest and best organised in his time. He built Transport House in Smith Square, and housed the Labour Party headquarters in it – a significant accommodation. Labour had no voice in the daily press whatever, except George Lansbury's lively *Daily Herald,* which had a small circulation and regularly lost money. Bevin made a deal with Odhams Press to make the *Herald* a big Labour paper, went all over the country putting it across (I attended one or two of his meetings) and helped to build it up to a two million circulation: '*My* paper.'

Bevin came to the fore in the aftermath of the disaster of 1931, as if to fill the gap left by the loss of Labour's leaders and to repair some of the damage. In the financial crisis itself, he emerges as the only public figure who knew what to expect and the right measures to take. For this he had been equipped by his experience on the (Lord) Macmillan Committee on Finance and Industry, upon which the other historic figure was Keynes. Meeting throughout 1930 this had a profound effect on Bevin: it gave him a grasp of the working of the financial and economic system such as no other politician had, certainly not Snowden, Chancellor of the Exchequer, fixed in the Gladstonian orthodoxy of Treasury and Bank of England. Keynes challenged this intellectually, though he did not dare to draw out the logical conclusions for practical action. Bevin was not afraid to; it is astonishing how right he was, in the light of all that has happened since. Nobody thought that at the time.

Briefly, Bevin agreed with Keynes that the return to gold parity in 1926, with the pound at $4.86, had been a great mistake, damaging exports, creating unemployment, indirectly responsible for the disastrous Coal Strike, a whole train of ill consequences. (Ironically, Churchill's intuition had been against it, but as Chancellor he had been overborne by the weight and expertise of Bank and Treasury.) It emerged that these experts – Bradbury of the Pound notes and Montague Norman of the Bank – did not consider the effects on industry and employment: their blinkered vision was confined to finance, and the currency, the maintenance of the gold standard, the parity of the pound to maintain the City's prestige as the international money market. The strain on the country and its internal economy was intolerable.

Bevin urged that any necessary sacrifices should not be inflicted alone on wages and unemployment benefit, and the *rentier* class go scot free. He was not afraid to contemplate a temporary tariff (I was in favour of a tariff on luxury imports, e.g. wine, tobacco etc, to correct the imbalance of payments); and he was the only one to envisage the devaluation that was inevitable. His biographer says that Keynes 'shied away' from this, and wonders mildly, in the stagnation of Britain's economy throughout that dreary decade – when the *rentier* class never had it so good – 'whether the untrained layman did not show more understanding than all the experts who sat on or appeared before the Macmillan Committee.' I think he did, and Bevin thought so too. We may except Keynes and Lord Brand of All Souls, who understood the technical minutiae; oddly enough, Brand was less unsympathetic than the rest to Bevin's views. However, he was an international banker.

What should MacDonald have done in the *impasse* of the (to us minimal) crisis of 1931, a mere matter of raising a deficit of £75 millions? He could not throw over the immovable Snowden, plus the Treasury and the Bank of England. Having a majority of Tories and Liberals against him, he should have handed the 'poisoned chalice' to Baldwin, who had the majority with him. Instead of that he allowed himself to be flattered into remaining a figurehead of a bogus 'National' government. He was a lost man, a deserter, never forgiven by any of us.

Already during MacDonald's second Labour government Bevin was moving into the foreground with his revitalisation of the *Herald* as a Labour daily paper. In his agreement with

Odhams he was careful to keep control of political policy, and no less careful to place Trade Union members, not Labour party nominees, on the board. He had a great nose for *power*, the real stuff of politics, himself a figure (and speaker) of tremendous, indeed vehement, power. By 1933 the *Herald* was the first paper in the world to reach a two-million circulation, Bevin beating Beaverbrook.

To supplement it Bevin planned a weekly, a more reliable *New Statesman,* utterly undependable under Kingsley Martin, whom Keynes had placed as editor. This took the form of *The New Clarion*, echoing the title of Robert Blatchford's famous broadsheet, *The Clarion*. It was Bevin's brain-child; he raised the money for it, became the chairman and wrote articles for it anonymously, keeping in the background. I think that at this time he did not want to come forward into politics – though Colonel Wedgwood told him he ought to be Prime Minister. (Would that he could have been in 1931!)

Again he worked hard, this time behind the scenes, to recruit support, and I was invited to write regularly for it. I do not seem to have kept a file of the paper, as I have of the *Cornish Labour News* which I founded. But Bevin's biography tells me that I contributed twenty articles, as also did G. D. H. Cole and H. N. Brailsford, Harold Laski even more. Among other contributors were Morrison, Lansbury, Stafford Cripps, H. E. Bates and Phyllis Bentley – not however Attlee, never much of a writer. I have forgotten my articles, except that, knowing Germany and a friend of Adam von Trott, I was obsessed by the Nazi danger, and saw very early that it was all over with European Disarmament. I have not forgotten that for this foresight, obvious enough, I was occasionally labelled 'Fascist' by some young fool. *The New Clarion,* however, failed to reach a circulation to make it pay; here it was unfortunately outrun by Keynes's *New Statesman and Nation.*

Bevin now made a surprising move. G. D. H. Cole had started the New Fabian Research Bureau and the Society for Socialist Inquiry and Propaganda, and Bevin decided to give the latter his full support. Lord Bullock says, 'with their strong flavour of Hampstead, Bloomsbury, and the University Labour Clubs, neither was the sort of body with which anyone would expect Bevin to be connected.' He even consented to become Chairman of S.S.I.P. and take the lead in it; it showed how much he recognised the need, with the growing economic crisis and the failure of the Labour government to deal with it, a refusal to look at any new ideas, Snowden blocking the way, and MacDonald's faltering lack of decision, which angered even Attlee.

Attlee was a silent member of S.S.I.P. – I never saw him at its meetings – along with Cripps and Pritt, Dick Mitchison and his wife Naomi Haldane, and the deleterious, semi-Communist Postgates. 'Bevin's willingness to join such a group marked a big change of attitude on his part and, if the partnership had proved successful, it might have strengthened the Labour Movement at one of its weakest points, the gap which separated the intellectuals from the trade unionists.'

For Cole it was a chance to repair some of the damage he had done years before by leaving the Fabians – as Beatrice Webb said to me, he had taken with him all their younger generation. Fond as I was of Douglas, especially when later he came across from Univ. to All Souls, I gradually came to distrust the facile way in which he would lay down the law about the running of the coal mines or iron mills – had he ever been in one to know how?

Myself, I wasn't much of a socialist when it came to economics – I always believed in work, and properly differentiated incentives. The old formula of the nationalisation of 'the means of production, distribution and exchange' meant nothing to me; as for nationalisation of the land, could one see the Labour Party running agriculture! I believed only in the extension of public corporations, such as the Port of London Authority, or the BBC, or the London Transport Board – as Morrison and Keynes did. (And why couldn't Keynes work with us to that end?) For the rest, I was obsessed by the growing threat from Germany; while Chamberlain and Co. regularly sold the pass to our enemies as well as the interests of Britain, when we should have supported and gathered together our friends – even reaching an understanding with USSR, with both under threat. Churchill always thought that it need never have come to war – we should simply not have allowed Hitler to re-arm. Fundamentally, it was the ineptitude – worse, the sabotaging of our own interests and those of the democracies – to play the game of Hitler, Mussolini and Franco, that kept me on the Left in all that evil decade.

What was S.S.I.P. supposed to be doing? Bevin himself put the purpose – 'that of projecting ideas. It is not a ginger group to the Party, or anything of that kind; it is an attempt to work out problems and to give the new generation something to grip. A good many of us feel that the younger people are just drifting; there is a kind of apathy which is appalling.' I had just produced my *Politics and the Younger Generation*, in time to have it caught in the disaster of 1931; but there was a good deal of talk about the younger generation and the gap in leadership with a whole generation of the best lost in the holocaust of 1914–18. (What we have to thank the Germans for!)

Oxford was good recruiting ground for the new generation: there Cole was our leader. I brought along my friends from All Souls, Richard Pares and G. F. Hudson (who knew about the Far East), and I recall from our body the beautiful, but serious-minded, Elizabeth Harman, to become well-known later as Lady Longford. We foregathered for several meetings at Lady Warwick's Easton Lodge at Dunmow. This was the inheritance of that extravagant beauty, a Maynard, mistress of Edward VII.

How well I remember it all: the big house with its Edwardian flavour, palms and aspidistras. In the grounds was a summerhouse, the 'temple of friendship', dedicated to those bygone days, photographs of Edward and his 'exotic entourage', to which the favoured were permitted access. There was the old lady herself – she had been converted to socialism years before by the condition of the chain-workers of Birmingham: still beautiful, violet eyes, ample velvety bosom, pneumatic bliss. She and Ernie Bevin sat there peaceably overflowing their armchairs together; I don't know which was fatter.

My mind was distracted by the scene and her, I don't know what we talked about, mostly hot air – 'What I am thinking in terms of . . . ' Cole would begin, Bevin looking benevolently on, saying nothing. When we got back to Oxford, Pares directed my wandering attention to an item in a Brighton book-catalogue: a cheap French novel by Paul de Kock, morocco bound and inscribed 'For lovely Warwick, from

Albert Edward, Xmas 1894.' It inspired me to send her, for her kindness to us, a little book I valued (and could not replace), François Mauriac's *Vie de Province*.

Then misfortune struck S.S.I.P. Among those seeking to give a 'new lead' after the disarray of 1931 was Stafford Cripps. A good deal of a crank himself, for all his forensic ability, he had the faculty of attracting cranks around him, along with them a break-away group from the hopeless I.L.P. The Independent Labour Party had had a distinguished past, as the nursing ground for leaders like MacDonald and Snowden. It had now dwindled into a pathetic faction, with long-haired Jimmy Maxton as leader, going round asking, 'Tell me what I am to do, and I will do it.' Talk about 'making bricks without straw'! – a sickening exhibition of ineffectiveness.

There now came up a proposal to unite the Socialist League they formed with S.S.I.P. Initially Bevin was not opposed, he suspended judgment. I was all along in favour of the widest front possible against the unspeakable Old Men of the 'National' Government. But, an unimportant young man in the ranks, I knew nothing of the negotiations, or that the crackpots of the Socialist League were so hostile to Bevin that they refused not only to have him as Chairman but to accept him in any office at all! Talk about sense of power – lack of it was the endemic disease of the Labour Party, one of the things that had sickened MacDonald, as it was sickening me. (It was also the fatal disease of the Social Democrats in Germany, and enabled Hitler, who knew all about power, to brush them aside with the greatest ease.) Here were the crackpots of the Left alienating the most powerful, and biggest-minded, man in the Trade Union Movement, and Cole – reluctantly – capitulated.

The effect on Bevin was permanent: it confirmed his distrust for intellectuals for good and all. His attempt to work with them in a common effort went by the board. To Cole he wrote, 'How could anyone have followed you in the last ten years?' – referring to Cole's book on the Next Ten Years. 'Really, old man, look how you have boxed the compass.' 'When we have tried to associate with the intellectuals, our experience has been that they do not stay the course very long. . . . You see, the difference between the intellectuals and the trade unions is this: You have no responsibility, you can fly off at a tangent as the wind takes you. We, however, must be consistent and we have a great amount of responsibility.'

As usual, Bevin's case was unanswerable. I was an intellectual myself, but not a middle-class one with no roots in the Movement, and I did 'stay the course' until the bitter end in 1939–40. However, I did not follow Cole again. Margaret Cole wrote me a kind, patronising letter approving my 'loyalty to the Executive' at this juncture; but I was not wholly apprized of what was afoot, and may have been wrong – as they were. Cole should have stayed with Bevin at all costs, instead of allowing himself to be pressured by the semi-Communist Postgates. I always remained on personally affectionate terms with him, and managed to persuade him not to stand for the University seat at Oxford at the election which returned Arthur Salter. I got him to back Salter, with the widest range of support against Chamberlain – anything, anything to get rid of the Old Man before too late. Ultimately it was too late.

There now came up something vastly more important: Mussolini's invasion of Abyssinia and the first crucial test of the 'National' government's sincerity in its foreign policy. Would they allow him to get away with it, or would they make effective the declared policy of Collective Security – i.e. that of the democracies – against an obvious aggressor? The Trade Union Congress was solid on the issue, led by Bevin and Citrine, who declared: 'There is only one way of dealing with a bully, and that is by force. Moral resolutions are no good.' The Government sought the support of the Labour Party, in the cause of unity in case of war.

After 1931 the 'National' government had some 550 MPs in the Commons – they could have done anything in the nation's interest – to 55 Labour MPs. All the experienced leaders of the Party were out of Parliament; the leadership fell by default to George Lansbury, a secondary figure who commanded much affection for his overflowing heart, with Attlee as Deputy Leader, an unknown quantity.

Labour's support in the interest of national unity was responsibly given by the Trade Union Congress, and by the

resolutions of the Party Executive. Lansbury as leader had
accepted this, and then his 'conscience', his emotions, got the
better of him and he went back on his undertaking – really an
old Pacifist sheep. He was supported by Stafford Cripps, no
Pacifist, but with the clever argument that the 'National'
Government, having been given the confidence of the Labour
Party, would use it for another snap election and catch the
Party at maximum disadvantage. There *was* that danger;
nevertheless it was the duty of a responsible Party to incur it if
necessary.

The issue came before the Brighton Conference, the most
dramatic in the Party's history – until 1940 – and it was debated
all day. Bevin was justly angry at Lansbury's exposing a rift in
Labour's leadership at a time of crisis – to him it was like 1931
over again with MacDonald. Bevin gave the Conference a lead
with a vehement speech which raised protests from sentimen-
talists, who thought he was brutal to Lansbury – Bevin in
effect was giving him notice. 'If he finds that he ought to take a
certain course, then his conscience should direct him as to the
course he should take. It is placing the Movement and the
Executive in an absolutely wrong position to be hawking your
conscience round from body to body to be told what you
ought to do with it.'

It was a most dramatic moment when this direct challenge
to the old man was made: I held my breath, many people were
shocked by Bevin's words. But there was no getting away
from it: his argument was unanswerable. By the time he
finished the Conference did not want to hear any more
bleatings from Lansbury: he had to go. Bevin's anger was
directed no less at Stafford Cripps; and in his own defence he
could argue, 'the great crime of Ramsay MacDonald was that
he never called in his Party; and the crime of these people is
that they have sown discord at the very moment when
candidates want unity to face an election.'

For, of course, Baldwin – a party-politician before anything
– having got the green light from the Labour Party took the
opportunity to catch it out, as Cripps had foretold. The Tories
won another disproportionate majority – some 450 seats to
Labour's 155. L. S. Amery was a Conservative figure whom
the Old Men kept out during the whole of that decade, because

he consistently opposed Appeasing the dictators. He admitted to me that the Election of 1935 was a deception.

Baldwin's government put up a half-hearted token resistance to Mussolini, while privately determined not to topple him over. Hitler immediately drew the conclusion as to what he could get away with, and in 1936 militarised the Rhineland. He was thereupon allowed to get away with that and the aggressions that followed: Austria, then Czecho-Slovakia, which overturned the whole balance of power in Europe. – Until, eventually, it took the might of the United States and Russia to overpower Germany and save us. For – though no one states the fact – in 1940 Britain was defeated as well as France.

It was not merely the ineptitude of the British governing class during that decade, which brought this about: it was their connivance. They sold the pass because of their fear of Communism. Opposition to Communism was understandable and right enough; no one was more anti-Communist than Churchill. But he had the strategic sense to see that the immediate threat came from Germany – Soviet Russia was no danger in the Thirties. We should in fact have joined with her in containing Hitler's Germany, as Churchill thought. Then, as he also thought – he always called the Second German War the 'Unnecessary War' – Hitler would have been unable to break out: the abscess would have burst inside.

In 1940 Labour joined up with Churchill to save the country. He made Bevin Minister of Labour and National Service, and from that moment his enormous career became part of the history of Britain. The story of it is told, possibly in too much detail, in the second volume of Bullock's three-decker biography (two volumes would have been enough). Party politics were over 'for the duration', and the Minister passed out of my ken. I have to offer no more than what those who worked with him have told me, though I did see him occasionally in London and he told me a thing or two in chats with him – I noted them for the record.

Briefly, what Bevin did in 1940–5 was a tremendous job: he re-created the Ministry of Labour to organise bit by bit the whole man-power and woman-power of Britain for the war effort. He did it by his own principle of 'Voluntaryism', as he called it clumsily, against all those, like Beveridge, who wanted industrial conscription. Bevin knew better. Paradoxically this great Trade Union boss was more of a democrat: instinct and experience told him that he would get better results from the workers if he brought them willingly into the war effort, consulted them, kept touch with them, journeyed round over war-scarred Britain, gained their confidence and shared with them what was involved. He was much criticised in Parliament – and always resented criticism personally, especially ill-informed criticism. He was more in touch with the working class, belonged to it, and spoke their language. (His forceful, ungrammatical way of speaking, dropped h's and all, were an advantage in talking to the men in the works: he was one of them.)

His technique worked, and he gradually won his battle. He would content himself with 80 per cent of what he wanted, and at the next opportunity slip in the remaining 20 per cent. He was full of ideas, his civil servants realised that he had more than anybody, and *knew* more of the subject – he had been in it all his life. They too rallied to him with enthusiasm, as later at the Foreign Office, where the eminent civil servants were grateful for a Minister who knew his own mind.

An important point that is overlooked is that Bevin was always a social reformer. Educationally he had had no chances at all – so he was keen on raising the school-leaving age. In his colossal task of organising the whole of British humanity to fight the evil thing – in Germany they did not make use of woman-power to the same extent and the German people fed well enough by starving the rest of Europe – Bevin kept working-class conditions in the front of his mind, food and health, hours and wages, and housing as far as possible in all the destruction going on from the German mania. (Once, he let out that he really hated the Germans – understandably – but that he strove to keep an impartial judgment.)

Bevin had always been concerned about the health and well-being of his men. He once told me that 'his' London bus-drivers had a high incidence of duodenal ulcer (no doubt from strain, irregular meals, stooping over their steering-wheels), and that he had got his Transport Union to vote a considerable sum to the Manor Road (Trade Union) Hospital for research into the causes and conditions of duodenal and gastric ulcers. I noted then how characteristically imaginative of him.

As Minister of Labour his most strenuous battle was with Beaverbrook as Minister of Aircraft Production, who wanted priority for aircraft and, even after he had achieved his targets, pushed to extend his empire at the expense of other urgent necessities. The hostility between the two is well known; Bevin himself told me that Beaverbrook exerted himself all he could to get him out of the government. The irresponsibility of that, and at such a time! Bevin, with the support of the Labour Movement was immovable: it was Beaverbrook who went. Bevin went from strength to strength; Churchill well realised his essential contribution to the war effort, his patriotism and loyalty, his indispensability, and came to lean on him, treating him with exceptional consideration as no one else.

Those two great men balanced each other, each a heavyweight in the scales: Churchill in the conduct of the war, Bevin in home affairs. It is ironical, after the vacuity of the Thirties, that the inner cabinet in charge of home affairs during the war consisted of three Labour men and one civil servant: Attlee, Bevin, Morrison and Sir John Anderson. As the end of Germany's preposterous effort approached, the government became concerned with post-war plans. Rab Butler assured me how much he learned from Bevin, serving under him on the committee to consider these questions. Butler succeeded him as Minister of Labour in Churchill's Conservative government, both men made it clear that Bevin's plans for demobilisation and re-settlement would be adhered to.

The great men who had saved Britain – Churchill, Bevin, Attlee – were all in favour of maintaining the national union until the war with Japan was over, in perhaps six months, and that that was the proper time for an Election. Those three were looking at it from the standpoint of world affairs and Britain's influence in them. The party politicians thought otherwise; and in the Labour Party Morrison and Aneurin Bevan joined forces to precipitate an Election.

From the Party point of view they were proved right: there was an immense overturn in the country, and Labour won a disproportionately large victory to compensate for the historic injustice of the Thirties. Since this is a personal account, personal recollections, I may say that Ellen Wilkinson, 'Red Ellen', told me that when she toured the Occupied Area in Germany and asked British soldiers why they had all voted Labour, they replied blissfully, 'Well, miss, – anything for a change!' In the constituency where I had worked as a candidate for so long, which now went Labour, people told me that they had voted Labour but were 'sorry for Mr Churchill' – decent of them.

Churchill was angry at what he considered the British people's ingratitude. He had, however, warned Stalin that it might happen: in Britain there were two Parties and he might be voted out. Stalin was able to assure him that 'one Party is much better.' At Potsdam Molotov complained to Attlee that he had told them he expected only a small majority. They simply could not understand the working of a democracy, were convinced that it must have been arranged – and what was the explanation? (Like Talleyrand at the Congress of Vienna, when the Russian ambassador died: 'Dear me, I wonder what was his motive?') Churchill met his Conservative Ministers with only one consoling thought: Bevin was going to be Foreign Secretary, and 'he is as firm as a rock.'

Bevin himself wanted, and expected, to be Chancellor of the Exchequer; after his long and formative experience with the Macmillan Committee he considered that he knew 'all about' economic and financial questions. And indeed his hunches, his instinctive understanding of them, were more reliable and sound than those of the economic experts, themselves always divided, often giving contradictory advice. Attlee's chief motive in preferring Bevin to the Foreign Office was that he would be firm as a rock in dealing with the Russians – he had had a lifetime's experience in dealing with Communists and fellow-travellers.

At the Party's Victory celebration Bevin encountered Kingsley Martin, editor of the factious *New Statesman*, mouthpiece of the intellectuals: "'ullo, oogly – 'ow long before you'll be stabbin' us in the back?' It was only a matter of weeks. Malcolm Muggeridge, with his usual Christian charity, says that he could not stand Kingsley Martin's physical proximity. Myself, I could not stand his intellectual proximity. Kingsley Martin was not a bad man, nor a Communist; he was just inside-out: whatever his own country did was always wrong, the other side (usually USSR, never the USA) right; and, of course, his own Party under Bevin's leadership always wrong.

Never a good word for, or even an attempt to understand, Bevin's policy the whole time he was Foreign Secretary, and a great one. It sickened me, as it sickened George Orwell. We do not need to go into the record here: Bevin personally turned Marshall Aid – the American offer of help to Europe – into a measure for the complete economic Reconstruction of Europe. Even Molotov inclined to favour it, until Stalin brutally vetoed it. Bevin had the measure of Stalin, and was left alone in the breach to stand up to him, while the Americans still suffered from Democratic illusions about the Russians under a hopelessly ignorant Secretary of State, Byrnes. Not until President Truman himself, new to international affairs, tumbled to the facts, did they get it right.

Stalin complained that Bevin was 'no gentleman': a *petit-bourgeois* himself, he encountered a real working-class man in Bevin. Molotov – a middle-class man, cousin of the composer Scriabin (which was his own real name) – complained that Bevin did not treat Soviet representatives with proper respect. In a good humour Ernest would occasionally slap the monster on the back, though he always called him Mowlotov, even after being corrected. Privately, Ernest regarded him as a murderer, and indeed he had connived at Stalin's multiple murders – though Molotov's own wife was held under arrest for several years. What a society!

In Dean Acheson, Bevin had an opposite number in Washington worthy of himself: a great American Secretary of State. Acheson's tribute to Bevin was that he 'could lead and learn at the same time.' To Ernest the youthful-looking Dean was always 'My boy'.

The Left Intellectuals backed the Communists to win in the Civil War in Greece, and attacked Churchill, then Bevin, bitterly for their resistance. (The Americans were at sea about the issue in Greece also.) Bevin had no illusions, he knew Communists only too well, and the appalling massacres they were perpetrating in Greece (this is not to deny that there were massacres on the other side too). What the Left Intellectuals did not know was that Stalin himself had given over the

Communists in Greece. An utter realist, he had made a deal with Churchill as to respective spheres: Roumania and Bulgaria the Russian sphere, Greece that of the West. Loyal to the agreement, Stalin left the Communists in Greece to their fate.

Their endless nagging abuse of Bevin merely confirmed his distrust of intellectuals. A propos of Dick Crossman, to whom he had given his chances on a Palestinian Commission – during which he crossed sides – Bevin said that he wouldn't have university men in the Cabinet: 'you can't trust 'em.' Loyalty was a keynote of his nature – loyalty and responsibility. Though Attlee was not his creation as Party Leader – as I used to think – Bevin came to appreciate from working with him his exceptional qualities.

These were not obvious to the world outside, for Attlee would never push himself or put himself across: extraordinarily selfless for a politician. In consequence there were several attempts to replace him. Morrison always thought that he ought to be Leader, and several times tried to nudge Clem out. Actually, Attlee did not like Morrison; he liked Aneurin Bevan better, though he gave so much trouble. Nye, as a complete Celt, had a warm, lovable personality. Morrison was the Party's best tactician; Bevin did not appreciate this, he considered Morrison an intriguer. I am bound to own that, though I admire Bevin more, he was unfair to Morrison. He would never serve in government under Morrison, and that effectively excluded him from the leadership. Herbert could never reconcile himself to this and, for all his splendid career of achievement, died a disappointed man – as most politicians do.

There was a funny scene when Cripps and Dalton joined forces to lever Attlee out and get Bevin to take his place. One of them put it to the lumbering old fellow getting out of his car in Downing Street – by this time eyes and face twitching with overwork and strain: 'No. I'm stickin' with little Clem.' When I had a chat with him about this time at the Garrick Club, of which he enjoyed being a member and where he used to lunch companionably, he told me that he hadn't been to bed before 2 a.m. for years. By that time he looked it.

An essentially constructive mind, a builder, Bevin was

often angry at the frustrations and abortiveness of international relations. When one reads Bullock's detailed third volume, devoted to Bevin's five years as Foreign Secretary, 1945–50, one is appalled by the complexity of the events Bevin had to deal with – a world smashed-up by the German mania (Tacitus knew it, *furor teutonicus*) – and the weak hand he had to play. He made the most of it: no-one could have done more, not even Churchill as much, in the conditions that prevailed. As an historian I doubt if any Foreign Secretary before him ever had to operate under such difficulties. For his achievement consult that volume: here I confine myself to my last glimpses of him. In the early complications of the Palestinian issue, he told me that he was within an ace of clinching an agreement between Jews and Arabs, had in fact an understanding with the US State Department, when it was thrown over by Truman, who had an election to consider in New York with its large Jewish electorate. Such are the amenities of politics.

Bevin made a great Foreign Secretary – he grew to that job and had an instinctive grasp of international affairs, as I am afraid my friend, Herbert Morrison, showed that he had not, when he insisted on succeeding Bevin. As with Attlee himself, the extraordinary thing about Bevin was his capacity for growth. His lifelong experience as a Trade Unionist had made him a formidable negotiator; and the international contacts of Trade Unionism, the conferences, had initiated him into world affairs. And he had travelled. Morrison suffered from the disadvantage of lack of education. I knew him better than I did Bevin. It was pathetic that, when Morrison was Foreign Secretary, he was trying to learn French. Ernie would have known better than to try; he had the instinct and the knack for foreign affairs, and the decision. No wonder his officials adored him; one of them described him to me, squaring himself up: 'I won't 'ave it.'

All the same, though Bevin spoke freely and unreservedly to me, one had no sense of intimacy with him. I was never close to him. Few people were. Lord Bullock sums up fairly, 'Even those who agreed with him . . . often found him difficult to approach. He was reserved in private life, suspicious and slow to give his trust or admit anyone as a friend. His ability, his strength of character and determination were obvious and admitted; but he was respected or feared rather than loved, and his position in the Labour Movement, although powerful, left him personally isolated.' I am afraid that he had not the upper-class ethical high-mindedness of Attlee; he was working-class, and apt to be vindictive.

Then, too, 'like Churchill, Bevin enjoyed being a Minister and exercising power with that uninhibited enjoyment which shocked the conventional but was one of the hallmarks of both men's strength.' Why should it be inhibited? Why should the dull and conventional set standards for remarkable people? Practically all remarkable people have a strong ego, the source of their strength. Attlee wrote of Bevin, 'like Stafford Cripps he was a tremendous egotist – Ernest having the egotism of the artist, Stafford the egotism of the altruist.' And then, 'Ernest looked, and indeed was, the embodiment of common sense. Yet I have never met a man in politics with as much imagination as he had, with the exception of Winston.'

Though we all admired him, Bevin did not have a personal following, as Morrison had, and even Dalton, both of whom did their best to encourage young recruits to the Movement. I recall traipsing round the China Clay area in Cornwall as a candidate, with Bevin speaking; but he was there as a Trade Unionist, not as a Labour Party politician, and I do not suppose that he was interested in my candidature (or anybody else's). When I told him some years later that I was giving it up, all he said was, 'Get another constituency.'

By that time I had had enough – or, rather, too much. All the same, as I go over the ground at home today I often think of that great lumbering figure, who became a statesman on the stage of world affairs, coming down to speak to the men in the works, at a street corner, or at the cross-roads, when only half-a-dozen would turn up to hear him in those days, the paralysis of the Thirties over all the land.

4

C. R. Attlee

Attlee has this in common with President Truman that he turns out to have been a much bigger man historically than anyone realised at the time. Of course each of them attained the summit of power to become leader of his nation, as Prime Minister and President respectively; but this was largely by accident – politics is full of accidents – and no-one expected it. Truman did not want to become President of the United States; he was perfectly content to be Senator for Missouri; and Attlee can hardly have expected – perhaps hardly wanted – to become Prime Minister of Great Britain.

Each of them proved himself a greater man in office, and paradoxically each has reached a higher pinnacle of estimation after his death. This is not the usual way with political figures, let alone ordinary politicians. A famous tag of Tacitus may be applied in reverse. A Roman who everybody thought capable of ruling before he came to the job was found to be no good at it: *capax imperii nisi imperasset*. With Truman and Attlee, no-one would have thought beforehand that they would prove so good at it – and now, we know, even better. In fact they grew with the job, coping with events increased their capacity to deal with them. As Churchill put it, in his own way, when someone remarked how much Attlee had developed: 'If you take a wasp and feed it on royal honey, in time it becomes a queen-bee.' This points the contrast with his earlier remark, when someone defended Attlee as a 'modest man', 'He has plenty to be modest about.' Churchill himself was far from modest: why should he be?

Even at the end of Attlee's life – with an historic career behind him and all the events of history into which he had entered – his estimate of himself was absurdly modest. He had got a Second Class in the History School – appropriately awarded, by my old friend Sir Charles Grant Robertson of All Souls. If he had got a First, he would have stayed up at Oxford and tried to become a Fellow of a College. 'I've no regrets, but in fact it has been the second-best thing', he said to an interviewer. 'If I could have chosen to be anything in those days I'd have become a Fellow of Univ.' It was an extraordinary summing up. He was blissfully happy at University College, across the High Street from All Souls; his second year there was the happiest in his life – though he made no impression as an undergraduate, just a quiet, good sort of fellow, whose only prize was for playing billiards.

He remained always loyal to Oxford and loved coming down for a break from the unceasing grind of politics – for he was always a conscientious hard worker. Thus it was at Oxford that I mostly saw him to speak to, a man of few words; I had glimpses of him publicly at Labour Party Conferences, and once or twice he came down to Cornwall to speak for me during the ghastly Thirties when I was the Labour candidate for Penryn and Falmouth. It was an uphill struggle, though the decade of work I put into it (not entirely wasted, for I learned a good deal about politics and people in the course of it) turned it into a Labour seat in 1945. Clem's brother, Tom, lived in the constituency at Perranarworthal. He took no active part in politics but dedicated himself to the W.E.A. (Workers' Educational Association); however, his correspondence with Clem kept his brother apprised of affairs in Cornwall.

It is typical that I cannot remember when I first set eyes on Attlee, for his was an appearance so unstriking as to be almost invisible. Most leaders stand out by their appearance: Ernest Bevin, that huge bulk, once seen never forgotten; Ramsay MacDonald, with handsome looks, mop of waving hair and glowing eyes; George Lansbury, with old-fashioned ginger mutton-chops and Cockney accent, like a Victorian cabman; Philip Snowden, crippled, with narrow, wizened face, marked by pain, sharp chin and hissing s's, with a sudden sweet wintry smile; Mussolini, with the heavy ill-shaven jowl and bald scalp of a convict; Bukharin, copper-red beard. (I never saw Hitler with his mesmeric eyes.) Attlee looked like the Average Man and merged with the background.

One used to see him, one of many on the platform at Party Conferences, smoking his pipe and doodling, hardly ever looking up or listening to the waffle poured forth on such occasions. But, when Ernest Bevin spoke, Clem woke up and was all attention; for Bevin was powerful horse-sense incarnate, and he, with Walter Citrine, another commonsense man, commanded the Trade Union block-vote which held the majority and decided issues. I never heard Bevin speak but I felt it was self-evidently right.

The catastrophic Election of 1931 was decisive for Attlee. Labour was deserted by its leaders – MacDonald, who certainly had charisma; Snowden, generally respected; Jimmy Thomas, the Railwaymen's leader, un-admirable but popular (even with King George V: their language had much in common. 'Your Majesty, I've got an 'orrible 'eadache.' 'Take a couple of aspirates, Mr Thomas.' I do not believe this story: George V would not have known what an aspirate was). The 'National' Government got 550 MPs behind it; Labour's representation in Parliament was reduced by the panic to some 55. The consequences were disastrous. The 'National' government took every wrong course: contraction of social services, increase of unemployment, instead of expansion; severe deflation when a dose of moderate inflation would then have been the right course; a ruinous foreign policy that enabled first Mussolini to get away with aggression, then Hitler following his example and taking the measure of the nerveless lot he was confronted with. Attlee condemns the record wholly and justly in his autobiography, *As It Happened.*

The Parliamentary consequences were hardly less deleterious. The Panic Election of 1931 repeated that of 1924, when the Labour Party was framed by the Red Letter scare. A very young man then, I was astonished that people could be such fools as to be taken in so easily. But again in 1931 – with a mere rump of an Opposition of 55, this unbalanced the working of Parliamentary institutions, and confirmed distrust throughout the Labour Movement. Baldwin, the most powerful man in British politics from 1924 to 1937, claimed that he encouraged the maturing of the Labour Party towards responsibility. In fact, the sequence of fraud Elections, 1924, 1931, 1935, which enabled the Tory Party to hold power through most of the period between the wars, gravely under-mined the sense of responsibility and increased distrust of whatever came from the upper classes – even when they were right, as they were (belatedly) over Re-armament. (Neville Chamberlain was mainly responsible for holding it up.)

George Lansbury, a secondary figure in the Labour Party, became Leader of the Opposition in these disheartening circumstances. Major Attlee, a quite unknown quantity, became Deputy Leader and worked doubly hard to cover all the subjects left bare, unprovided of any qualified speakers – they were all out of Parliament. It was this accident that gave Attlee his historic opportunity, and he conscientiously made the most of it. A naturally laconic man, he covered more columns of Hansard in those depressing years than anyone.

In the country at large the Party needed pulling together, re-organising from top to bottom by a first-rate administrator. Herbert Morrison was just the man for that job, when Arthur Henderson stepped down as Treasurer, the key post in the structure – as Morrison showed when Labour won the London County Council and he gave it efficient and inspiring leadership. (I recruited Douglas Jay's wife at this juncture for social services on the L.C.C., to which she devoted years of work.)

Morrison could have done much the same for the Labour Party's organisation in the country. Careful steps were taken to see that he did not get the chance. He was the leader of the constituency parties, i.e. the political wing of the Movement, in which I was his convinced supporter. He was opposed by the Trade Unions, which were determined to hold up his advance; and at the Leicester Party Conference, where I was a delegate, I watched the manoeuvre with a sickening heart.

Before it I had gone over from Oxford to Inkpen to urge Hugh Dalton to back Morrison for Treasurer. To my astonishment Dalton declared himself against – when he must have known that Morrison was the best man for the job. Much disheartened, I privately concluded that Dalton was being careful to keep in step with the Trade Unions, especially with Ernest Bevin, Morrison's inveterate enemy. At Leicester the manoeuvre was worked. The motion brought forward was drafted to exclude anyone of Cabinet stature from being Treasurer – quite obviously designed to exclude Morrison. Laski, popular as a speaker but a light-weight politically, of no judgment, was brought in to speak for the motion; naif as he was, he may not have realised who was pulling the strings. I watched Morrison, white with suppressed anger at the game being played to exclude him. The Party went without the re-organisation it so badly needed, stumbling on as inefficiently as before. The game of 'making bricks without straw' I used to call it biblically, more and more sickened as I watched it.

Attlee had nothing to do with these manoeuvres: he was not that sort of man. Altogether he put in fourteen years of solid good work in the East End, at social services and then administration as Mayor of Limehouse, for which he was elected MP. So that he was a London figure, hardly known in the country at large. As his official biographer (my early protégé), Kenneth Harris, says: 'Few people thought much about Attlee at all.' He was almost H. G. Wells's 'Invisible Man'.

Another accident, or chapter of accidents, made him the Party's Leader. No-one expected it. At the Brighton Party Conference the overriding issue was Mussolini's invasion of Abyssinia: should Labour support the National Government in a showdown with Mussolini, the threat of armed intervention if necessary? The responsible elements in the Party – as against the lunatic fringe of pacifists and cranks – brought the Conference round to support a direct confrontation with Mussolini, if it came about. What gave serious trouble was that the Party's leader, George Lansbury, was a declared Pacifist, which played straight into Mussolini's hand, as it did Hitler's.

Attlee himself says the last word on this issue: 'Socialist pacifism was a product of the optimistic Victorian era when the British Navy ruled the seas and when the idea of a world war seemed remote. Liberals and socialists held to this idea.' Again, on the general issue so much debated today in connexion with Nuclear Disarmament: 'Non-resistance is not a political attitude: it is a personal attitude. I do not believe it is a possible policy for people with responsibility.' This is put characteristically – not at all controversially, but unanswerably. However much one might wish to be an absolute pacifist, in an ideal world – in the real world, with human beings as they are, it is not practical politics; i.e. as Attlee says, it is an individual attitude, not a political one – really not relevant to politics.

This was what Ernest Bevin meant when he challenged Lansbury's conduct as Party Leader. The conference overwhelmingly supported Bevin; Lansbury resigned and Attlee was elected Leader, again unexpectedly. We of the constituency parties, the political wing, all wanted Morrison. So now did Dalton, too late: he regarded Attlee's election as 'a wretched disheartening result! And a little mouse shall lead them.' Bevin wanted Arthur Greenwood, a good-hearted fellow, but too easy-going. It was the MPs in Parliament, mostly Trade Unionists, who had seen Attlee's day-by-day devotion to his work there, who made him Leader.

That evening I spent mostly alone with him in our hotel. I was far from enthusiastic, all my hopes had been for Morrison. Attlee sat there glumly smoking his pipe and said practically nothing. I thought that he had plenty to worry about; now I realise that he was a great one for not taking his hurdles till he came to them.

Thereupon Stafford Cripps's cynical expectation of the National Government was fulfilled: having been given the trust of the Labour Movement to do justice on Mussolini, Baldwin took the chance to declare a snap election and catch out the Labour Party yet again. The Election of 1935 was just as fraudulent – as a leading Conservative, Leo Amery, admitted to me. The Labour Party returned only 155 MPs; the 'National' Government commanded an overwhelming majority and could have led the nation in accordance with its interests and those of the other European democracies. Instead, it betrayed both, beginning with Italy, continuing with Spain and Hitler's Germany.

Its inner guiding line was, quite simply, anti-Communism, for which it followed what it took to be its class interests, and sacrificed Britain's. It put up a token show against Mussolini, while anxious not to topple him over. His Abyssinian war could have been easily stopped by sinking a ship in the Suez

Canal, then under British control. When this point was put by Sir Reginald Coupland at All Souls to Sir John Simon, then Foreign Secretary, Simon replied, 'But that means Mussolini would fall!' This gives their game away. Attlee knew Simon well – he had served for months with him on drafting a constitution for India (whence Attlee learned much about India for himself). He later summed him up: 'Simon was a lawyer – justify anything, believed in nothing.'

The next crisis that came up was the Abdication of King Edward VIII in 1936. Here the Parliamentary Labour Party, informed of the facts of the case by Baldwin, were in agreement with him and his government. Attlee pays this Old Man of the Sea a generous tribute for the way in which he handled the awkward affair. 'The Party – with the exception of a few of the intelligentsia who can be trusted to take the wrong view on any subject – were in agreement with the views I expressed.'

This was one for the likes of me and my (then) younger generation, who were not informed of the facts, who did not take an old-fashioned moralistic view of the matter and were inclined to think of Baldwin, Archbishop Lang and Co as humbugs. I freely admit now that I was wrong; but my attitude was not a sentimental one. I had no sympathy for Edward VIII and Mrs Simpson; my motivation was political. – Anything, anything at all to get rid of the paralytic Old Men of the 'National' Government, Baldwin, Chamberlain, Simon, Sam Hoare, the lot. This was Churchill's motive too, not simply emotional loyalty to an unsuitable monarch. They, however, stuck to power; Churchill, and the Labour Party, *out*, until in 1940 it was virtually too late.

Hitler's conquest of Western Europe was the culmination of seven years of Appeasement – not even then did the architect of it lose the support of that unspeakable House of Commons, where he still had a majority. Enough of them however deserted him to demand a real national union at the crisis of our fate. The Labour Party would never serve under Chamberlain after the experiences of the Thirties. But who was to lead the nation? The King apparently favoured Halifax, as many Labour people did because of his record in India. Once more we were wrong, and Attlee was right.

He favoured Churchill – as Churchill himself did. The men both on the Left and on the Right, who had been kept out during that dreary decade – Churchill, Eden, Attlee, Bevin, Morrison – came together to save the nation. Attlee became Deputy Prime Minister. During the First German War he had served as an officer in Gallipoli, and was always convinced that Churchill was right over the Dardanelles Campaign – that it was only by accident that it did not succeed, as it should have done. This made for an unspoken bond of understanding between the two. Attlee had been a good officer; a Public School boy, he had enjoyed the discipline and his O.T.C. training. So that he had – unlike most Labour people – a natural habit of command. This is an important clue to his success as leader, presiding over the snakepit of the Labour Party for so many years, when no-one else could have done. This clue most people missed, and wondered how he managed to hold on, when several times challenged. Again, in government, it was important that he was a member of the governing class (as a child he had succeeded to young Winston Churchill's governess).

I once asked Lord Strang of the Foreign Office how Attlee compared as an administrator with Chamberlain, whose chief claim was that he was a methodical, orderly administrator, unlike the indolent Baldwin. Strang answered that Chamberlain was not in the same class: Attlee had a natural instinct for running the machine of government. Montgomery regarded Attlee as far superior to Churchill as chairman of the Cabinet – a man of genius, Churchill had too many ideas and talked too much. And, as Lloyd George noted, Attlee had much safer judgment.

All this was invisible to us. Attlee remained a mole in the background – actually an indispensable link in the machine – though he had none of the magic of Churchill's oratory or was capable of his inspiration. So we continued to underestimate him. I remember a meeting in my rooms at All Souls, where I had succeeded G. D. H. Cole for a time in running his socialist group, the 'pink dons'. Attlee came down, sat with the others on the floor of the crowded room, and never uttered a word – he might as well not have been there. I remember thinking, suppose if Hitler's Deputy, Göring, were here, he would make his presence felt all right!

It was a defect in a political leader to have so little presence, and no charisma at all. MacDonald had had too much, and in Labour's reaction to him in 1931 it was a commendation of Attlee that he had no 'side'. In fact he disliked any 'side' in people, and did not care for that element in Churchill, an essential part of his dramatic personality and of his appeal to the people. On the other hand, it was thus that Attlee conserved his energy and never wasted a word. Though a wiry man, he was not strong physically, and led a controlled, disciplined life – with the bonus of a happy marriage and family background, happy and contented at his Public School (unlike so many rebels who came over to the Left in consequence). Thus he was an exceptionally well-balanced man, no 'personality' troubles; hence his extraordinarily trustworthy judgment (though even he was belated about Re-armament, while Dalton was right).

Attlee had a dislike of volatile intellectuals, like Harold Laski or Dick Crossman. His public rebuke to Laski, with his itch for the limelight, is well known: 'A period of silence from you will be welcome.' After which Laski curled up and eventually faded out. Attlee put paid to Laski's prolific outpourings on politics with a quiet phrase to me: 'He never did get the hang of it.'

Crossman, who once hoped to succeed Laski at the L.S.E., was a more serious case. Actually the Attlees had been friends with his parents. Dick's Achilles' heel was that he had a German grandmother: Richard Pares, who had known him from Winchester days, used to say that his trouble was that he was just a German. He had their daemonic energy and, just like them, no sense of direction: he spun round like a top. Hence Maurice Bowra's soubriquet, 'Double-Crossman' – unfair, it was just that Dick charged round and was liable to change horses in mid-stream. When Hitler came to power, Crossman said to me that National Socialism meant socialism and that Hitler would bring it into being. What judgment! – I was furious with him. At Attlee's College Dick defended Hitler at high-table: 'At least he is sincere.' On one occasion Crossman treated Attlee to a twenty-minute long tirade about foreign policy – at the end of which Attlee said, not unkindly,

'Dick, how's your mother?' He had simply not wasted time listening to it. Another time Dick caught Attlee in the Smoking Room of the House of Commons, and told him that he thought that the Party's latest statement on foreign policy was a very good one. 'And, do you know', Dick reported to Douglas Jay, 'he never said anything at all! I wondered whether he had heard me; so I said, "Mr Attlee, I thought that the Party's statement on foreign policy was very good." And all he said was, "Did you?" '

I hope this gives the reader an idea of what Attlee was like to know – not very encouraging. This kind of thing meant that Crossman hadn't a good word to say for him. Neither had G. D. H. Cole, whom Attlee described as a 'perpetual undergraduate'. Of Stafford Cripps, he is 'no judge of politics' – quite right, as usual. Hugh Dalton slipped up as Chancellor of the Exchequer, by imparting to a journalist on the way into the House to make his Budget speech that there would be no rise in taxation: the news was in the City before his speech was ended. Attlee sacked him at once. Herbert Morrison told me that he was not in favour of this drastic action, but 'the Prime Minister took a different view.' Attlee on Dalton: 'He always was a loud-mouthed fellow.'

I suppose it must have been on that visit that Clem reported to brother Tom at home in Cornwall, 'I saw Rowse the other day at Oxford. He is maturing a bit, but should certainly stick to history.' This was what I was making up my mind to do; in spite of wasting time and health on being a political candidate, I had carried on with historical research and teaching, and was already writing history. In fact, nearly killing myself with overwork and overstrain. Continual ulceration had practically blocked the food passage into my stomach – peritonitis twice – critical operations (when my nurse kindly informed me after a second that she 'didn't expect to see me leave the operating table alive'). I survived; but when I had a severe haemorrhage later, my doctor ordered me to give up an active life and reconcile myself to an invalid's. So I gave up politics – and was happy ever after.

How I had hated the chore of being a political candidate, trying to open the eyes of fools to the idiocy of Chamberlain's Appeasement of Hitler! It had all ended as anyone of sense should have foreseen; but few did. In the Foreign Office itself, Cadogan who had been promoted by Chamberlain to carry out his policy in place of Vansittart: 'It has all happened as Van said it would, *and I never believed it.*' So there need be no further argy-bargy about Appeasement: it was hopeless from the start. The only correct policy was the historic one of a Grand Alliance against the overwhelming threat to us and everybody else which Germany constituted, both the Kaiser's and Hitler's. This both Churchill and Attlee understood; I had been arguing for it, writing for it – all in vain – ever since Hitler came into power in 1933.

Attlee, as a historian, understood clearly and simply who had been responsible for 1914, as Churchill did – another historian. Attlee wrote, 'One can see now that the German and Austrian ruling classes, by their ill-considered action in making war, destroyed the class society which gave them their privileged position'. Few people understood the sinister dialectic between Germany's backward social structure and the threatening policy of her dominant classes: they meant war. Then, as Henry James despairingly said, 'Nobody ever understands *any*thing.' I had had enough, and was willing, though sad, to give up.

In any case, when the nation was fighting for its life, there was no point in party politics any more: it was a question of survival. In a nuclear world, dominated by the appalling danger of the spread of nuclear armaments – the black cloud over all our lives – I have ceased to be interested in mere party divisions, between Labour and Conservative, Democrat and Republican, between Britain and the United States: we are all involved in the human tragedy together.

Up to the turning point of the Second German War and the formation of Churchill's government backed by the whole Labour Movement, I had been a straight Labour Party man, no fringe-man like so many fellow intellectuals, let alone joining the Communist Party as many of them were such idiots as to do, and later repent. Strictly speaking, I was a follower of Herbert Morrison, whom I had hoped to see Leader; I have letters from him saying how sorry he was that I was giving up. I had many twinges of heart when I went round my former constituency and ran into old supporters, particu-

larly when one of the fishermen at Mevagissey said sadly,
'You don't come to see us much now.' More than that, I had
had so much to put up with one way and another, that I turned
my back on Cornwall: they had had their chance: they would
hear no more from me for the next twenty years. Their loss
rather than mine.

Active politics being blessedly over – which I made absolute,
with the absolutism of my temperament – I nevertheless kept
in some touch with the friends with whom I had had so many
contacts over those wasted years. (I hated that decade so much
that I have written little about it in all my writings; however,
the evidences remain *pour servir à l'histoire*, as the phrase has it.)
Here is a letter from Attlee, from 11 Downing Street, 15
September 1941: 'Thank you for your admirable suggestion of
the O.M. for Beatrice Webb. My general rule is not to
recommend for any honours except those which, like Privy
Councillorships, are part of our Parliamentary tradition; but
this is certainly a justifiable exception. I am, therefore, mentioning the matter to the Prime Minister.' A couple of years
later Churchill gave the O.M. to Sidney Webb; he should have
given it to Beatrice, the most remarkable woman of the time.
But Winston was always rather anti-feminist. Earlier, when
the formidable Beatrice had planned to make him her instru-
ment for the expansion of the social services, he 'declined to be
shut up in a soup-kitchen with Mrs Sidney Webb.' I still think
my suggestion was a right one; so evidently did Attlee.
    Next year he wrote of *A Cornish Childhood*, 'It seems to me a
most happy conception to give at the same time a picture of
past Cornwall and an impression of the journey from Tre-
gonissey to All Souls, which is itself a symbol of the new age.'
Actually, that was the way the book had begun – not as an
autobiography, but as a picture of the life of the village before I
was born, from what my father and mother and old great-
uncle had told me; I remember feeling rather self-conscious
when, halfway through, I realised that I had to begin on
myself. Attlee went on, 'It makes one feel a bit old, for your
early days at school coincide with my beginnings in the
Labour Movement. I can never escape from the Victorian era
in which I grew up – an era which, in the light of the last thirty

years, had some points of vantage in the way of tranquillity.'

That was saying a lot for him, always laconic, and also characteristically sober. What a blissful era of security the Victorian age was! We shall never see the like again. Attlee inherited, and carried on into a hideous world the good standards, the devotion to duty and public service, the incorruptible uprightness and honour, of that better age.

Myself, I was now immersed in the still more inspiring Elizabethan age, when we were a small 'people such as mend upon the world' (Shakespeare): we were then going up in the world, at the beginning of that wonderful historic arc of achievement, which has left its traces across the oceans, though we, alas, witness its end. I put together a harmless little book, *An Elizabethan Garland*, to celebrate the coronation of Elizabeth II. Attlee wrote, 'I started reading it in the train this morning and much enjoyed it. I liked the chapter on Coronations. I wonder what kind of celebrations they had in the country in Elizabeth's reign. The street parties were a great feature in London this time. I wonder what the Elizabethans did in the little towns and villages?'

The answer to that was – nothing. A Tudor coronation was a London and Westminster affair, with a procession from the Tower to Whitehall the day before. There grew up spontaneously the custom of celebrating the Queen's Accession day, 17 November, with bell-ringing all over the country, for a century or more, so great was her fame.

In November 1951 Attlee reported to Tom, 'I have read Rowse's last book – very good in parts, with curious little strokes of egotism coming in.' This would have been *The England of Elizabeth*. I don't in the least mind that comment. He wasn't a writer and wouldn't know that a writer's ego is where he gets his inspiration from. The little strokes are there to keep the reader on his toes – irritation, better than sending him to sleep. If they were not there I should deliberately put them in. Nothing of that in Attlee's own writing, like a civil servant's. He was a dull writer, and not inspired as a speaker, unlike Churchill – most egoistic of men, fortunately.

Attlee was a quick and widely read reader, especially of history. At Oxford he had taken the Renaissance as his Special Subject in the History School. Appropriately, in taking pos-

session of 10 Downing Street and Chequers, he quoted Leo
X's 'Now that we have the Papacy, let us enjoy it.' And, with
all the worries of politics, he never lost a night's sleep over
them.

One day after a crucial division in the Parliamentary Labour
Party over the Government's Re-armament programme during the first phase of the Cold War, he presided over a debate
which was a very close-run thing and would have overthrown
his leadership if it had gone against him. His motion was
carried by only two or three votes. At once he snapped, 'The
motion's carried – meeting's closed.' Not a moment allowed
for reconsideration or recrimination. Douglas Jay caught up
with him hurrying down the corridor. Not a word about the
critical meeting, the narrow shave he had had. All he said was:
'My wife has had a small sum of money left her. How would
you advise me to invest it?'

I find, in my immense Archive, a last letter from him in
retirement, from Cherry Cottage, his home at Great Mis-
senden, in 1958. 'Thank you so much for sending me your
book on the Churchills with such a charming inscription. I
always think it is interesting where an old stock suddenly
burgeons with brilliant blossom. There is a parallel case in the
Cecils, where after the first two nothing happens until we have
the old Marquis; and in the next generation what the present
Salisbury once described to me as his harlequin set of uncles;
and of course himself and David. I suppose a geneticist cannot
throw any light on the problem, any more than they can
explain the flowering of genius anywhere. I am reading the
book with much delight here in bed, but I expect to be out and
about by the end of the week.'

During the intervals I had met and chatted with him several
times, usually on his visits to Oxford, and each time there was
some memorable point in the exchange. One night we were
talking about Labour Party figures, in the candlelight over
dessert at All Souls. I had been amused by old Trade Unionist
Tomlinson, whom Attlee had made Minister of Education,
speaking at a Foyle's Literary Luncheon: ' 'amlet – ah've always
liked 'amlet.' I thought this rather good from a Minister of
Education. Attlee said, 'I always like to hear what Tomlinson

has to say.' No doubt he was right: he would get plain, working-class commonsense from old George – Attlee didn't want to hear what the Crossmans had to say.

Curiously enough he was more sympathetic to Aneurin Bevan than he was to Morrison. Attlee wished that Aneurin Bevan could have made a Leader of the Labour Movement: he had the gifts, if it had not been for his irresponsibility and fatal lack of judgment. It was Aneurin, seconded by Harold Wilson, who brought down Attlee's second administration, in 1951. This had very ill consequences. If Attlee had been there, there would have been no Suez fiasco. He was always friendly with Eden, went into 10 Downing Street, and warned him: 'Now, Anthony – no getting caught out on a limb with the French.' This is exactly what happened: the French Prime Minister and Foreign Secretary came over and gave Eden the final push. After the collapse, Eden said to me in Cornwall that it would not have happened if Ernest Bevin had been there. I suppose he meant that Bevin would have rallied Labour behind the government. Doubtful.

I happened to be on a cruise of Lady Waverley's down the Thames on one of her husband's Port of London Authority's vessels. There in the party was Clem, just before he was due to leave for Russia with Aneurin Bevan and others in the delegation. It was obvious that he didn't want to go, but was going to keep an eye on Aneurin and prevent any mischief. An exhausting affair, for they were going across Siberia to Vladivostok, and out via Japan. I hoped that he had had proper inoculation. Yes, he had had inoculations against every sort of thing. He did not need any inoculation against Communism: he had had too much experience all along of what it was and what its leaders really were. He described Stalin, *tout court*, as a 'barbarian'. A barbarian of genius, of course, like Hitler. At the Potsdam Conference Stalin had his first glimpse of Attlee, and said, 'He doesn't look a greedy man.' A sharp insight. The same could not be said of Stalin.

In Moscow, at a reception at the British Embassy, there they were, the people involved in Stalin's crimes; Aneurin engaged in friendly talk with Malenkov, the successor, Clem planted in the middle of the room, alone, stolidly looking on the ground. Wouldn't he like to come and talk with Mr

Malenkov? Or Mr Mikoyan? Or . . . ? Clem: 'No, sick of the lot of them.' When they emerged into the light of day and civilisation, and were interviewed by the world press, Aneurin was able to enthuse about Malenkov: a most intelligent man, he was sure we could reach understanding and do business with him. When Attlee was asked for his opinion, he replied glumly, 'Very able man.' Within a matter of weeks Malenkov was out of power. It offers a typical contrast of judgment between the volatile Celt and the sobersided Englishman: Aneurin was very Welsh and Clem very English, almost to the point of caricature, reserve, shyness, understatement. However, the English are more intelligent than they pretend to be, and that takes others in.

Few other occasions do I remember. Attlee had a close understanding with Edward Bridges of All Souls, secretary to the Cabinet and Head of the Civil Service – to whom the country owes an immense debt for the maximum efficiency with which he ran the machine of government. After a hard day's work, each night he took home work till midnight for next day; every morning Cabinet business ready for decisions in order of priority. Nothing like it at Hitler's headquarters, where all depended on the inspiration of the divine Führer. Attlee persuaded Bridges to stay on after his term – he was expected to come back to All Souls as Warden. I shared rooms with him in College, and one day remarked what secrets of state he had shared; 'Yes, and they will remain in the deep freeze.' Like Attlee – and unlike Churchill – he gave away nothing.

But Bridges did describe to me Churchill's curious way of reaching a decision; he thought it must be something like that of Elizabeth I, for he would delay, and procrastinate, and hum and haw – until eventually the thing came clear to him, emerging as from a pregnancy. With Attlee, I suspect, the process was less intuitive and more rational, crisp and clean from the first. As also with President Truman (in contrast with Roosevelt), whom Churchill described as 'the man most full of decision that I have ever met.' Edward Bridges told me a remarkable dream he had, which tells its own tale as to the burden of responsibility he carried. He took over as Secretary to the Cabinet, from Hailey, under Neville Chamberlain. He dreamed that at his first Cabinet meeting a man crawled out from under the green-baize table, ran out of the door and down the stairs of 10 Downing Street. Bridges pursued him, but lost him in the street. When he came back, Chamberlain said, 'But didn't you look under the table? Hailey *always* looked under the table.'

Attlee came down to Oxford to persuade Oliver Franks to come back into government service. Franks had made a great name for himself as a recruit to the civil service, much trusted by Ernest Bevin, highly thought of by everybody, with an unrivalled gift in negotiation. After the war he came back to academic life, and was comfortably installed as Provost of Queen's, next door to All Souls. I remember this visit too, where Attlee was successful in persuading Franks to become Ambassador to the United States.

A later glimpse, on a visit to the gallery of the House of Lords, revealed the two old rivals, Attlee and Morrison, retired from the hurly-burly of the Commons, to the plush dignity of the Upper Chamber. There they were, lounging side by side, feet up on the bench, nothing to do. What a life! Last glimpse of all was in the course of some publishing occasion, at the Tower of London: there was, unexpectedly, Clem, old and looking frail, taking the opportunity to sit down, but alert and keeping his interest in what was going on, to the end. We exchanged a few words; I felt it was a kind of farewell, and in that historic place.

I hope I have given a fair, recognisable picture of this man not easy to conjure up, so little was in evidence, so much under the surface. Where bigger, bulkier men – Bevin or Churchill – provoked opposition to their ebullient personalities, Attlee threaded his way like a needle, creating the minimum of resistance. No doubt theirs were richer and more humorous natures, Aneurin Bevan's and Gaitskell's warmer and more eloquent, yet Attlee's was sharp and incisive, with an edge of wit. Of Chamberlain he said that, where Baldwin gave the House of Commons an impression of being in touch with world affairs, with Chamberlain their minds were tuned in to the Midland Regional. This was his parallel to Churchill's funnier *mot* that Chamberlain looked at world affairs 'through the wrong end of the municipal drain-pipe.'

A deeper element in Attlee's achievement was his capacity to grow with events. This is where we had been wrong earlier to underestimate him and prefer Morrison as leader. Attlee had a capacity for growth much beyond Morrison's, as was shown when he insisted on following Bevin at the Foreign Office: 'the worst appointment I ever made', Attlee concluded.

This has become clearer than ever – since the publication of Kenneth Harris's biography, a notable contribution to the history of our time. We used to think that the dominant man in Attlee's government was Bevin: we now know, what was not apparent at the time, that Attlee was the master. He took all the major decisions as they came up himself. I once asked him in the early days of Labour rule what chance there was of planning ahead. He said, none – things kept 'boiling up' the whole time. A good thing he was a pragmatist: he met each problem as it came up; all the same, under his aegis the Welfare State came into being.

He had a vein of idealism in him; as he says in his auto-biography, *As It Happened* – a significant title – his family had a strong tradition of social service. This is the way he came to socialism, that and the reading of Ruskin. His long years of service in the East End undoubtedly determined him to do all he could to improve the lot of the poorest and lowest-paid. He only once made a public plea that they should respond with some sense of service to the community. This was rather upper-class of him; a working-class man would hardly have that idealist expectation. Try it on the highest paid (and most selfish) of the Trade Unions!

He made the big decision to hand over rule in India: whether that was an advantage to the teeming millions of peoples there I doubt, but the end of the Raj was inevitable. He made the decision for Partition between Hindu India and Moslem Pakistan, overriding Stafford Cripps who was under the influence of Congress – Nehru's – demand to keep Moslems under Congress rule. (Nehru succeeded in holding on to Moslem Kashmir, contrary to justice, humbugging the issue: hence the two or three wars since Britain left.) Congress had always played down the inveterate hatred of Moslem and

Hindu, and blamed it on Britain – no longer there to blame. Even Churchill came to accept the inevitability of the hand-over, persuaded by Attlee, so Beaverbrook told me resentfully.

When it came to the decisive issue of an independent Nuclear deterrent for Britain, Attlee again took the onus himself, without consulting either the Cabinet or Parliament in so urgent a matter that had to be kept secret. Finally, he saw to it that Hugh Gaitskell became his successor as Leader of the Labour Party, the right man for the job – his early death a grievous loss to the Party and the nation. For he too had the capacity for development, as well as absolute integrity and public spirit.

These qualities and Victorian standards in Attlee gave him his strength: it was the combination in one man in politics that made him exceptional. No-one else could have held together a government that contained the mutually exclusive Bevin and Morrison as leading members of it. For long it was unknown why Bevin went to the Foreign Office – a surprise to himself, for he had expected to be made Chancellor of the Exchequer, the field in which his interest lay. None of us knew. It eventually transpired that it was a characteristic decision of Attlee's to keep him and Morrison apart: one in home affairs, the other in foreign. It would never have done to have them competing and wrangling in the same field: it would have rent the government. Thus Attlee held the field and himself con-trolled it.

There is a charming story of the Attlees towards the end of his life. His wife – who had driven him thousands of miles electioneering in their modest car, somewhat unsteadily, but in the end not fatally – came from a Conservative family, like the Attlees themselves. (He always had the old Tory dislike of Gladstone.) 'Clem was never really a socialist, were you, darling?' she said. Clem, preoccupied with *The Times*, mumbled dissent. 'Well, not a rabid one', she said comfortably.

Clem was a good socialist, and a kind, civilised man – unlike his German and Russian contemporaries, who ruined the world we live in.

5

Lionel Curtis: 'The Prophet'

Of all the eminent men who foregathered at All Souls in the old days – Viceroys of India, Governors-General of Dominions, archbishops, Cabinet Ministers, political figures – Lionel Curtis was perhaps the most remarkable (along with his friend there, T. E. Lawrence). Curtis was to some extent a mystery man, who deliberately chose to keep out of the limelight, while seeking to influence public affairs more effectively as an *éminence grise*. This was not only policy on his part, it became almost an affectation – when, for example, he organised a large dinner of prominent people to advance some cause he had in mind, the one person absent being himself.

His entry in *Who's Who* was similarly characteristic: it doesn't tell one who his parents were or where he was born; it doesn't give his full name, and supplies hardly any dates. All that mattered to him was 'the Cause' – the overriding Cause to which he dedicated his life, and of which he considered himself the Prophet, along with the lesser causes he took up and promoted. He might have said of himself as Napoleon did, 'J'avais le goût de la fondation, et non de la propriété.' He was a promoter, propagandist, constitution-monger, schemer, planner, founder of bodies and institutions – of which Chatham House, the Royal Institute of International Affairs, is perhaps best known.

I remember his coming back from London one evening, throwing himself down on the long bench in our smoking-room (from which they liked to think the affairs of the Empire were governed), with: 'Thank God, Chatham House is safe! I've got Abe Bailey to give it £150,000.' Curtis had a magic wand where big-minded business men were concerned – he had several of them among his submissive followers and disciples; he could do nothing with small-minded dons.

This habit of mystification means that it is hardly possible to write his biography; several people have tried their hands at it and fallen down on the job. Geoffrey Dawson – the notoriously pro-German editor of *The Times*[1] – Curtis's associate for many years from the South African war onwards, once told me that only he could write the Prophet's life. One would think him a pure innocent in the ways of life, Dawson said; not a bit of it, and he retailed an example of Curtis's technique. One follower subscribed a large sum of £25,000 for one of his causes, and was promised an honour for it. Under MacDonald the honour was not forthcoming, nor under the next Prime Minister. The poor rich man began to be restless and to complain; nevertheless, after an interval and yet another administration, it was eventually forthcoming. One element in Curtis's technique was persistence: he never gave up. A more important weapon was his personal disinterestedness: he wanted nothing for himself, and this gave him power with others. I used to think, watching him with affection (for he was also lovable), that with him absolute disinterestedness became absolute interestedness.

Again Dawson was right that, though Curtis was a Christian gentleman, one would think butter wouldn't melt in his mouth – yet he knew the shady side of public life all right, he knew the score and people's price. He told me of some disagreeable transactions regarding a Secretary of State for India and the Indian Princes. He was well informed about the financial dealings of a behind-the-scenes wheeler-dealer in these matters (knighted of course; forgotten today, but not by the historian, whose business it is to remember). He himself was not the least interested in money.

As for Lionel's innocence of the facts of life – he regarded the Johannesburg millionaires of the time of the South African war as a vicious lot. As Town Clerk there he visited the hospitals, where one woman was affected by syphilis in her eye. She had been regularly paid by one of these infected miscreants to ejaculate in her eye. And Lionel knew all about

---

[1] For him v. my *All Souls and Appeasement* (fuller version the American edition, *Appeasement: A Study in Political Decline*).

Lord Randolph Churchill, similarly infected, on his visit to South Africa in his last years, 'crawling in and out of kaffir kraals.' Thus Lionel, by no means the innocent – though a deeply good man – the innocent themselves might think.

In any case he would never write an autobiography, though I wished he would. To my mind his life was far more interesting than the 'Causes' to which he dedicated himself. To people who urged him to write his Memoirs he would reply: 'My job lies with the future, not with the past.' Portentous – he really thought of himself as a prophet; but we see that there were many things in his life that he really couldn't tell.

In his last years he did allow the early Diary he had kept to be published under the title, *With Milner in South Africa*. It turned up unexpectedly, 'and the diary records much which in fifty years had passed from my own memory.' He did not set much store by it – after all, it was the past. To a historian, however, it was the most interesting thing he ever wrote; this would be heresy to him, and I should be excommunicated for saying it – except that our relations were of mutual affection and he allowed me to be a licensed libertine, which was certainly not allowed to his disciples in the faith.

The Diary is not only a fascinating record, but one of the most revealing documents of the South African war, which has had such tragic consequences. One certainly sees the tragedy of it. But there is a great deal else with it: wisdom, insight, foresight; the charm of the handsome boyish young man the photographs show him to have been (he always retained that handsome presence, his distinction of manner, unfailing good temper in fractious circumstances); the generosity and warmth, the good fellowship and camaraderie. On top of everything else Lionel was a good scout, impossible to resist.

I laughed at myself at what happened when I determined to resist, in early days. He had a rambling thatched house beside the Cher at Old Kidlington. There was to be a Kidlington historical pageant. Alice Buchan and various others were writing scenes, and Lionel called on me to write the Elizabethan one. I was quite determined that I would not – I had so much else to do, wasn't sure that I could, etc. Then

Lionel called in Arthur Salter's brother, who was a parson out there, brought him to lunch – and of course I ended by doing what Lionel intended I should do. There it all is in print; I do not remember ever seeing the Pageant.

In addition to everything else, there has been a kind of hoodoo about a Curtis biography. Practically all his immense collection of papers went up in flames when that thatched house, Hales Croft, burned in 1933. He was stoical about that, quite unmoved by it. Dermot Morrah, of All Souls, was to have written the biography, and failed. Then somebody else. At length a woman scholar collected a great deal of material – and had her typescript, notes etc in two suit-cases stolen from her car in a London car-park. (Apparently she hadn't heard of the new social order, nor taken the proper precautions against its amenities. As if historical papers were of value to the depredators so characteristic of it! They must have been disappointed, but a loss to us.)

Though I lived for thirty years on terms of friendship and increasing affection with Lionel, and have memories and stories of him – he was an excellent raconteur, and did have a sense of humour – enough to fill a booklet, I know that I could never have written his biography. There was so much that was missing, and so much that he would not talk about – he would never betray the technique by which he gained influence with people, though I watched them fall with amusement. I realised that the South African experience, over those crucial years 1899–1909, had been the formative one in his life, had fixed him in what he regarded as his call from God – he did not bore me with it, or even attempt to. His friends of Milner's Kindergarten – no less than five of them were Fellows of All Souls – were constantly coming to and fro; so one was fairly *au fait* with that part of the story and the characters. But one knew nothing about his part in the Irish negotiations that led to the Treaty of 1922 and the setting up of the Irish Free State (that led to a breach with Kipling, who had donated a large sum for arms for Ulster). Or about Curtis's invention of Dyarchy for India, the compromise that held the field for some years, granting a measure of responsible government in the provinces while retaining authority at the centre in Delhi. Curtis would be the first person to recognise that historic compromises do not work for long: the Prophet was an Either-Or man (in Keirkegäard's terminology).

Curtis's childhood was spent at Ledbury in Herefordshire – John Masefield's home background: Lionel told me how shocked local people were by *The Widow in the Bye Street.* I suppose Curtis was born there, in 1872, his father an Evangelical hot-gospeller, whose sermons about Hell-fire made the young Lionel quake as a boy – and the Gospel influence remained with him all his life. When he came to marry, lateish, in 1920 it was to the daughter of a Devonshire parson, who exchanged her original name of Gladys for 'Patricia', a handsome piece, fine brown eyes, sexy voice, a rather heavy sense of humour. She had been his secretary. Earlier he had proposed to the eldest daughter of the great Lord Salisbury, though making it clear that marriage to her was not to interfere with his prophetic call. This was not thought good enough for a daughter of the House of Hatfield.

Like Attlee – I don't know whether they knew each other – Curtis was at the Anglo-Indian Haileybury. Then New College, where at evensong in Chapel his eyes fell on the tall upstanding Lionel ('Nel') Hichens. 'It was love at first sight' – Curtis said innocently to me, registering naughtily that one couldn't say such things nowadays. I have often wondered whether there was an unconscious homo-eroticism among Milner's Young Men, the atmosphere was so emotional, and towards the great man, a life-long bachelor until towards the end of his life. Completely repressed and virtuous, of course; though Lionel knew the facts of Public School life, 'in my time perfect sinks of iniquity'. All the same, it is clear from the Diary that Lionel loved and admired Nel Hichens, constant tributes to his charm and comradeship, the ability with which he surmounted all difficulties.

Hichens returned from South Africa to become chairman of the shipbuilding firm of Cammell, Laird and Co. He is almost the only member of the Kindergarten I never met; I regret this the more because he was a fellow Cornishman, from Falmouth. He was killed in 1940, when a bomb hit Church House, Westminster. Lionel wrote biblically of him: 'It was fitting that he should pass from the earth in a chariot of fire.' I think otherwise: one more fine fellow extinguished by the German mania that ruined our century.

Those two had had a wonderful time together in South Africa. If we can forget for a moment that the Boer War was a tragedy, and should never have happened, those young fellows had a high old time, were tested, brought to maturity, and gained large responsibilities in the course of it, and the reconstruction thereafter. Modern Johannesburg owes much to young Curtis, though he never spoke of it. His wider experience in South Africa as a whole was a formative influence upon his mind, and fixed it – the word is deliberate, he had a 'fixation' – upon imperial federation, and later 'world-federation'. It is typical that Bertrand Russell should get a Nobel Prize for his abortive campaign in that direction, while Curtis got no recognition for his – equally abortive.

Curtis's career in South Africa is part of history, and vastly more constructive than anything the useless Russell ever accomplished. I do not need to go in detail into it here. But as Town Clerk Curtis took over the direct administration of Johannesburg when it was a chaos of mine dumps and workings, shacks and slums, dotted with *nouveaux riches* properties on the margins; with no proper water supplies, drainage or sewage systems, etc. No wonder typhoid, enteric, dysentery were widespread. (Lionel's elder brother died of enteric at Ladysmith, Lionel himself contracted dysentery.)

He laid the foundations of the great modern city and brought that kind of thing to an end. On horseback he surveyed the district, following the contours and watersheds to co-ordinate an area equal to that of modern London, laid down what was to be a splendid city park, appropriated sites for schools and hospitals, and set proper municipal government going following the procedure of the London County Council. And in thirty years of constant discourse he never mentioned his extraordinary achievement as a young man!

Lionel Curtis is known as an Imperialist, but a historian should point out that he was also liberal-minded – about the blacks, for example. Indeed, that was an issue in the War itself: the Boers really believed in Biblical slavery, the British did not. John Buchan, as another young man working for Milner, held that the British were 'only just right' in the War. With the advantage of hindsight, I should say that they were 'only just wrong'. Beneath the two immovables, the Boer Kruger and the Germanic Milner, was the conflict for power. The simple fact is that the Boers, the Africaners, regarded – and regard – South Africa as *their* country (they were there before the blacks largely moved south) – and, in spite of a deplorable war, they eventually won the peace.

A considerable number of the British ended up, chivalrously – the young Churchill among them – as sympathetic to the Boers. One is struck by the wisdom and foresight of the young Curtis similarly. After his brother's death, he wrote home that 'we must think of them as given as they gave themselves that, after the War, we might have a South Africa where men have learned to bear with one another.' Alas, for his hopes! At home the Jingo *Times* was then edited by Buckle (another Fellow of All Souls); his brother, a private in South Africa, remarked, 'We who are fighting are mostly pro-Boers. The really bitter people have stayed at home to write articles.' Curtis continually inveighs against the appalling inefficiency of the military and the War Office, the criminal ineptitude of the farm-burnings, the never-to-be forgotten tragedy of the disease-ridden refugee camps.

Curtis – a high-minded Christian gentleman – wrote home with equal distaste for the behaviour of the looting soldiery, 'the sweepings of the Empire', and the Joe-Chamberlain line of *The Times*: '*The Times* seems to me to represent all that mass of respectable moneyed opinion against which Christ came to wage war.' Modern wars come about largely because of ignorance or blindness as to the intentions of the other side; here the Boers and British were equally at fault and should have known better. At home the War was popular with the mob; Curtis understood, 'about fifty years ago it was a common belief that popular government would mean the end of war.' No democratic illusions of that sort with him. Nor did he regard the idea of an 'independent United States of South Africa' as discreditable to the Dutch: 'It may ultimately be realised in the dim centuries to come.'

It has come about in this very century; for, in fact, at the Peace of Vereeniging the British capitulated to the Boers, and the ablest of the Boer leaders, Smuts, dominated the drafting of the constitution of the Union of South Africa – for which Curtis led the propaganda on the British side. In return, Britain gained South African support in the two German wars that threatened her existence; in the first, the quarter-German Milner made an inestimable contribution in the War Cabinet, as Smuts gave invaluable help and counsel in both wars. Such was the reward of politic generosity. Curtis himself brought both Smuts and Herzog to All Souls.

He saw the conflict in South Africa partly in terms of the struggle between North and South in the American Civil War. He points out at the time that Southern 'rebels' were being rounded up in Texas only quite recently. 'Had the South and Slavery prevailed, America would be a decaying nation instead of the most vigorous one in the world. English predominance in South Africa is to save it from the worst, *and that is all.*' Alas, for English hopes, once Boer predominance was re-established! Meanwhile, 'The more one hears of America the more one is inclined to think that she will eventually inherit the earth.' Curtis was writing that in 1901, at the beginning of 'the American Century': good for him.

The South African War was Kipling's apogee, the most famous writer in the world, still young – except perhaps for old Tolstoy at the opposite pole. Curtis told me that on the march they would recite 'Boots':

> We're foot-slog-slog-slog-sloggin' over Africa . . .
> Boots-boots-boots-boots-movin' up an' down again!

The Leftist poets of the Thirties talked about taking poetry to the people – can one imagine them marching to *their* over-intellectualised verse, Auden's 'Spain', for instance? Kipling didn't talk about it, he just did it.

Nor, ardent Imperialist as he was, was he without sympathy for the gallantry of the fighting Boers – many wartime poems like 'Piet' testify to it. Or there is his moving epitaph on the Boer General Cronje:

> With those that bred, with those that loosed the strife,
> He had no part whose hands were clear of gain,

But subtle, strong, and stubborn gave his life
  To a lost cause, and knew the gift was vain.
Later shall rise a people, sane and great,
  Forged in strong fires, by equal war made one;
Telling old battles over without hate –
  Not least his name shall pass from sire to son.

When Curtis accompanied Lord Milner to take possession of Pretoria, the Governor General recited the tribute to Cronje to his companions. Those were the days when the élite figures in public life could be inspired by poetry. (Curtis himself wrote not bad verse, and later gave me a little booklet of verses he had privately printed.)

He continues: 'Then we built castles on the air and on the kopje, and laid out terraces and avenues in imagination. Pretoria lay just at our feet, and we were looking right across it to the Magaliesburg.' Thus came into existence the magnificent Parliament buildings designed by Rhodes's favourite architect, Herbert Baker. The politics of it was that this was a concession to the Boers: if Johannesburg had been chosen for capital they would have regarded the government as being under the thumb of the Uitlanders.

Curtis got characteristic glimpses of Kipling, who, in February 1900, 'came into our camp at Green Point with his nose to the ground for subject matter, and examined every mortal thing from the Maxims to the officers and privates.' Curtis was capable of being critical of the much-publicised writer, who arrived at Bloemfontein, the capital of the Orange Free State, in the wake of the Army. Curtis hoped that the statue of President Brand of 1888 would make Kipling rethink his recent 'hasty' pronouncement – evidently too jingoistic for Lionel. At Cape Town Herbert Baker took him to see the beautiful house he had designed for Kipling, at Rhodes's expense, in an exquisite situation: 'Rhodes's idea was that Kipling would do his best work in such a place rather than living in an hotel.' Actually nothing stopped Kipling from writing wherever he was. A pal of Curtis introduced Kipling to 'a youthful looking commander of a flat iron called De Horsey, and shortly after he wrote "Judson of the Empire". In an abandoned tin hotel Kipling lay a little on all the beds

successively looking at the ceiling, and in the morning produced "The Ballad of the *Clampherdown*." '

Curtis was no less critical of Rhodes, whose appearance he
remarks on unfavourably, and 'how refreshing for that man of
iron will and muddled mind to blunder into a correct opinion.'
The greatest blunder of all was the Jameson Raid, which
precipitated the war. 'Jameson tried to conquer the Transvaal
with 500 men.' That affair was one of monumental ineptitude.
(My father's brother and a son, Cornish miners in Jo'burg, sat
up all night drinking whisky, waiting for the call which never
came.) In the War itself Curtis ran into a detachment of
Cornish Volunteers – I suppose miners. In later years he told
me a comic story about the mistake the military made in
arresting and imprisoning as a rebel, a fellow of the good old
Cornish name of Baragwanath (Anglice, Whitbread), which
they were convinced was Dutch.[2] Later, when the mistake
was cleared up, they had to pay the Cornishman a good sum in
compensation, I am glad to say; but I wish I could remember
the misunderstandings and complications of the story before
this happy consummation was reached.

Naturally Rhodes's Will and his imaginative conception of
Rhodes Scholarships, with the foundation of the Trust, more
than doubled the pivoting of the Kindergarten and its allied
interests upon Oxford. His architect was called in to design
Rhodes House, with its domed hall of approach, Zimbabwe
bird as totem, and the temple which a friend of mine described
as 'the tomb of the Unknown Rhodes Scholar'. When Kipling
came to visit it in later years – he who had been so celebrated all
over the Empire, and in the United States a special train
provided for him – he was shown round by the official Porter,
whom the great man thanked, and 'You may like to know
whom you have been so kind as to show round: my name is
Rudyard Kipling.' It did not register: unrecognised. *Sic transit
gloria mundi.*

Among all these Empire grandees whom Curtis brought to
All Souls, Kipling did not figure: there had been a breach.
Curtis would say of him that, on one side, he was an inspired

---

[2] Today the big hospital in black Soweto is named for a Baragwanath, no
doubt people think a black.

prophet; on the other a grousing reactionary. He told me a comic story of Leo Maxse's last illness, a spiritual brother of Kipling, editor of the *National Review*.[3] When Kipling inquired how he was – he had had a blood transfusion – Maxse replied, 'No better: I think they have injected into my veins the blood of a member of the League of Nations Union.' Kipling rushed to send a telegram with the consoling message: 'It's quite all right: no believer in the League of Nations ever gave his blood for anything.'

Working with Milner in South Africa and, after his departure, in accordance with his ideas for the reconstruction of the country, Curtis was in his element: from re-starting, practically re-founding, Johannesburg and giving it proper municipal government to Assistant Colonial Secretary of the Transvaal for Local Government, to Member of the Transvaal Legislative Council. He never talked about that later: it is true that he did not look back – he was no historian.

Though I once and again asked him what was the secret of Milner's extraordinary influence over the variously gifted young men of the Kindergarten – they were all devoted to him – Curtis never answered the question. With his well-developed technique for working people to his purposes, not only instinctively but quite consciously, I do not think that he was interested in them psychologically: he was a Victorian, pre-Freud. It is evident that Milner was a remarkable administrator, with a constructive mind, full of ideas; a non-party man, really contemptuous of party-conflict – he was above all that – he even came to look sympathetically on the Labour Party at the end of his life. I remember his surprising *Observer* articles to this effect. He might have been a Fabian – as, oddly enough, the Tory Amery was.

Amery was another Fellow of All Souls whom Curtis became friendly with in South Africa. It is extraordinary the number of people who made their mark later whose apprenticeship was served in South Africa. Among All Souls men,

---

[3] Milner eventually married Maxse's sister. Were they Germans too? I once met her, a deep-dyed, doctrinaire reactionary, whom nobody could agree with.

Bob Brand, international banker of Lazard's, influential in shaping the constitution of the Union, on which he wrote the standard book. Geoffrey Dawson – who had to change his name from Robinson (hence always 'Robin' to the group) on succeeding to his Yorkshire estate; he served his apprenticeship in editing the Johannesburg *Star* and as correspondent of *The Times*, of which he became editor. (In his day the paper was hailed as 'the All Souls Parish Magazine'; he recruited several of us to it, and was kind enough to ask me to join – I should have been sacked rather than accept his pro-Appeasement line.) Dougal Malcolm, who had defeated John Buchan for the Fellowship, most clubbable of men and devoted to College life, became Chairman of the British South Africa Company, Rhodes's great enterprise for Central Africa. Perry, who had been responsible for the native Protectorates, had been personally recruited by Milner and helped to bring Curtis out ('I was dying to get back to South Africa to work under Milner – as we all did'). Perry later hived off to Canada; I saw him only once in College, a handsome, amiable, remote fellow. Lionel did not speak of the deserter.

Philip Kerr – later Lord Lothian – was a close co-operator, the first editor of the group's propagandist journal, *The Round Table*, inspired by Curtis and him. With his facile pen he wrote profusely and, overworked, had a prolonged nervous breakdown. (There was mental instability in the family.) Hereditarily a Catholic, he was helped to recovery by Christian Science, a bonus from Nancy Astor with whom he was in love – platonically of course, but a bore to Waldorf. A man of charm, public spirit and generosity, he was hopelessly wrong about Germany, which he did not know. When he died in the Washington Embassy, without medical attendance, Lionel owned to me: 'Philip died in the knowledge that he had been wrong.' What was the good of that? The damage had already been done, and was irretrievable.

It was a tribute to Curtis that he did not go in with Lothian over Appeasement of Hitler's Germany; he never declared himself on the issue, he had more sense, perhaps of political expediency. For some of the friends he wished to keep in line with – or, rather, keep *them* in line – were not Appeasers. Brand was not: he knew Germany, in touch with Schacht.

Amery, who knew Central Europe and the Balkans (he was partly Hungarian) was absolutely sound and had a consistent record on the issue. Even Waldorf Astor at Cliveden was not so sold on Appeasement as his editors on *The Times* and *The Observer*, Dawson and J. L. Garvin, Lothian or the egregious Tom Jones, working away like a mole for Hitler; or Neville Chamberlain and his *éminence grise,* Horace Wilson, another mole; or Chamberlain's Tory Party; or Montague Norman and the City. In the event they wrecked their country. It was not only Lionel Hichens but Britain that went up 'in a chariot of fire'.

Curtis to me, at that appalling moment of the Fall of France, in 1940: 'We must go down with the flag flying.' (I had other ideas.)

Though not a Fellow, Lothian came regularly to College. Occasionally too came the mysterious John Dove, who succeeded as editor of *The Round Table*. He had played his part as Chairman of the Transvaal Land Settlement Board, and subsequently accompanied Curtis to Australia on his fact-finding plus propaganda mission for Imperial Union. Dove was an asthmatic and a valetudinarian: I remember him silently snooping about the papers in our Coffee Room, as if surreptitiously – he didn't belong.

Basil Williams was another of the group, who came to visit us: he became an eminent eighteenth century historian, a precursor of Richard Pares in that field. There turned up too in South Africa the deplorable Duke of Westminster, Churchill's buddy, 'Bendor', recently the subject of a superfluous biography: to Curtis merely 'a gilded youth'. Lionel had no use for him – as he had a use for most of us.

After Reconstruction Curtis devoted all his energy and single-mindedness to the cause of promoting the Union of South Africa. He was a man of an *idée fixe* – of a series of *idées fixes*, one at a time; this was what gave them force. Here the idea was sparked off by his reading F. S. Oliver's book, *Alexander Hamilton*. It is extraordinary to think what an influence that book, by a rich business man in Debenham's – no historian – had on the thinking of the group. 'I shall never forget the effect which *Alexander Hamilton* had on me when I read it', Curtis wrote. 'He came into our lives as a great inspiration at the moment when we most needed it in South Africa. Here we were trying to work out a new philosophy of the State, and behold an unknown linen draper who had done it all for us!' The more intellectually trained Amery realised that Oliver's *Alexander Hamilton* was the Bible of the Kindergarten.

Lionel recommended it to me. To us who were historians this was derisory; Oliver was no historian any more than Curtis was: both were propagandists. This was their point, and perhaps it showed how limited the unappreciative academic mind was, for it is men of a fixed idea who are apt to make the running in history (look at Hitler! look at Lenin!). I suppose Oliver's point was that Alexander Hamilton, even after the American Revolution, wanted to keep what had been the first British Empire together in world affairs. Historians, however, would draw the moral that when dominions arrive at a degree of maturity they want to run their own affairs their own way. This is the moral to us of the American Revolution – applied, perhaps rightly, by Attlee in the hand-over in India; and subsequently, with very questionable results, in Africa.

Oliver, the sage, an elderly man, did not appear at All Souls. But, among colonial administrators, Curtis brought to us one of the greatest, Lugard, under whom Nigeria was a source of pride: one could trek unarmed two or three hundred miles. Look at it today! – massacres running into hundreds of thousands, political and economic collapse, chaos. Similarly with the Sudan, Zimbabwe, or Uganda: black shambles.

Personally considerate as always, Lionel introduced me to Oliver's artistic son, a collector of pictures, who invited me to dine at his house, a fragment of the old Tudor Richmond Palace. There I saw my first Modigliani. But we did not keep up the acquaintance – I was much too busily occupied at Oxford, and one really couldn't keep up with all the people one met in those generous, hospitable days.

Curtis had inspired, and Philip Kerr largely wrote, the journal *State* which made the propaganda for Union in South Africa. Curtis also travelled incessantly in those years before 1914 putting the idea across, as forcefully as he knew how. What effectively brought Union about was the change in political circumstances. The Liberal government at home granted responsible government – prematurely in Milner's opinion, who saw that it would mean Boer predominance, and despaired. The Kindergarten, however, favoured responsible government, and did not despair; Union came about, within the Empire, until ultimately the Afrikaners moved out.

After Union, most of the Kindergarten, their work done, returned to England to their different avocations – Curtis, however, to carry forward the propaganda for Imperial Union. He became the 'Prophet'. Today it is easy for us to see that this was never a possibility, difficult for us to appreciate that anybody thought that it was. True, circumstances were very different. The Dominions had not yet arrived at complete jurisdiction within their own bounds; Canada and Australia had contributed notably to the Empire's effort in South Africa; one half of the Unionist Party supported Joe Chamberlain's campaign for Tariffs, allied with Imperial Protection. A practical politician like Amery saw that the only practicable step in this direction was the latter. Curtis did not declare himself on this issue, for most of his group were Free Traders. He was fixed on the idea of Organic Union. Amery resented his dominating all discussions within the group by his *idée fixe*, and withdrew.

When Curtis made his fact-finding tour, sponsored by the group, to Canada and Australia, he found the prospects more discouraging than he expected, though he managed to set up groups to study the problem and Empire questions generally, to be aired and discussed in *The Round Table*. He was the standard-bearer; but he had the sense to realise the strength of the movement in each Dominion towards self-sufficiency and running their own affairs, if not actual independence. It is true that, at that time, the Dominions were not independent from the point of view of defence: they were dependent on the British Navy. It was not until the Second German War that the United States succeeded to the leadership of the English-speaking peoples. As for an Imperial Parliament – an historian should have known that the Declaration of Independence, of 1776, put paid to that.

Curtis came to realise the strength of the Dominion movements to realise their own separate identities; but, an Either-Or man, he posed the exclusive alternatives of *either* Organic

promising settlement. Adams, who became our Warden,
a Scot who lived a good deal, and married, in Ireland. He
been secretary to a grand man, Sir Horace Plunket, w
created Irish Agricultural Cooperation and did much for t
rehabilitation of the land. The Irish Republicans burned dow
his house for him and destroyed his historic papers.

I must confine myself to Curtis at Oxford, which hence-
forth became his base with his election to a Fellowship at All
Souls. Warden Pember, friend of Grey and Asquith, was
really a Little Englander and did not like the 'Empire builders',
as we called them. (Though a Labour man, I did.) I fancy that
Geoffrey Dawson put Curtis across – as Estates Bursar he
wielded much influence at the time. T. E. Lawrence had also
been elected, to write his famous book. It is again a tribute to
Lionel that Lawrence confided in him more than in anyone.
When one reads Lawrence's remarkable Letters, one sees that
the most intimate and revealing are those written to Curtis –
Lawrence poured out his secret heart-aches to him as to no-
one else.

When Lawrence joined the R.A.F. and ceased to live in
College, he left his few possessions with Lionel, who
exercised a kind of guardianship over his interests. When
Lawrence sometimes arrived at night, with Curtis away, he
would sleep in his rooms and away again on his fatal motor-
bike at daybreak. Lionel was involved in Lawrence's affairs at
his death, and was much moved, though he had seen too much
of death in South Africa to show it. I remember Lawrence's
appearance on the night his Fellowship expired. It was All
Souls tide, and my first Gaudy Night. There suddenly
appeared in the Smoking Room, crowded with Fellows i
dinner jackets and black ties, and Quondams in white ties a
tails, a slim lance-corporal in R.A.F. uniform, looking lik
boy of eighteen, only his blazing eyes and tortured m
betraying him. Lionel pushed me forward to meet h
would not intrude, as usual I was content to watch and r

Curtis brought the most interesting people to All S
don't remember Brand or Dawson or Malcolm doi
much richer: Lionel was the hospitable one, the e
He had some private means, not much, and later he
bit of property; he used his small Fellowship stip

Union *or* the dissolution of the Empire. Milner, with his Germanic mind, agreed with Curtis at heart. They set too much store by having things set down on paper, framing constitution, etc, and insufficient store by instinctive unspoken affiliations, the consoling fact that blood is thicker than water, that all round the globe were Britain's kith and kin, who did not need constitutional formulas to come to her rescue at the two crises in her destiny in the twentieth century – above all from the United States. (It must be gall and wormwood for German historians to reflect upon, but Germany showed herself altogether too uncivilised for any leadership in the world.)

The 1914–18 War ended even discussion, let alone prospect, of Imperial Union. Curtis must have felt that his mission had failed, though his *sense* of mission remained; he had other irons in the fire, causes to promote, people to push forward, followers and disciples. I do not know what his part in the Anglo-Irish negotiations amounted to, though he was closely involved. All he said to me was his oracular: 'The history of Ireland is something all Englishmen should remember, and all Irishmen forget.' (So typical of human affairs, the contrary is what prevails.) It was like his pronouncement that the history of South Africa was 'much too interesting'.

Curtis knew the Irish negotiators, and in South Africa had known Erskine Childers, who adopted the Irish Republican cause and was shot, by former comrades, then in the Free State government. Lionel did tell me that Childers was driven into his desperate extremism by his fanatic of an Irish-American wife, a cripple devoured by hate. Childers was condemned to death by Kevin O'Higgins, who was then assassinated by the Republicans – the usual sickening amenities of Irish politics. I once asked Curtis if the boundaries of Ulster in the Irish Treaty had not been drawn too widely: would it not have been better to include fewer Catholics? He said that only thus was the Province viable. I wonder. In Thrace, only an exchange of populations made peace possible between such humans (Swift in this regard doubly to the point: he knew Northern Ireland). Or perhaps a Chinese Wall?

In those negotiations W. G. S. Adams proposed the most

his books. As I have said he brought Smuts and Herzog to us, and also Smuts's right-hand man, highly intelligent young Jan Hofmeyr, whom his own Africaners would not have at any price to succeed Smuts: as an Oxford Rhodes Scholar, much too liberal-minded about the blacks. Dick Feetham came over too, by now (I think) Chief Justice in the Union. I do not recall Sir Patrick Duncan, who became Governor-General, whose early promise Curtis had observed admiringly, if patronisingly: 'a great man sprung from a Scotch peasant home.' Lionel was nothing if not a patron.

From Canada he brought the retired Prime Minister, Sir Robert Borden: a fine old-fashioned Canadian gentleman, crinkly curly hair parted in the middle, elastic, springy gait. He was good to me, very much a junior, and on his return kept writing me letters, and sent me the Collected Poems of Archibald Lampman. A terrible highbrow, I could not enthuse over sub-Swinburne – a devotee of Eliot, I didn't much care for Swinburne in the original. It was rather a case of –

> There was a young man in the States,
> Who so greatly admired Mr Yeats
>   That he sent him some books –
>   An edition *de luxe*
> Of Wilcox, with portraits and plates.

Then came André Siegfried, with whom I became more friendly. A tall, harsh Lorrainer, with grey complexion, staring blue eyes and grinding voice, he was distinctly *raide*, but interesting to me as any Frenchman would be. He had made a name in the English world with a book on New Zealand, and followed it up with something of a best-seller, *America Comes of Age*. In France he was regarded as an authority on the Anglo-Saxons. Of a rigid cast of mind, in his way as pontifical as Curtis himself, he had no subtle or flexible understanding of the English, as Elie Halévy or André Maurois[4] had. Siegfried was astonished when I told him that the then Leader of the Labour Party, a Leftist Socialist, George

---

[4] For Maurois v. my *Memories of Men and Women*.

Lansbury, was a practising Anglo-Catholic: unthinkable in France, he said. (However, I remembered that at least the wife of the great Socialist, Jean Jaurès, was a *dévote*.)

Siegfried, a rich man in his own right – the family were manufacturers in Normandy, from which his father had been a Senator of the Third Republic – had political aspirations, but settled for an academic career, becoming a professor at the Collège de France, eventually attaining to the French Academy. He had imbibed Anglo-Saxon habits of hospitality, entertaining me at his home in the Rue de Courty, just round the corner from the Chambre des Députés, where perhaps his heart was.

An interesting example of what Curtis could do with and for a man is provided by the case of Reggie Coupland – to become Sir Reginald. A New College Wykehamist, he was stuck as Ancient History tutor at Trinity, bored in the well-trampled field of Greek history, nothing in mind to write about. Curtis persuaded him into the field of the Empire, and he eventually became Beit Professor of Colonial History. As such, he wrote a series of standard historical works, mainly on the history of East Africa, such as *Kirk of the Zambesi* and its successors. He may be said to have laid the foundations of research in this field, though he wrote also on Nigeria, William Wilberforce and David Livingstone. Somewhat overlooked by the narrower and stricter academics, he produced some of the most creative and fertilising historical work of the time, and in a significant field.

Coupland became a distinguished public figure, member of important government commissions on Palestine and India, and ended up with an ambitious (unfinished) work on the Nationalities within the Empire. A pure academic like Richard Pares derided Coupland's avowed business of bringing colonial governors to Oxford; and there was a *Zwiespalt* between Coupland and E. L. Woodward. (My sympathies were with Coupland. G. N. Clark realised that though I was the protagonist of the Labour Party in college, a supposed Left fanatic, in fact I was more ready to compromise; Pares not, a sea-green incorruptible. Contrary to academic opinion, I also thought Coupland a better historian.)

Then came a sad breach. Coupland refused to follow Curtis

in his last campaign, for World Federation, announced in *Civitas Dei*, and its sequel, subsequently published as *The Commonwealth of God*. Coupland thought, as others did, that the Prophet had gone off the rails. But Prophets are ruthless, and Coupland was never forgiven for his defection. Lesser men were forgiven minor offences, Lionel took no notice; but this was the Ark of the Covenant, he held the key to it. The world must come together, or perish in flames. If Curtis was wrong, he was no more so than Bertrand Russell, who received all the acclaim. Curtis remained, as always, in the background.

We of the younger generation in College were very irreverent about *Civitas Dei*. According to his custom with earlier (influential) memoranda for circulation, Curtis had it printed with a blank page opposite each page for comments by the Chosen whose opinions he sought. Pares and I, like a couple of schoolboys, used to steal surreptitious readings in Lionel's absence. We were convulsed by his introduction to the Problem of India: 'The ground is damp, difficult and dangerous to sit upon.' We felt confirmed by Bernard Shaw's Comment, ending up, 'In short, the British Empire is Christ's Kingdom on earth, and Lionel Curtis is its Prophet.' This was no worse than the Red Dean of Canterbury's conviction that the USSR, *The Socialist Sixth* – a best-seller, which made a fortune for him, already a rich man – was Christ's Kingdom; or Sartre's pronouncement that the USSR was the incarnation of human freedom.

'Lord, what fools these mortals be!' – William Shakespeare was not given to such prognostications. Lionel's brought him a fresh crop of devotees. His book was translated into several languages; gifts were laid at his feet from various countries. I recall a consignment of magnificent sponges from Cyprus; Lionel gave me a huge one, which has lasted me to this day, more than thirty years after. And the faithful turned up – some of them fearful bores – to follow in the steps of the Master.

However much we laughed, he had not ceased to be able to pull off a trick or two. He brought Arthur Salter back, retired from the International Labour Office at Geneva, to become Professor of Political Theory and Institutions. Salter was an eminent civil servant, but he knew no political theory – none the worse for that; so I was given the job of deputising for him and giving his lectures on it, tying myself in knots to square Marxist theory with common sense.

China came up as a chief question on the international chess-board, and these various authorities tootled off to see what they could do to put things right. Curtis went, and wrote his portentous book, *The Capital Question of China*; Salter went, and came back with that curious Chinese look about the eyes, as also did R. H. Tawney. I think Lindsay of Balliol went, so did Warden Adams. The more these great and good men put their shoulder to the wheel, the more the thing fell apart, till it collapsed totally. When I made the point irreverently to Salter, he was nonplussed for a moment, but saw the humour of it.

Another creation of Curtis' was H. V. Hodson (my first election as examiner for the Fellowship). Lionel lifted him on to *The Round Table*, of which he became editor, thence on to *The Sunday Times*, meanwhile writing on the economic aspects of the Empire, and books like *The Empire in the World, The British Commonwealth and the Future* – very much in the idiom of the Master; or a more factual study of disintegration, *The Great Divide: Britain – India – Pakistan*. He ended up as Provost of beautiful Ditchley.

Hodson is descended from the Hodson of Hodson's Horse. His career makes me think of Lionel's charming children's story: of the hunter who spared the life of a baby elephant in Africa. Elephants never forget, and when this one grew up to be a circus elephant, years after, it one day recognised its saviour, extended its trunk and carefully lifted him from the sixpenny seats into the half-crown stalls. There was something elephantine about Curtis, and something of the hunter in Harry Hodson.

Did Curtis recognise defeat? He gave no outer sign of it. There were always minor causes to take up: at one time a campaign against Ribbon development – Kidlington was being ruined, a hideous mess. No doubt he was right, but – a Canute against the tide of modern 'civilisation': in vain. At another time, a campaign against sky-writing. A modern young man with modern tastes, the Duke of Windsor – then Prince of Wales – was all in favour of it. Curtis's campaign got through to old-fashioned King George V, who carpeted the

Prince, and enforced that the Royal House should speak with one voice on the matter. I rather think that the nuisance was abated for the time.

Academe was allergic to Curtis. A typical don, Robin Dundas of my old College, Christ Church, described him to me *tout court* as a 'bore'. Of course Lionel could be a bit of a bore, but he was so much else; Dundas was unaware that he was a bore – and nothing else. And Lionel did good work for Oxford, unbeknownst, and in spite of discouragements.

Among unforgettable scenes at All Souls, some of them comic, here was one that was rather shocking. Lionel brought to dinner rich Mr ffennell of Wytham, woods and all, a valuable lung to the city. Lionel had known him as Schumacher in South Africa, and now had his eye on him for a prospective benefactor. E. L. Woodward was in the chair – I as a junior the only other witness; he held forth against bringing rich people into Oxford, holding out the prospect of honorary degrees, etc, for what they might do for the university. I was rather shocked, though hardly surprised at anything from Woodward – he was lower middle class, envious of his betters, rather ill-bred. Lionel was appalled, but said not a word, except to me afterwards. Patience, persistence, public spirit received its reward: eventually the university got Wytham, park and woods, from generous Colonel ffennell. I think Woodward walked in them.

Another such scene occurred one evening when Lionel was entertaining Tom Jones. 'T.J.' had been immensely influential as secretary to Lloyd George, then to Baldwin, eventually to the Cabinet. He was a regular habitué of Cliveden; I have a photograph of Lionel, T.J., and myself out walking on a winter's day there. I am bound to own that T.J. was friendly, and I liked my fellow-Celt. One evening the three of us were in Lionel's rooms with Douglas Jay, then Junior Fellow, when he launched forth into a violent diatribe against the Welsh – he was really reacting against recent experience with Goronwy Rees, unreliable and undependable as any Celt could be. Again Lionel kept utter silence – always under control, as I was myself (an unpopular trait with juniors).

There were also comic scenes. Lord Faringdon was coming in from Buscot to present a book to the Codrington Library through Lionel: he was never my guest, though I had been his at Buscot. On the other hand, Lord Berners, who lived at Faringdon, was frequently my guest. We were sitting around the smoking-room fire with Quintin Hailsham, not expecting Gavin Faringdon to be brought in.

> Lionel, portentously: 'Why am I mixed up between Lord Faringdon and Lord Berners?'
>
> Quintin, wickedly: 'Ask Leslie: he knows.'
>
> Lionel: 'But I don't know. Which is which? Why do I confuse the two?'
>
> Quintin, with a meaning look at me: 'Ask Leslie. *He* knows.'
>
> Lionel, thinking this over, raising his voice: 'Do you mean that he is an Enemy of the Family?'
>
> The butler, appearing round the screen: 'Lord Faringdon to see you, sir.'

— Had he heard the exchange from behind the screen? Lionel hastily arose and scampered off with him; Quintin vastly pleased at his own naughtiness, and both of us tickled by Lionel's old-fashioned phrase, 'an Enemy of the Family', for it.

Lionel's last protégé before the War came down on us was the splendid German, Helmuth von Moltke, great-grand-nephew of the famous Field Marshal and head of the family with its vast estate in Silesia. Lionel came to know him through his South African connexions, the Rose Inneses (of Scottish descent). It fell to me, one sombre autumn evening before dinner in Hall, to introduce those two noble figures to each other: Lionel's friend Helmuth and my friend, Adam von Trott, each of them 6 feet 6 inches tall; Helmuth, dark, erect and glittering, like a sword; Adam fair, blue-eyed, more supple and willowy. I watched them give each other a momentary look of doubt. Both were condemned to death by Hitler after the Generals' abortive plot in July 1944, though Helmuth had no part in it. A devout Christian, he belonged merely to a circle which discussed the shape things should take in Germany *after* the evil thing was defeated — by others. Foreign Office people had a certain sympathy for Hitler at that moment: after all, the Generals, the

German Army and people had supported him all the way, so long as he was successful. Historically, he had done a marvellous job in organising his idiot people for a second attempt at *Welt-Macht*. No wonder Stalin remarked to Eden that he was 'a very remarkable man — only he had no sense of moderation'; and then added, 'I see you think I have no sense of moderation. That is where you are wrong.'

Lionel celebrated his friendship with Helmuth in a booklet, *A German of the Resistance*; I celebrated mine with Adam in *A Cornishman Abroad*: a certain parallelism in our experience. It was General Swinton who first brought Adam, quite young, to All Souls. Lionel had known Swinton in South Africa. I helped to bring Adam to Oxford as a Rhodes Scholar. These things connect up. And what scenes there were at All Souls in those historic days!

Lionel and I were both countrymen, a bond between us; neither of us was urban, and certainly not suburban – where the mass of English people today inhabit suburbia, physically and mentally. At Johannesburg his idea was to ensure 'a girdle of green country around the city.' Then, 'we found a lovely little nest of dead grass on the ground with two warm eggs in it, exactly like lark eggs.' On the veldt 'the flowers defy description, B. & L. were quite carried away, and I, not knowing by what names to address them, remained speechless.' He had an eye for everything country-wise: here 'a mimosa bush with strange green flowers or fruit in the shape of arrow heads hanging downwards. . . . The pendants were the houses of creatures made in imitation of a product of the tree.' Or, there, 'an immense area of drainage amongst the hills all runs down to a narrow neck, which could be blocked at slight expense giving immense storage for irrigation.' Then, 'I went to see the 1500 graves of the English soldiers before we left Bloemfontein. I noticed Tom Hichens' fresh grave with a rough wooden cross.' Both Lionels left a brother in South Africa. I often notice the memorials of the Boer War in English churches: the price of Empire. Had it been worth it?

At Kidlington Lionel created a garden behind the house, planted a whole field of willows beside the Cher beyond, and lived a rural life. I can see him now canoeing alone along those sedgy waterways, looking like a tramp. And indeed, as an undergraduate, he had taken to the roads as a tramp to see what it was like to live as such folks lived. Once he overplayed the part and arrived at a village at night in a downpour, dirty and famished, utterly penniless, and had to throw himself on the mercy of the local vicar for a night's lodging, declare who he was and what he was up to, to help him to get back to Oxford. Sometimes he would organise a Sunday morning tramp across the fields – in those days there were fields – ending up at hospitable Kidlington for lunch.

On our after-lunch walks round Christ Church Meadows or Magdalen Lionel was always first to see spring announced in the rose-flush of the willows, or to admire the first chestnuts coming out in flower. Along the city wall in front of Merton there used to grow clumps of ivy-leaved crowfoot – the French have an imaginative name for it, *les ruines de Rome*. Lionel noticed that the gardeners had scraped it all off (the people never *see* or understand anything). One afternoon in Addison's Walk I pulled down a superb chestnut bloom for him to sniff; at once there popped out a bee, which stung him on the inside of his nostril. He charged me with doing it deliberately, to tease me; but by the time we got back to All Souls his nose, that fine organ, looked like a pudding.

He was not accident-prone, but he told me of a comic happening to him when coming through the Mediterranean on a liner during the 1914–18 War. There was an alarm of a submarine about, and Lionel, going below to console a hysterical old lady, sat plump down on her crochet-bag; the needle hooked on to his bottom and couldn't be got out. So Lionel had to step up the companion-way with the crochet-bag fixed to his backside to get hold of the ship's doctor. Everybody laughed so much that they forgot the submarine for the time.

The most accident-prone of the Fellows was Geoffrey Faber, to whom something similar happened. He was fly-fishing on a stream on the Welsh Border when the wind blew his line back into his face, and the barb hooked itself into the gristle of his nose. The more he tugged at it the worse it got. Nothing for it but to mount his motor-bike into the neighbouring town, riding uphill with rod, line and hook fixed to his face, to seek the doctor, while the boys in the street jeered and cheered.

I have said that Lionel was a good raconteur – I wish I could remember more of his stories. Here is one from South Africa, where Bishop Colenso (a Cornishman) was a doughty defender of the blacks, particularly the Zulus, even of Cetewayo, a rather murderous old barbarian. The Bishop's daughter, a rigid six-footer of an unmarriageable sort, had gone thoroughly to the good. The joke was put about that she was to marry Cetewayo, and she was supposed to have said, 'What? And he a *king!*'

It was Lionel who told me the story of an irrevocable brick dropped at the Bodleian. Bodley's Librarian was Craster of All Souls, of a Northumbrian family so ancient that his name originally had an apostrophe, Cra'ster, and with a cleft palate he had an apostrophe in his speech; his hair sprouting from every orifice, he resembled the sculpted gargoyle of himself over a Bodleian gateway. He was the soul of courtesy. However, one day he was showing round the Bodleian a party which included a former Foreign Office diplomat who had had to resign for dealing in foreign currencies. This gentleman put the question to Craster, who had no idea who he was, 'How did Sir Thomas Bodley come by his money?' To which Bodley's Librarian replied innocently, 'He was – ah – in the diplomatic service.'

Craster came off better when, at the time of the Abdication, Lionel was saying that a statue should be put up to Mrs Simpson for ridding us of an unsuitable monarch. Lionel laid down that what was needed above all in a king was punctuality – and Edward VIII was always late. Craster, who had the Edwardian taste for puns: 'So he became the – ah – late king.'

Curtis had a nice story, which reflected absurdly the conflict between the philosophers over realism and idealism, and put it in its proper perspective. He had come back from more urgent affairs in South Africa, and went to New College to take his former tutor, the philosopher Joachim, out for a walk. Joachim had been a friend of his fellow philosopher, Pritchard. Pritchard was now living in one of those delightful eighteenth-century houses in the Broad, destroyed to make way for the architecturally third-rate New Bodleian. Curtis proposed that he and Joachim should collect their old friend too, but noticed a distinct coolness, and asked why. Going down New College Lane, Joachim pointed to a tree saying, 'He thinks that that tree is *real*!'; and then, his voice rising to a scream, 'And not only real, but *green*!!' Lionel, who had more important things on *his* mind and been through a war, said, 'Come on, now; let's call on Pritch.'

Dear Lionel, his last days of decline were rather sad. He had developed an addiction to snuff, with a little admixture: where had he got the habit from, whence the addiction? I wondered whether it wasn't, at the end, an unspoken admission of defeat, a recognition that the Prophet's mission was over.

6

John Buchan at Elsfield

I

When John Buchan died, the Editor of *The Times* told me that never had they received so many tributes to a public figure, sheaves of them pouring in from men of all walks and conditions of life, only a tithe of which could be published. That gives us some indication of the man himself; it is testimony to the extraordinary range and variety of his contacts and friendships with people. It also shows that these contacts were not merely formal; John Buchan belonged to the rare class of public figure who comes across to people as a friend, with whom they feel a personal bond, and in whom they feel a care for them and their concerns.

I can testify from my own experience. When he was on his last leave from Canada and already ill – within a year of his death – I was ill in London of the same duodenal complaint of which he was a victim, and he found time amid all the innumerable claims on him and in his own illness to write me encouraging letters in his own hand. Hundreds of people have had similar experiences of his kindness and thought. I appreciated it much then – how much more now; perhaps only a busy author, with writing of all kinds on his hands, knows so well what it means.

No doubt he paid some price in concentration of achievement for his readiness and willingness, his constant services to all and sundry. What he gained in stature was unmistakable; he gave himself away, right and left, with no thought for his own strength, like the man in the fable, *L'Homme à la Cervelle d'Or*.

With that there went – and perhaps from it came – the

catholicism of his sympathy. A Tory himself, his instinctive conservatism rooted in his sense of history – though that did not mean that he was not a progressive – his sympathies and affections were extended in every direction politically. In fact, I believe it was a recommendation with him that one was on the other side. I remember the particular regard in which he held, and always spoke of, Maxton, then much in the public eye as leader of the I.L.P. and a notable figure in Parliament. With one young neophyte of the Left, ardent and touchy, he was patience and courtesy itself.

Alas, with what can one reward his kindness now? Nothing – except to cherish the memory of the man he was: that quick, spare, gallant figure, with the grave face and frosty Northern eyes that could yet sparkle with liveliness and good-humour, with his old-fashioned Scots courtesy and birdlike quickness of movement, walking cap in hand and in loose-fitting tweeds along the lanes and up the hill from Marston to his home on the brow of Elsfield overlooking Oxford; or walking on the terrace in the green shades of a summer evening, looking down upon Otmoor and, in the gathered blue of distance, his beloved Cotswolds; or again, sitting on a low chair in a corner of the library at Elsfield, the firelight leaping up and gleaming in the ranks of books, himself the heart and soul of the talk.

The foundation of his life, I realise now, was the principle of Christian love. He really loved people. Everything, apart from his gifts – though they derived strength from it – sprang from that. There was the secret spring of the two qualities that were so marked in him: the unsleeping sense of duty, the breadth of his sympathy. His devotion to duty was obvious in every sphere of his life. He was stern with himself in his work; always beforehand with his engagements (like Trollope), never failing to perform what he had promised – in that so unlike the ways of authors in general. He was a good deal of a stoic – except that, to balance that strain in him, no one had a greater natural gift for the enjoyment of life. Only someone who knows the physical anguish and pain that accompany that illness from which he suffered, knows what such devotion to work and duty must have cost.

Perhaps I may say something of him as a writer, though it is a disadvantage not to know the Scottish background, the society and tradition out of which he sprang and against which his work must be seen. I appreciate all the more the importance of that background, the inspiration that came from his native region, the memories and associations that went back to his childhood there, since a writer should have roots. His were vigorous and idiosyncratic, at once hardy and nourishing to the life of the imagination; the beginnings in the manse in Fife looking out upon the Forth; the summer holidays in the Border country, that was Sir Walter Scott's own country too, the beloved Tweedside. The memory of those hills and streams is never far away in his writings, and his best books are either inspired by them or somewhere carry their stamp. When he came to sum up his own work in *Memory-Hold-the-Door*, he wrote: 'The woods and beaches (of Fife) were always foreign places, in which I was at best a sojourner. But the Border hills were my own possession, a countryside in which my roots went deep. . . . The dying shepherd asked not for the conventional Heaven, but for "Bourhope at a reasonable rent", and, if Paradise be a renewal of what was happy and innocent in our earthly days, mine will be some such golden afternoon within sight and sound of Tweed.'

One can appreciate what he owed to that distinctive background and the life of its people. For a writer, it was an advantage too to have been born a son of the Manse; he knew what it was to be poor, to share the life of the people; at the same time, the standards that he imbibed from childhood were the educated standards of ministry and gentlefolk. It meant, as with Kilvert or Crabbe, that all doors were open to him, the ways of life of all classes. There was the freshness and vividness of the Border country itself, the sense of the soil, the love of its solitary spaces, above all the historic memories and associations with which it is crowded. Nor should one forget the importance attached to intellect and the things of the mind – which Scots are apt to feel more keenly than English people – to appreciate learning, scholarship, intellect as such. A further strain in him was the tradition of Adam Smith, Lockhart, Caird, and of so many generations of Scots coming up to Balliol. He told me that he should have come up to Balliol in the usual way if it had not been for his intense admiration in his undergraduate days at Glasgow for Walter Pater. Out of that romantic devotion he chose to come up to Brasenose. (By the time he came up Pater had died.)

He started as a follower of, and inspired by, Robert Louis Stevenson. There could be no better school for a beginner; for Stevenson was a careful craftsman and Buchan had a mastery of words – an initial gift which greater writers have sometimes been without and some writers never achieve. His romantic temperament, his preference for the life of action, admiring the heroic and stirring deeds, responded to Stevenson; one sees the influence on his early stories – among his best. Buchan has told us how potent that influence was over the young men of his generation, especially at the universities in Scotland. R.L.S. was 'at once Scottish and cosmopolitan, artist and adventurer, scholar and gipsy. Above all he was a true companion. He took us by the hand and shared in all our avocations. It was a profound and overmastering influence.'

Eventually Buchan grew out of it. In time 'Stevenson seemed to me to have altogether too much artifice about him, and I felt a suspicion of pose behind his optimism and masculinity.' That helps to define a point for us about Buchan's own work: he was an admirable stylist. His own style was the reverse of artificial or affected; it was vigorous and natural, athletic and spare, running beautifully clear like one of his own Border streams, with an occasional coloured pebble in it to arrest the attention, some infrequent word that was yet authentic, coming out of the life of the land and the language of its people. He had a discriminating use of words, sensitive and scholarly. He was, by nature and inclination, a scholarly writer, having both a classical education, with its accompanying training, and strong historical feeling. Since style is a preservative element in literature, his best books will be read so long as we care for good standards.

Of his novels I am not qualified to speak; but to his gifts we must add – what is not very common – the sheer faculty of telling a story. John Buchan was a Tusitala in his own right. He loved the story for its own sake; he understood suspense, the art of excitement, in such stories as *The Thirty-Nine Steps*; that he was sensitive to atmosphere may be seen from a story like 'The Grove of Ashtaroth' in *The Moon Endureth*. In his autobiography he tells us how from early days he told himself stories, or rather stories told themselves in his head; one recognises a born story-teller – just what Trollope says of himself in his *Autobiography*.

Buchan kept a clear distinction in his mind between his lighter efforts, his thrillers and tales of adventure, and his more serious work, whether in fiction, *belles lettres* or in the field which came to weigh most with him, historical biography. I remember him telling me that he wrote his novels at dictation speed; but that he never could write more than fifteen hundred words a day at serious history. He took biography as serious history, devoted himself to it with all the application of his mind, working hard at sources, making himself into a professional historian – a professional who could write: there is the difference.

He says of his *Montrose, Sir Walter Scott, Cromwell* and *Augustus*: 'All these four books were, indeed, in a sense a confession of faith, for they enabled me to define my own creed on many matters of doctrine and practice, and thereby cleared my mind. They were laborious affairs compared to my facile novels, but they were also a relaxation, for they gave me a background into which I could escape from contemporary futilities, a watch-tower from which I had a long prospect, and could see modern problems in juster proportions. That is the supreme value of history.'

Above all, there is the Life of Scott. There he had a magnificent subject, to which all his impulses responded. 'It is a book which I was bound one day or other to write, for I have had the fortune to be born and bred under the shadow of that great tradition.' He had the noble background of Scott's country, Edinburgh – the most striking, the most sharply-etched town in this island, with its mingled sharpness and sweetness, like the cold showers and rare lights of a Northern spring; and the shared experiences of Tweedside: 'Above all, Scott had that kindest bequest of the good fairies at his cradle, a tradition, bone of his bone, a free life lived among clear waters and green hills as in the innocency of the world. . . . The world opened to him as a wide wind-blown country, with a prospect of twenty miles past the triple peaks of Eildon to the line of Cheviot, the homely fragrance and bustle of a moorland farm, the old keep of Smailholm as a background, and a motley of figures out of an earlier age. . . . He had mingled intimately with every class and condition of men, he had enough education to broaden his outlook but not enough to dim it; he was familiar alike with city and moorland, with the sown and the desert, and he escaped the pedantry of both the class-room and the drawing-room; above all, he had the good fortune to stand at the meeting-place of two worlds, and to have it in him to be their chief interpreter.' From the country that gave him birth to the man himself: the poetry, the peopled imagination, the nobility of Scott, one of the most magnanimous of men.

Of his historical biographies, *Montrose* and *Cromwell* have special claims: *Montrose*, because Buchan had a lifelong devotion to that gallant figure out of the Scottish past, and because he had an inner sympathy with his point of view. It is true that he sees the history of that time through the eyes of Montrose, but he gives a just estimate of the character of Montrose's grim opponent, Argyll. In all these books he has a firm hold of the personalities of the historical figures, whether his sympathies are with them or not. This book must be regarded as his chief contribution to historical research; it is written from original sources and he had various additions and corrections of his own to offer in writing it. He had an intimate knowledge of the countryside over which Montrose fought, all those marches and counter-marches in and out the Highlands, the Homeric battles. He had an intimate knowledge of the literature, even of the pamphlet literature, of the seventeenth century; he collected the traditions and stories, what there was of verbal tradition.

The Life of Cromwell covers a less original track, a more trampled field. It is a bigger subject, a larger canvas crowded with figures, and Buchan made of it a fine book. It sprang out of his abiding interest in the seventeenth century, where he was most at home. He read all the sources and authorities; he visited, as an historian should, the places and studied the battlefields. He had a good understanding of military history. (An historian friend of mine, who fought in 1914–18, told me that Buchan's account of trench-warfare in his *History of the Great War* was true to the fact.) He brought something more to his study of Cromwell – his own turn of mind.

We see the breadth of his sympathies enabling him to thread

his way with fairness and understanding through the maze of sects and sectaries, the parties and factions. There is justice of mind in his treatment of the men on both sides, Cromwell and Charles, Laud and Strafford, Ireton and Vane. For Cromwell himself, that extraordinary man, Buchan had an inner feeling that makes him at least clear. Then there is the firm composition of the book, well conceived and built up, the sense of scene, the practised rendering of action, the gift of phrase. Of Cromwell's religion, for example: 'He has been called a religious genius, but on his genius it is not easy to be dogmatic; like Bunyan's Much-afraid, when he went through the River none could understand what he said.' On the constitutional dilemma of the Protector's government, its inner contradiction: 'He was to be a prince, but a prince who must remain standing, since he had no throne.'

I remember meeting Buchan on his way back to Elsfield the afternoon he came down into Oxford to send off the manuscript of *Cromwell*. (He did all his writing in his own hand; hence the high standard he maintained.) It was early summer, June over the Oxfordshire countryside, the long grass lush in the water-meadows, the elms of Marston in their full panoply of foliage. He was feeling sad, he said, at parting with someone with whom he had lived for two years now. Not a word about the immense labour and effort that had gone into it; he took all that for granted.

He lived in the realm of the historical imagination. How naturally it came to him may be seen in an essay, 'Thoughts on a Distant Prospect of Oxford', full of feeling for the place and its memories; printed in a volume in which the sense of history illumines the study of literature, *Homilies and Recreations*.

Of his classical biographies, *Julius Caesar* and *Augustus* – the latter his last big work – I am not able to speak. But they have this element of authenticity, that they go back to his youthful interest in Roman history, to the ambition of his undergraduate days to paint a portrait of Augustus. 'I had already done a good deal of work on the subject,' he wrote amid all the distractions of being a Governor-General – 'and my first two winters in Canada gave me leisure to re-read the Latin and Greek texts.' 'I have rarely found more enjoyment in a task,' he adds, 'for I was going over again carefully the ground which I had scampered across in my youth.' What boyishness, what verve! – and from a man in highest office and often in pain.

It testifies to the width of his reading and culture; a man of a type all too rare in public life today. For he was a great reading man. 'Reading has always filled so large a part of my life', he says disarmingly – as if there were not a score of other interests and avocations: fishing, bird-watching, walking; the Empire – first South Africa, then Canada; publishing, Reuter's, serving on the University Chest at Oxford; becoming a Member of Parliament, Governor-General of Canada. In addition to being one of the most prolific authors of his time. Yet – reading filled a large part of his life. You will get some idea of his powers in this direction – along with a retentive memory – from an essay on Scott in *Homilies and Recreations*. During his serious illness and duodenal operation in 1917 he read through a dozen of the Waverley Novels, the Valois and d'Artagnan cycles of Dumas, then Victor Hugo's *Notre Dame* and the immense *Les Misérables,* almost a library in itself, ending up with half a dozen of Balzac. How he contrived to get through all the reading and writing he did, let alone everything else he accomplished, beats me; though he owed a lot to the watchfulness and care of his wife: a rare comradeship in life, in work and public service.

When in those days one went up to Elsfield, one always found him abreast of contemporary reading as of affairs, interested in all that was being written and thought. Alas, being young, one took so much for granted! It is only now that one knows how remarkable that was, such generosity of spirit in it: he was by nature an admirer, an encourager of others' work. He had nothing of the denigrator about him: I never heard him utter depreciatory words of anyone – a rare attitude in literary circles. He did not move in literary circles; he was by nature a man of action, who happened to have the gifts of a writer. I remember how he won me early on by his warm appreciation of 'Q.' 's novels and stories – absurdly under-estimated.

Now, when one thinks of Elsfield, something rare has gone from the familiar landscape. Everything there reminds one of him; the way up the hill, the little bridge and culvert at the foot, the road winding between the elms and ash trees, the elder I once saw in blossom-time gleaming like a ball of snow in the frozen moonlight, while a parachute-flare slowly descended over Otmoor. There is the little church, hipped up on its platform, with bell-cote at the west end overlooking the road; then around the bend to the tall house with its eighteenth-century core, and something Scottish about its rigid vertical lines – that ever-hospitable house with its friendly welcome for the young.

On Sunday afternoons in those days there was always a crowd and good talk. Out of a kindly thought for my shyness, I used to be asked on quieter occasions, when there was just the inner circle of the family, a few guests, the domesticity and firelit charm which those two, John and Susan Buchan, gathered around them. Evening wore on; the firelight leaped on the hearth and made a comfortable glow in that square shelved room with its cargo of books. Now it is autumn and the trees outside are turning lemon and gold; mellow evening light comes across the green spaces of Otmoor and in at the western windows. Or it is winter and there is a winter stillness outside – darkness in the trees, snow-light upon the slopes, the village street moonlit as in Arnold's poem. At the door one takes leave of that friendly house; it is time to go downhill, back to the spires and colleges waiting down there in the night. As one recalls that so familiar routine, the village on the brow, that hospitable house, time slips away and one is there again, the circle rounded and complete once more.

II

What are we to think of John Buchan today?

When a well known writer dies, his reputation, and even knowledge of him, dip into a trough for a time, perhaps for a whole generation, and the more popular he was in his lifetime the longer and deeper the trough. The most notorious example of this is the case of Trollope, and the more spectacular the recovery. A writer as distinguished as he was popular, Quiller-Couch – properly admired by John Buchan – has not yet emerged from eclipse. Buchan himself, in the shade for a time, has made an early recovery, especially with his thrillers – which he himself set least store by.

My original tribute to him was written under the immediate shadow of his loss. Since then much more has emerged about him. He has had the good luck of one of the best literary biographies of our time, by Janet Adam Smith; and recently a Memoir by his son, William Buchan, hardly less good. Yet neither achieves intimacy; each author, even the son, is conscious of a certain distance from the subject. What was it that was so reserved about Buchan, when so many people thought they knew him? Where was the centre of the man? What made him tick?

His son entitles his concluding chapter, remarkably, 'A Very Queer Fish Indeed?' He says, 'JB had always seemed to me a mysterious person. For all his openness, courtesy, kindness, his geniality, his great knowledge which he was ready to share, his charity and his questing, eager spirit, together with his pains and disappointments and very human foibles . . . I believe that he held always a certain part of himself apart, inviolable and inviolate.'

I don't regard Buchan as a queer fish at all. He was above all a writer; and one answer to his son's question is that a writer instinctively keeps the seed-bed from which he creates secret and inviolate. With no-one was this more obvious than with Trollope, who protected his inner life with a gruff, abrasive manner. John Buchan had beautiful manners, and was courteous to all and sundry; his eminent qualities his son denotes justly, but about his inner life the writer was as close as a clam. Not deliberately, but quite naturally; that was what made him a secret man, the essential man no one knew (except possibly his wife: she understood him).

His inner life was dominated by his imagination. Wherever he was and whatever he was doing – and he was doing a hundred other things besides writing (that was what was so remarkable) – he was telling himself the stories that welled up in him, talking to the characters that came to mind and demanded to have their stories told. Just like Trollope. The characters in his fiction were sometimes suggested by, or had touches of, real people he had known, as with any novelist. Sir

Edward Leithen, especially in *Sick Heart River*, comes closest to himself; and Auberon Herbert has had a distinguished biography under the title, *The Man Who Was 'Greenmantle'*, for his career suggested it. The great men of history and literature were no less real to Buchan – they were heroes to him, Montrose and Sir Walter Scott especially (for they were Scots), but also Cromwell, Ralegh and Augustus; and he wrote about them all.

Paradoxically Buchan started as a writer of the Nineties in the *Yellow Book*, the organ of the decadent aesthetes, and as reader for John Lane, their patron and publisher. Q. distinguished in the Nineties two schools: the writers of action who looked up to Robert Louis Stevenson, and the aesthetic movement around Yeats and Arthur Symons. Q. belonged to the first; when it came to the decadent Symons, 'I could do nothing for him', he said to me, and would not put a single poem of his into *The Oxford Book of English Verse*. In spite of the aesthetic book jackets of Buchan's earliest volumes, poems and essays, he was no aesthete and realised himself in the school of action.

These writers had a view of life in which action came first; their aim was a well-rounded, balanced life, making their contribution to the life of the nation – as both Q. and John Buchan did – in which writing was only a part of the whole. Both of them devoted a large amount of time unsparingly to public causes. This stands in marked contrast to writers who dedicated their whole lives to their writing – contemporaries like Henry James, Hardy, Kipling, Meredith, Conrad; these emerge as greater writers, single-minded, concentrated on their work.

Public life has many disillusionments, and demands sacrifices all the greater from a writer, who has better things to do. Perhaps Buchan's son has this in mind when he writes: 'Contrary to the widely held belief that John Buchan's life was a story of unbroken successes, he had in fact many disappointments. After his failure to win a Fellowship at All Souls, the first real setback of his life, he was to endure many other blows, to feel sometimes a sense of rejection. There was his failure to make the kind of mark in British politics which, once, he must have been sure of making. There was the noticeable lack of recognition of hard and valuable work for his party.'

John Buchan was a small, spare man. I sensed among the bigger, bulkier figures who took up so much more room on the public stage in their day, were so important and self-important – and are now forgotten (as he is not) – a condescending attitude towards him on their part: after all, he was only a writer. They did nothing for him – until Canada asked for him to be Governor-General; Canada and John Buchan put that right: he became the best and best-loved Governor-General Canada ever had.

There remains the question of the man as such. William Buchan tells us: 'The world of my father's family was an innocent one, and the quality in him that I see most clearly is a kind of innocence, a real simplicity of heart. Giving people all his kindness, perception, even his admiration, he was unaware that they were not always so generous in receiving as he was in giving. His faults were the faults of innocence. If he dropped names, or seemed to rejoice in close acquaintance with important people, this was only an expression of his pleasure in the richness and variety of the English society in which he, a Scotsman and a historian, had found a place: to call him a snob would imply that he used his grand acquaintance to impress or humiliate others. . . .'

The important thing here is that Buchan was a historian, and a historian has, in the course of his work, to drop names like Henry VIII and Oliver Cromwell, the Duke and Duchess of Marlborough, the Marquis Curzon, Ernie Bevin or Winston, names like those I am dropping in this book. Not to drop names, to please conventional muffs, would put a historian out of business, and 'name-dropping' can be seen to be an absurd (and very recent) American cliché. It is usually the dull and inferior who resent one mentioning more interesting people than they are.

Once at a dinner of the Annenbergs at the American Embassy, I was engrossed in conversation with the lady on my left, when at length the lady on my right said, 'Are you particularly interested in the lady on your left because she is Curzon's daughter?' I said, 'Of course, Curzon was a historic figure, and I am a historian; one was always hearing about him at All Souls, though I never knew him.' She said, 'Well, I am descended from Sir Gervase Elwes.' I was at once interested, knowing all about the murder of Sir Thomas Overbury in the Tower of London, when poor Elwes was Lieutenant.[1] So then we had an equally interesting conversation on the right, instead of pointless chat.

Snobbery is a wide subject, and again most people think nonsense on the matter. There are intellectual snobs (I am one), garden snobs (not one), social snobs, family snobs, snobs about the royal family; democratic Americans are apt to be luggage snobs. Something is to be said for most forms of snobbery; it testifies to a sense of values and, if the values are good, so is the snobbery. I once came to the defence of Archbishop Lang on this score, against one of his own confraternity, with this: 'It only meant that he found interesting people more interesting than *un*interesting ones.' Logically irrefutable, and anyway interesting people *are* more interesting – though the uninteresting may not like the fact.

This was John Buchan's case: he was so generous-minded that he found almost everybody interesting, a Scotch fisherman or ghillie as much as a duke or T. E. Lawrence. It was part of his inexhaustible human interest – of the greatest value to a novelist – part of his kind nature as a man, and also (like Cosmo Lang) he was a Scots romantic at heart. It was also charmingly naif of him. Early in our acquaintance he asked me at dinner, Did I know the Duchess of Marlborough? Of course this young neophyte from the people replied equally naively, 'Do you mean Sarah?' To John Buchan the Marlboroughs and Blenheim Palace, past *and* present, were part of the romance of English history.

His son concluded his account of his father: 'Yet he eludes me still, as I believe he has eluded everybody.'

John Buchan does not elude me. He was, first and foremost, a man of genius, and that does make a man 'mysterious'. Secondly, he was a normal, even conventional family man; that does not usually go with genius, which is apt to be abnormal, sometimes scandalous. John Buchan was also an innately good man, with the highest standards of conduct,

[1] v. my *The Tower of London in the History of the Nation.*

both public and private. That quality is hard to write about; it is much easier and more exciting to write about a bad man. Then William Shakespeare says,

> They say best men are moulded out of faults
> And, for the most, become much more the better
> For being a little bad.

John Buchan had nothing bad in him whatever; perhaps it is that that makes him more difficult to recapture.

There is nothing that I wish to alter in my earlier tribute, written at the request of his widow, under the immediate impact of his loss. Only one word: I always thought that there was something sad about John's countenance and expression – Susie made me substitute the word 'grave' for 'sad'. But why shouldn't he have looked sad? For all his enjoyment of life he was often in pain from duodenal ulcer; he had had a Calvinist upbringing and knew the tragic side of life – his nearest friends and youngest brother killed in the holocaust of the First German War, so ruinous to English life.

I am proud that G. M. Trevelyan approved of my evocation of him, and should like to add a description of his appearance from a woman's sharp eye, Catherine Carswell's. 'The scar from an accident in childhood drew attention to the strikingly noble contours of his head. The long queer nose, questing and sagacious as a terrier's, was in odd contrast with the lean, scholarly cheeks and with the mouth narrowed as by concentration or the hint of pain subdued.' That tight-lipped mouth speaks to me of inner discipline and determination, a hint of repression, constant exertion of the will, and perpetual strain.

Some things now can be added. I never quite realised how deeply his failure to become a Fellow of All Souls affected him, how much he missed all through life the camaraderie of that unique freemasonry, of which several of his early friends – from Milner's Kindergarten – were lifelong members. He spoke to me of it, told me that he had tried twice, came nearest in the examination on the first occasion; his second attempt came after a year when he was already so hard at work in

London that he could not keep his scholarship, or perhaps examination technique, up to scratch.

He spoke without any rancour or resentment against the College – unlike some people who have failed to be elected. In Buchan's case it was the College rather that failed by adhering too closely to examination marks. Buchan was beaten by a fellow Scot, an Etonian, with a special aptitude for Greek verse – undoubtedly a better classical scholar, but with nothing of Buchan's promise already fully evident. Everyone expected that he would carry it off, like his friend Raymond Asquith.

The Prize Fellowships of All Souls were the Blue Ribbon of an Oxford career, even more so then than today, when there are more of such opportunities about. Naturally, when only one or two of the twenty to thirty candidates are chosen, one could construct a College of as much distinction from those who were not elected. For myself I used to regret that, among all the public and academic figures, there were not more writers. We might have had Belloc, instead of H. W. C. Davis, a better historian but no genius – just a professor; we might have had Aldous Huxley or David Cecil, Namier or John Buchan. It is a consideration that goes against too rigid an adherence to examination papers.

Actually it was at All Souls that I first met the Buchans at lunch with the Pembers in the Warden's Lodgings. Warden Pember was a handsome figure-head for the College, first-class classical scholar, an Harrovian friend of Stanley Baldwin, but a closer friend of Edward Grey and Asquith. Well off, an admirable host and raconteur, Warden Pember was a dear kind man (he did not recover from the loss of his only son in the War, had never believed he would be killed) – it was good of him to include this proletarian recruit to the College so often in the private gatherings at his table.

I used to be asked out a lot, for those were the days when people still had servants, were not taxed to the bare bones, and there was a great deal of hospitable, civilised entertaining. (Today impossible – only trade unionists have the money for that: whether the entertainments are civilised is another matter.)

Shortly I was recruited to Elsfield, the house and company

as I have previously described it. Little to add – except that, as Alice Buchan writes, I felt rather shy there, for Susan herself was shy; tea-time was all very well, but I found dining out rather a chore. In later years I became a devoted friend of Susan in her long widowhood – when she found herself as a writer. While John was alive she had a very full life with the family, beautiful Elsfield to look after, and John to protect. It was the writer who was the magnet for me.

Only on the historical side was I on Buchan's wave-length, for I did not read his thrillers or his novels, and, a Left intellectual, I was devoutly highbrow. In any case he did not go in for literary chatter. In his nostalgic autobiography, *Memory-Hold-the-Door* – no one knows where he got the title from – he says: 'As a writer it was my misfortune to be too little in the society of writers.' Like Kipling, he was all for men of action. He goes on: 'A writer must inevitably keep the best of himself for his own secret creative world.' That corroborates my diagnosis of him.

He was a man for a telling anecdote, perhaps germ for a story. I remember the *frisson* I got from his story about the Old Man of the Cairngorms. Buchan was a tremendous walker, and one day he was on those ominous mountains, late and alone, when he heard footsteps behind him; the faster he went the closer the steps tracked him, and he came down off the mountains right quick! No doubt it was the echo that was following him. All the same those mountains are sinister. The mother and sister of an Oxford contemporary were out on them, when there was a thunder clap and a flash of lightning which threw them to the ground; the sister did not rise again. The month in which I write this, the winter of 1983–4, five men were missing on those hostile hills.

Buchan could never resist a challenge. When Governor-General of Canada, an elderly and a sick man, returning from an exhausting tour in the Arctic, Bear Mountain above the Mackenzie River confronted him. 'The face had never been climbed, and up he had to go.' 'The rock was rotten and slanting the wrong way, but I took it cautiously and had no difficulties, except at the very top where there is an overhang. I managed to drag up an Indian so that he could give me a back, and wriggled my way up. The rest of my staff, including an inspector of police, got stuck on the lower rocks and had to be rescued by ropes!'

Now, why had he to do everything, be everything, taking every challenge and so much out of himself, life such a strain? – that is the question. I suspect the little man had to *show* them. I feel sure that the grandees of political life, the pomposities, disconsidered him, rather looked down on him – until Canada; that showed them all right, made up for everything. Others envied the success he had achieved, entirely by his own gifts and hard work, Scotch grit and will power. He did not allow it to sour him – too Christian a spirit for that – but he knew it well enough, and said one day to Susie: 'It is only when you are successful that you discover the world is not a very nice place.'

I have forgotten most of his anecdotes, but one Scottish one had a characteristic theological flavour. He was out fishing and was engaged hauling in a catch, when his old boatman said something to this effect; in the receiving of Divine Grace, would you say that the initial impulse came from above, or from the believer below? Catch an English fisherman entertaining such thoughts!

Buchan was not in sympathy with the writers of the Twenties and Thirties, whom I did read: Eliot, D. H. Lawrence and Joyce, the whole of Bloomsbury. He writes in a rather stuffy way about them, evidently not able to come to terms with them. 'One section of this class, very vocal in speech and writing, cherished modernity as its peculiar grace, regarding the word as descriptive of quality, and not merely as denoting a stage in time.' A good historian's debating point, this – and as a stylist he was himself equal to the best of them. He clearly detested Lytton Strachey, 'their fugleman', as G. M. Trevelyan did; and then goes on uncomfortably: 'they were much concerned with sex, and found sexual interest in unusual places, dwelling upon it with a slight titter.' This makes me laugh; for of course I was much more in accord with their view of things. Dear John, how innocent he was! Married to Susan, 'the only woman I have ever been in love with, or ever shall love' – it was just like Q., married to the only woman in *his* life. Each of them wrote to his wife every day that he was absent from her. To us and my generation, simply extraordinary: it made for such utter simplicity.

Nor, as a Labour Party man, with my intellectual obsession with Marxism, was I in sympathy with Buchan politically. I realised that he was naturally a romantic, historically minded Tory, but I did not give him credit for being much less of a party man that I was. He was genuinely friendly with the Red Clydesiders, Jimmy Maxton and David Kirkwood. Scotland was a bond, and that held too with Ramsay MacDonald. When MacDonald's eyesight began to fail him, Buchan had the new biography out specially printed in large type, for MacDonald to read on the rest he was ordered to take from politics. I don't suppose that in all Buchan's wide reading he had ever read Karl Marx.

I can see in the mind's eye that comfortable square library at Elsfield, his books all round him; behind his big writing desk was a bottom shelf of the manuscripts of his own books, beautifully bound. When I eventually graduated to a house of my own, I took that tip from him and had my bulky manuscripts similarly bound – John wrote everything longhand, as I do. Above the chimney piece hung a portrait of Sir Walter Ralegh, an early subject of John's – I doubt if he knew how faulty a hero he was. The Victorian chimney piece had been replaced and put away in the attics of that rather gaunt house, with the label – Susie said – 'Disapproved in 1930', perhaps to be rehabilitated in the next century.

I always thought there was a Scottish look about that abrupt Victorian house fronting directly on the village street. The back of it was older, with its magnificent view over all Otmoor, where John loved to walk, and across to the Cotswolds, which he wrote about and in which he placed, I think, *Midwinter*. Later the Buchans added an upper story to the eighteenth-century wing at the back, making a drawing-room and a private study for John's writing, away from the interruptions of family and visitors – for hospitality was incessant. How generous John was, with money, time, people – part of his innate and schooled generosity of mind. Money poured in from his books, though money was neither motive nor objective with him. I suppose he was a good business man, he was so methodical, and was a publisher from early days – when he could keep himself as an undergraduate from his writing. I remember how shocked Lionel Curtis pretended to be, at a publishers' session with John, when masterpieces of literature were swapped and bandied about like saddles of mutton. Money simply accrued, in those good days when a writer could hold on to his own earnings, instead of having them confiscated for people he disapproves and causes he detests.

The library was really the centre of the life of that house. I recall the new grand drawing-room being used only once, on the threshold of the Buchans' departure for Canada, for a dinner-party for Elizabeth Bowen, a friend of Susie rather than of John. We were sad at their impending departure – a consummation for him, a *corvée* for Susie. She was planning how she meant to keep it informal; but, of course, when they got there, in the Thirties, Vice-regal state had to be maintained: one sees it in the photographs – not for nothing was her Excellency a great-grandniece of the Duke of Wellington. Still, kind and warm-hearted as ever, they invited me over – though in those duodenal days I wouldn't dream of going: quite beyond me. A fellow sufferer – fellow member of the Duodenal Club of 'the best people', as a doctor described it, i.e. those who strained themselves working to the limit – John went through all the demands of the job, all the ceremony and ritual, the duties and chores, as he undertook everything, patience, good will, anxious to do his best and prove himself. In the end it killed him.

The historic, the essential, thing that remains is the remarkable way in which John and the whole Buchan family identified themselves with Canada. To be a Scot was a tremendous advantage: there were Scots everywhere. I gather that Buchan was asked for by Mackenzie King – and that would have been agreeable to the romantic Scot in Ramsay MacDonald. Mackenzie King, 'soft-centred spiritualist' in constant touch with his dead mother and a calculating party politician, was a queer lonely man, who expected to find a buddy in his Governor-General, whom he could lean upon for long heart-to-heart talks into the night. That was not to Buchan's mind or taste: those long Canadian winter nights were for work, and he used them to work harder than ever at his writing, free from the incessant calls and interruptions of life in England.

Elsfield was never the same without him, the whole spirit of the place for me had gone. After his death the family dispersed and left, and in later years I have rarely been up that beloved hill from Oxford – each time to watch for a moment beside his grave under the Round Table, to which did he, after all, belong?

7

Rebecca West; H. G. Wells

My subject is really my friendship with Rebecca West over many years, not her famous *liaison* with H. G. Wells. Others have written about that affair, including both principals; it will be seen that Rebecca wrote to me about it, and now their son, Anthony West, has given us his version. Actually I had had a contact with Wells some years before I met her, and the fact that I had known him was a bond with her. Thus I have placed a semi-colon between them to divide them – as early Saints would place a sword between them and their women in bed (far from H.G. and Rebecca in life); my title is not Rebecca West *and* H.G. Wells.

Let us dismiss him first.

I had seen and heard enough of him at various Leftist gatherings in London, New Fabians, or G. D. H. Cole's S.S.I.P. He was singularly unimpressive on the platform: a dumpy, bright-eyed chirpy little man, with an unregulated wispy moustache, and a pipsqueak of a voice. It was obvious that he was no gentleman, and no proletarian either (which I prided myself on being); he was unmistakably lower middle-class. In contrast to Bernard Shaw, ineffably an Irish gent. – at any rate Anglo-Irish; tall, slim, lithe, erect, on many years of vegetarianism; a carefully cultivated appearance to make him look like nobody else in the world, grizzled beard that had been copper-coloured, quirkish eyebrows; courteous manner and a most effective mastery of speaking and of the art of projecting his public persona.

Shaw had all the advantages, and this gave Wells an irritable inferiority-complex in regard to him; for he too had 'an overmastering determination to impress himself upon his time.' Even Rebecca, years after her disillusioning experience with him, wrote of him as 'master of his time'.

Well, he wasn't. He was a man of genius – that may be taken for granted; but he was not a 'master-mind', in the sense of the British Academy's series of lectures on such. On the other hand, before and after the First German War, he was famous, both in Britain and the USA. Those were the days when writers would incur fame (and garner the rewards) – in an elect world where standards counted for something; and where British writers had positive advantages, a bias in their favour in the USA, where we today have to work our passage the hard way.

Wells made something like £120,000 out of his *Outline of History*, when the pound was worth something too, and taxation not confiscation. But he was not a historian, and I did not think much of his history. I was even less interested in his science, more his field. Nor was I responsive to his novels: *Mr Kipps, Love and Mr Lewisham, Tono-Bungay, Ann Veronica*, were not for me: suburban, lower middle-class, Cockney comedy – not my world. I did appreciate *The Invisible Man*; it made me laugh uncontrollably – Wells had a rollicking sense of humour. I remember quite liking *The History of Mr Polly*.

However, a young Marxist on my high horse, I had no opinion of him as a thinker. I thought – and still think – that Marxism gave a clue to society, its structure and conflicts, a penetrating approach to history. The high-minded Christian, R. H. Tawney, was the better as a historian for imbibing a little Marxism. Wells had nothing of this, and was superficial (and supercilious) enough to think it unimportant and could be ignored.

That did for him in my eyes as a social thinker, and somewhere or other in print I said this. Wells was bent on influencing the mind of my younger generation; Leonard Woolf reported my remark to him, and Wells was concerned enough to write to ask me what I meant. Comically enough, it led to a row between Woolf and Wells. Woolf couldn't find the *locus classicus* of this youthful indiscretion, and I had forgotten where I had said it. It wasn't in a book, as Woolf thought; he couldn't find it in an article – had it been in a letter? Eventually, some years later, he did run it down; it appears somewhere in his Autobiography.

Meanwhile, I had to write and explain myself to Wells – and he carefully kept my letter. For, years after, when Gordon Ray was going through the Wells Archive at the University of Illinois, he came upon it and gave me a copy. I don't remember the content, except that I put what I considered the necessary historical approach to the understanding of society, an indirect way of defending what I *had* said.

Wells was interested enough to want to meet me, and began by asking me to lunch at his Reform Club. I was not charmed: he wanted to talk all the time, and I wanted to talk all the time. We were at cross-purposes: he laid down the law about Science and Society – not my subject and I didn't want to hear about it. I tried to lay down the law about Marxism and Society – he didn't listen. I was put off by his studying his plump, pink, well-manicured little hands. Then he made a mistake: he tried to shock my Marxist purism by telling me about the sexual goings-on of Claire Sheridan, sculptress (Winston's cousin), with the Bolshevik leaders. I said that I wasn't interested in the goings-on of men and women. Then Wells thought to score: 'In that case, you are not interested in half the human race.' I could have told him that, an unreconstructed Swiftian, I was not even interested in one half per cent of the human race.

However, he was obviously interested, for he swore me to let him know, when he got back from France, so that we might meet again. (I had no intention of doing so.) He was on his way to Grasse, where he and Odette Keun had neighbouring properties and, for more than neighbourly convenience, he made a communicating door between the two. When they had had more than enough of each other, he tried to close the aperture.[1] She went to law about it and defeated him; he thereupon wrote a novel about her as *Dolores*. I didn't read it; I merely made a *mot* about her having dropped a 't' from the end of her name and gone all over Europe looking for it.

Wells continued to send me inscribed copies of his books: I

[1] I leave this as I wrote it for the sake of the joke; but it appears that it was more of a *fracas* than I knew. According to Wells's son, Anthony West, Odette managed to throw Wells out of his own house. What a mug he was about women – another contrast with Shaw.

recall the vast (and boring) *Health, Wealth and Happiness of Mankind,* and various brochures and pamphlets planning the future of society. I set no store by them and used promptly to sell them. In later years I have occasionally felt – or thought that I ought to feel – sorry. After all, he had been kind to me, and he was a man of genius. But he just wasn't my type; I was all for history and poetry, my mentors were G. M. Trevelyan and T. S. Eliot. Perhaps my instinct was right; nothing could have come from an association with him, nor was I in fact very sociable.

This happened some years before I met Rebecca, I do not remember how or where. Her first book, *Henry James,* I bought when I was young and poor, I suppose because it was cheap, but I did not read it – beyond me. Nor did I make much of *The Strange Necessity,* not caring much for Lit. Crit. – I prefer creative writing, poetry and the novel. In later life Rebecca said that, if she had had her time over again, she would have written more novels. Her own early novels passed me by. The best of them was a novella, *The Return of the Soldier*: an original theme – the shell-shocked soldier who could not remember his previous existence or family – and an authentic one of that terrible First German War, with its innumerable casualties: a holocaust from which neither Britain nor France fully recovered. We owe that to the Germans.

Still, I have sometimes wondered whether Rebecca was not too cerebral, too much of an intellectual critic, for a novelist. The first thing about her was that she was extraordinarily clever, and hers was a discursive, argumentative intellect, too much interested in everything to concentrate in one field. Unlike Elizabeth Bowen, or Barbara Pym. (I wonder now what she thought of *them?*)

Thus Rebecca was first and last a journalist, and of the most brilliant – that ill-used word, so often used by American academics of books of leaden consistency. It means shining – and Rebecca's journalism shone and scintillated, spluttering with wit. H.G., as we both referred to him, put his finger on its special and curious quality: it was an *intricate* wit. How she carried those elaborate sentences in her head to their explosive conclusions, I cannot think.

Then there was this young woman's breath-taking
impertinence, the dash with which she attacked 'The Gospel
according to Mrs Humphry Ward', the *grande dame* of English
letters before 1914, standard-bearer of women's rights, niece
of Matthew Arnold ('Why, Uncle Matt, will you never be
wholly serious?', of Max Beerbohm's caricature), mother-in-
law of G. M. Trevelyan, whose wedding-service she com-
posed, because the bridal pair were too high-minded to believe
in God; above all, the author of *Robert Elsmere*, so much
admired by Mr Gladstone, though its expressed doubts
alarmed the bishops. 'Barricaded from the fastidious craftsman behind the solid Tottenham-Court-Road workmanship
of her mental furniture . . . Mrs Ward reveals to us the
psychology of the clergyman class.' Or, 'Mr Harold Owen is a
natural slave, having no conception of liberty nor any use for
it. So, as a Freewoman, I review his anti-feminist thesis,
Woman Adrift, with chivalrous reluctance, feeling that a steam-
engine ought not to crush a butterfly. . . . He leaves one
wondering whether one can safely lend an umbrella to one's
uncle.' The author of a work on Eng. Lit. is 'a bishop *manqué*.
He writes in the solemn yet hiccupy style peculiar to bishops,
with a "however", or "indeed" interrupting every sentence.'
His book must have been written 'in apron and gaiters.'

No apron and gaiters for Rebecca at twenty: she was an
'Emancipated Woman'. 'Life ought to be a struggle of desire
towards adventures whose nobility will fertilise the soul. To
avoid the ordeal of emotion that leads to the conception is the
impulse of death. Sterility is the deadly sin.' Again, 'It is the
soul's duty to be loyal to its own desires. It must abandon itself
to its master-passion.' She refuses 'to accept the convention
that if marriage is denied to her so is motherhood.' As for
Shaw, he 'never brought anything so anarchic as an unmarried
mother on to his stage.'

One sees that this young woman at twenty was ready for
H.G. Wells at forty-six, the prophet – and exponent – of free
love, notorious for several affairs which had created scandal.
The latest, with Amber Pember Reeves, daughter of the
Director of the London School of Economics, forsooth,
Beatrice Webb herself told me about. The girl was pregnant;

Blanco White was in love with her, willing to marry her and
take on H.G.'s child. Mrs Webb, formidable woman, was
determined that the marriage should go forward and the
cracks be papered over. She forced Wells, who was reluctant,
to drop the girl: she warned him that, if there were a court-
case, she would go into court and give evidence against him.
This worked: the marriage turned out happily and the bride
turned against her former lover.

I used to wonder why women fell for Wells, so physically
unattractive. Of course Wells was keen, and the charity of
women is inexhaustible. He needed sex, and his otherwise
indispensable wife wouldn't have it, so he was impelled to
look elsewhere. One of his women told G. D. H. Cole that
Wells smelled like honey – and some men, particularly workers on the land, do smell well; women should always wear
scent. Wells, odd as it seems, was attractive to women, who
often enough took the initiative with him. No doubt fame
helped, it seems to go their – hearts. He himself said of Odette
Keun, whose eyes devoured him, that she made him feel that
his trousers were made of gauze.

I was never convinced by Rebecca's account of her affair
with Wells.[2] The 'eternally feminine' of Goethe, she was
entirely subjective, and, with her creative mind, inveterately
given to fantasying. She was not wholly unobjective but, with
her, objectivity was intermittent. Wells, who was already in
trouble on several counts, was cautious and held off at first. It
is obvious that she took the initiative and dared him to take her
on. Wells: 'You're a very compelling person. I suppose I shall
have to do what you want me to do.' They became passionate
lovers – and sex makes fools of us all.

Rebecca became pregnant, and I have never accepted her
account of the responsibility in the matter – which led to so
much continuing trouble. We all know that men are held to be
alone responsible and have to take the blame. Queen Victoria
blamed the Prince Consort for her too numerous children, and
we have had recent cases in public life where the men have had

[2] cf. Gordon N. Ray, who fell a victim to Rebecca's account in his *H. G.
Wells and Rebecca West*. This view is contradicted by Anthony West in his
book on his parents.

to carry all the blame. Men are more naif than women, and more easily taken in. Rebecca wanted to make H.G. marry her: that much is admitted. He was determined not to be divorced from his wife (his second); he was dependent on her to manage his affairs (Rebecca, an intellectual, was never a good manager). Mrs Wells was a *femme complaisante*: she told Beatrice Webb, 'I know H.G. is polygamous, and I don't mind.' Much more, he confided his 'affairs' to her and sought her advice on them. Rebecca said later that she would have settled for a *ménage à trois*. Like the Regency Duke of Devonshire, his Duchess Georgiana, and Lady Elizabeth Foster – whom the Duke married when Georgiana died. Mrs Wells died before many years were out. Suppose Rebecca had waited . . . by then H.G. would not have married her anyway. This was what rankled.

Meanwhile, there was the child to be provided for and brought up, a perpetual bone of contention between them, and a life-long complex to Rebecca, as may be seen from her later letters to me. Before the nuisance arrived, it was, from Wells: 'I think of that happy thing cuddled up in your soft flesh and your dear warm blood.' Or, it was, 'Nobody licks his fur properly 'cept her. Nobody yowls back same as she does. Wants to take Handsful of her dear soft hair and stroke her Magnificent Flanks and—. Ssh!' It is extraordinary to think of a grown-up writing like that, vulgar little man. What would Henry James think of it? – indeed did think of Wells the Vulgarian.

Soon enough the tune changed: 'I love being with my work with everything handy.' That was what Jane Wells provided. 'I *hate* being encumbered with a little boy and a nurse, and being helpful.' Odette Keun saw the perhaps inevitable truth about a writer, when the two women ganged up together against the male chauvinist: 'I've never known anybody in my whole life who, fundamentally, can do without others as he can. It's only a pose of his that he needs people: he only needs people to elaborate his ideas and spread them. And, so long as he can work, he'd master every kind of shock, however sorrowful.' There is the woman's point of view, the female freemasonry. Henry James knew the overriding demand of a writer's vocation, and accepted it. Wells was too mixed-up by sex to give himself wholly to his genius, and – everybody agreed, Henry James, Rebecca, Wells himself – his work suffered.

Then came the recriminations. After their separation Wells destroyed practically all her letters, but we may judge what they were from what remains. They nagged and raged at each other, and Rebecca admits that it was her nature to answer rage with rage. Wells: 'The thing goes on and on with you, and I am tired to death with it. I do regret very bitterly that I ever met you, but I have done what I could to make some sort of life tolerable for us. For ten years I've shaped my life mainly to repair the carelessness of one moment. It has been no good and I am tired of it.' And again, 'I do not love you and I do not feel the slightest stirring of jealousy about you.' Really, after all those expressions of love! . . .

Later came Rebecca's complaints. 'He treated me with the sharpest cruelty imaginable for those horrible years' – she was a great one for complaining and exaggerating. 'He has cheated me of all but one child' – after all the trouble that one was to them! It is extraordinary that people should write like that to and about each other – like the letters of D. H. Lawrence (Rebecca was a character out of Lawrence, out of *Women in Love*), or the denizens of Bloomsbury, analysing themselves and each other to bits. The lack of self-control is incomprehensible – very unlike the correspondence of Henry James or G. M. Trevelyan, or even Eliot or mine.

Then there was money, of course, hardly necessary to specify. Wells was generous to his mistresses. Rebecca opened her mouth for £3000 a year; he gave her $20,000 out of his American royalties; then Odette insisted on trusts for the child's education. (What mugs men are about women!) When Wells died, she came out with: 'I loved him all my life and always will, and I bitterly reproach myself for not having stayed with him, because I think I was fairly good for him. . . . The tyranny was the incorrigible part of him – I could not have submitted to it all my life; nor do I think that he could have loved me or that I could have loved him if I had been the kind of person that could.'

What is one to make of that tangle of self-contradiction? It has the maddening feminine quality of inconsistency. Work was what mattered to a man; thus Wells: 'Your output of work has been trivial, my work has suffered enormously.' Rebecca's weakness in regard to him was that she thought – or at least assured him – that he was 'a great man'. Wells, for his part, assured her that '*The Outline of History* is going to change History.' I well remember the enormous *réclame* it had; but that was all. Fancy anybody thinking anything of the sort!

In her letters to me Rebecca gave varying accounts of her affair with H.G. Fairly early in our acquaintance, 'I write to you in a cold sweat of apprehension about a blithering paper I have received, suggesting that as a memorial to H. G. Wells an organisation should be formed to promote the publication of works which might be supposed to be in line with his ideas. I hope you disapprove of this as strongly as I do. H.G. was like Voltaire, he was master of his time, and ran beside it so assiduously that, when he broke with time, there was little to tell us what he would have thought of this world at this moment. I can see a committee being formed which would be indefatigable in their loyalty to H.G.'s ideas of, say 1910, and who make his name dusty in the eyes of a new generation by associating his name with the Joads who are yet to be born. I can see the dowdy progressive line which is bound to be followed. Look at the names on the list – Kingsley Martin, Vera Brittain, G. D. H. Cole, Dame Sybil Thorndike. Oh *God.*'

Twenty years later, after we had become much closer: 'Don't be apprehensive because I answer almost by return. You express wonder that I should have gone off with H.G., because he was so vulgar. But there was a very simple explanation. I had an aching need for affection and reassurance. While my mother and sister Winifred loved me very much, I nevertheless was emotionally starved during my adolescence. One of my family had always scolded and nagged me all day long. My sisters went out into the world, to school and University, and I was left at home with my mother, who then became a victim of Graves Disease (an exophthalmic goitre). She became unkind and ungrateful, and I had to use all my energy to keep her going, and got to school exhausted, upon which my teachers tormented me. When my sisters returned home I got no praise whatever, and indeed was nagged worse than ever. I simply wanted to be loved and cherished – the natural place to seek it was in a man's arms – and what arms I chose! But the point about H.G. that was, when he was not possessed by a devil, he delighted in and perceived one's good points as nobody else. And indeed all would not have been so bad if it had not been for—' and there follows a rocket against her son, which I omit.

It is no secret that Rebecca had a complex about Anthony, and went on about it in other letters; it was no business of mine, and I never reverted to it. I did not know him. I had met him only once, when Gerald Berners was staying with me in Cornwall, and John Betjeman brought Anthony to lunch. All I remember of the occasion was John's exclamation, seeing Johannesberger on the bottle of wine, 'And South African, by Jove!', to Gerald's reproach: 'he should have known better.'

After this meeting Rebecca wrote me a letter to say that she heard that I had taken Anthony's side against her. I was quite innocent in the matter and hardly knew what she was complaining about. (I hate complaints, another boring feminine trait.) Anyway I was able to reassure her of my innocence.

A later letter ended up, 'Thank you for the kind words about *The Birds Fall Down*.' (I thought this remarkable novel her best.) 'I could have been a good writer had I not been torn apart by a horde of devils.' I had been writing about Swift, a lifelong interest of mine. Rebecca was Anglo-Irish like him, and ended, 'An odd thing about Swift is that his biographers always write of the diseases inflicted on him by old age as if they were his normal state in middle age.' This, by the way, is not exact; nor do I suppose that her highly suggestive account of her youth is exact either. Nor perhaps her conclusion: 'People love you very much. I hear them saying so, often and often. Yours ever, with real love, Rebecca.' She was the most generous of women, but I did not count on that assurance – too sceptical and despairing of humans.

An earlier letter, of December 1947, throws light on her attitude towards her own writing. 'I have never been able to write with anything more than the left hand of my mind; the right hand has always been engaged in something to do with personal relationships. I don't complain, because I think my left hand's power, as much as it has, is due to its knowledge of what my right hand is doing.' Precisely: I should have thought that engagement in personal relations is the necessary equipment for a novelist.

She wanted to argue with me about my little *aide-mémoire*, *All Souls and Appeasement*, of which C. P. Snow had written, 'This is just as it was' – though attacked by a Junior Fellow, one Wolfenden, who had not been through the experience and did not know what he was talking about. Rebecca wrote, 'I am in the main in enthusiastic agreement: I think no analysis of the situation has come near to yours for shrewdness. But since I have been writing on Fascism and anti-Semitism I have wondered if Halifax and Chamberlain were not terribly representative.' She was right: they were; people supported them all the way along, and then were surprised when it landed them in war. She went on, 'The people who live in prefabs are valuable because they are living in houses which are apt symbols for their minds. But the minds of English people are often like that when they live in beautiful houses, large or small.

'There is a fact revealed by my correspondents which has interested me very much. The English correspondents present an extraordinary contrast to the Irish and the Jews, in their attitude to themselves: they do not seem to have any conception of themselves. The Jews write reams on what it is to be a Jew, and how wonderful they are. The Irish write reams on what it is to be Irish, and how much more than wonderful they are. "We are a people the like of which has never been seen," tells one, "for purity, generosity, courage, and simple wisdom." But the English never say what they are; they talk about the Union Jack and wanting to be worthy of England, but they hardly ever express an opinion of what they are. If you ever think of what you are, it is obviously more difficult to mobilise yourself for action, than if you were absorbed in a picture of yourself for twenty minutes out of every half-hour.'

Kipling has a perceptive poem on just this theme, but I doubt if he was a favourite with Rebecca, too much a Left Intellectual for him.

By 1957 I had become her 'favourite dreaming spire', and I would reply flirtatiously, 'Come down, O maid, from yonder mountain height'; for she was now happily married to Henry Andrews, a rich banker, with a large house at Ibstone on a ridge of the Chilterns. When Henry couldn't come down into Oxford and I suggested that she could come alone, it was, 'I couldn't trust myself.' (Dear Rebecca, at her age! And how little perceptive of her: she would have been disappointed.) Or she would bid me up to meet the siren Violet Trefusis, famous Mrs Keppel's daughter. I think she liked to have people think that she was Edward VII's, and indeed she had the figure. I rather think that clever Alice Keppel played the game properly by her husband, the Colonel. I have always been enchanted by the knowing Italian who, seeing them together on the Piazza in Venice, was able to inform his companion: 'See that man – Queen Victoria is his mistress.' I was not able to make much of Violet Trefusis, except to compliment her on her romantic Cornish name. Oh, no; she could never change that, she assured me. I registered 'disingenuous'.

A letter of February 1961 has some autobiographical interest. 'As a woman I have a great grievance on the physical plane, because I was born at a time which meant that the periods when I was young, and not so young that I was miserably shy, and when I had money to spend on clothes, coincided with the period when the best clothes were made by Chanel. The dresses that she made, or that other makers copied, were unbelievably hideous. I had to wear a hat bashed down on my head, and skinny and shapeless sacks that looked bad if one was made like a choirboy, and worse if one was not! Exactly the same thing seems to me to have happened in my time in literature, with T. S. Eliot preaching that you must not have three-quarters of an idea to every ten pages, and Leavis using fastidiousness like a *nouveau riche* who buys asparagus tongs for eating asparagus. All this dreary nonsense has made the world more grey than the Galilean succeeded in doing.'

I remember an earlier *contretemps* of hers with Eliot, to which he had replied with his usual courtesy by inviting her up to 24 Russell Square to discuss the issue over a cup of tea. She did not respond: Eliot was not her cup of tea. Quite right about the dreary Leavis, of course. I was to come up to lunch: 'I have a couple of sphinxes on the terrace that I did not have when you were last here, and I think you might like them.'

Rebecca had married Henry in 1930; he was able to support her in style: not only a largish Georgian country house, with farm attached, but a London life as well. Would I disinter myself from historical research to come up to the Picasso party at the Tate, dinner beforehand? No, I would not: London life was not for me. The domestic life of All Souls was more to my taste.

Both Henry, a New College man, and Rebecca were always willing to come down to All Souls with me. As she got grander and more at ease with society she became more and more interested in her Anglo-Irish descent and, since I was so very West Country, would insist that she had West Country blood through the Champernownes of Dartington. She wrote me reams about it. As time went on her letters show her clearly as Irish, or Anglo-Irish; hardly a word about her Scottish family, though she had been brought up in Edinburgh and very well educated at George Watson's Ladies College. I noticed that she had the Scots-Irish use of 'will' and 'would' for shall and will. (Today hardly anybody has the correct usage, and American writers don't know it.)

In earlier letters she did not mention her father, a typically feckless Irish gent, a Fairfield, apparently gifted and scholarly, a gambler, who could not bear the chains of family life. He deserted it, leaving his wife, an excellent Scots woman, whom Rebecca adored, to bring up three daughters. One sees why Rebecca needed a man so much: she as good as had no father. The ardent feminist all her life had been reared in an exclusively feminine environment. The clue to Rebecca is that, though her brain and *bildung* were Scotch, her temperament and character were Irish. This too is where she got her verbal wit, her sheer gift for words – like Cyril Connolly, who would scarcely recognise it, and claimed to be English, in spite of his all too visible characteristics. One notices this specific gift for words in the best writers of the language in America: Scott Fitzgerald, Flannery O'Connor, Eugene O'Neill, perhaps Edmund Wilson.

On one occasion, when Philip Magnus was staying with me, she was looking forward to discussing her family connexion with Edmund Burke, about whom he had written. In 1962 I had published *Ralegh and the Throckmortons,* based on the invaluable find of the Diary of Ralegh's brother-in-law, Sir Arthur Throckmorton, fullest and most remarkable of all Elizabethan diaries. It revealed the inner story of Ralegh's secret marriage, the birth of a child unknown to history – called after his West Country descent, D'Amory ('Damerei') – along with a great deal of fascinating information which has not yet seeped through into conventional textbooks.

Rebecca's alert mind was all interest. 'I have some interest in the Raleghs, being descended from Joan Champernowne who was Ralegh's aunt; but apart from that interest, I am delighted by the pace and concentration and warmth of your book.' With her rather bawdy mind she was struck by Throckmorton's intimate revelation of the horrors of regular Elizabethan purgations. 'The things which distinguish man from the brutes – the use of the hand, of course, but also surely distress over the bowels.' Who but Rebecca would have thought of that?

She goes on – so characteristic of her discursive mind: 'It has struck me as so odd that the Manichaeans, who were obviously more rather than less intelligent than the mob, were so worried about the discreditable contents of the intestines; and the contemporary African, who *loves* his little children, for their own good drives many of them straight out of this world by driving sin out of their little rectums by castor and even croton oil.' (Here by the way is an example of Rebecca's *intricacy* of mind and style.) 'Throckmorton was obviously trying to rid himself of those Tudor characteristics which he saw were making hell for him and his group, a self-made hell. But what an iron constitution he must have had.' Not so, Rebecca – too clever by half; Throckmorton's Spring purgings were just regular habit with Elizabethans. The historic truth was much simpler than Rebecca's fertile fantasyings; but then, I didn't waste time arguing with her, as H.G. had done – it would have been endless, she was all over the place.

There shortly followed a long letter about her Tudor ancestors. 'My collateral ancestress who is said to have been the source of so many peerages was Joyce, the eldest daughter of Sir Edmund Denny, King's Remembrancer to Henry VII, who married as her first husband, Sir William Walsingham, and as her second Sir John Carey, whose brother married

Mary Boleyn. [Correct: that was young William Carey, who became father of Lord Hunsdon, Patron of Shakespeare's Company, and protector of Emilia, *née* Bassano.] The brother of Joyce, Sir Anthony Denny, was my direct ancestor, and he married Joan Champernowne.' I omit more details.

'Her elder son, Henry, married Lord Grey de Wilton' – Spenser's hero in the *Faery Queene*. 'But that line died out in 1660. Henry's son was the original Earl of Norwich, and my cousin, Sir Henry Denny, an alcoholic rector sustained only by pride of birth in that unhappy position, ground his teeth at Duff Cooper for taking that title.' Fancy bothering! old Denny – I had no notion of his being related to Rebecca – used to bore me with fanmail about his ancestry.

Rebecca too. 'Henry's second wife was Elizabeth, daughter of Lord John Grey, and their younger son married a daughter of Piers Edgcumbe [of that Cornish family], and went to Ireland, and vegetated. Then some Denny girl had a daughter who married Charles George Fairfield, originally of County Longford: my grandfather.' – So that's who the Fairfields were. 'All this you know one way and another, but I thought it might interest you to see how it links up with the person who comes to lunch.' I didn't know it, and was interested only in herself the writer.

There followed another long screed, for 'here's a thing that has often seemed to me a wonderful example of the way events and personalities disguise their true nature.' Here was Rebecca the novelist of *The Birds Fall Down*, and her obsessive interest in *The Meaning of Treason*, spies and double-agents. 'There was an Irish General called Sir William Cuppidge, whose cousin was the William Burke who lived with Edmund Burke; the poor chap spent his life bailing out those two financial morons.' (They were worse than that.) 'Cuppidge's sister was my great-grandmother, or great-great. There could be nothing more English-sounding than the name Cuppidge; or more English, I understand, than the Cuppidges, who left Ireland and settled in Vancouver. But the founder of the Cuppidge family was a German soldier of fortune who came to Ireland, and his real name was Faustus Cuppich. The Cuppidges married mostly Scottish immigrants to Ireland, such as the Clydesdale Campbells [her mother's family, Celtic enough], and never any family domiciled in England. So the connection with England was purely institutional, school and army, and cultural.'

Altogether, one sees how un-English Rebecca was. Her obsession with her ancestry and family connexions reminded me of people of good family in the Southern States. There must have been something in this complicated link-up, for later I was to meet a Walter Raleigh Coppedge, when President of Charleston College, South Carolina.

Next month, she brought Curzon's daughter, Lady Ravensdale, down to All Souls. Curzon had been a great figure in the College, and when I was young his legend still lingered. 'Irene was enchanted by the visit to her father's haunts, and to bring enchantment into her sad world is really a deed that will let you off several thousand years in Purgatory. (Where both you and I may, I feel, spend some considerable time).' Note that Rebecca's lifelong habit of exaggerating everything was not an English trait, but Irish. (Nothing could be more English than Clem Attlee, by contrast.)

'I didn't know of the trouble you had mentioned. I knew her well in the Twenties and Thirties, and it was then threatened, but I have seen very little of her in the past fifteen years, and I hoped that like many of our friends she had shed that habit as she came out of those raffish years. My nephew dearly loved you. He is a genius, by the way, and also wildly interested outside his special field. As for Virginia [Cowles] and Bill, obviously Virginia is the attraction, and your frank, free prattle made me reflect that she is the object of deep affection on the part of two highly intelligent women. Polly Kahn, the wife of Gilbert Kahn, whom I think the most wonderful creature, lovely and intelligent, and Barbara Gimbel, the Californian schoolteacher, who married the chairman of Sachs, Fifth Avenue, and is quite something. I hadn't realised the pattern till you spoke of it.'

Well, the innocent historian, with all that feminism about, was alive to the possibility of a spot of Lesbianism. In earlier years, Rebecca had been an intimate of Lady Rhondda and her circle around *Time and Tide*. Why not? With Colette, it had been strokes all round the wicket, in Maurice Bowra's phrase; or in the French, *à voile et à vapeur*.

'What a unique tragedy the Curzon family have acted out – do you realise that Curzon's second and *quelconque* wife got through about half-a-million and there was nothing, nothing, NOTHING, to show for it?' Of course, I knew about it. I had been an undergraduate along with her alcoholic son, Alfred Duggan, whose historical novels Evelyn Waugh had boosted out of Catholic freemasonry. If only all that Duggan money had gone into saving Kedleston and its treasures, as no doubt Curzon intended! All I care about – the vanishing heritage, in our squalid society.

A few days later she received my *Ralegh* book: 'The relative to whom I lent my own copy – bought the day of publication, such was my esurience [what a vocabulary she commanded!] has asked me if she may keep it. Yes, Virginia did fall for the (not at all old) Professor, not that she's bored with Bill – they beat different records all the time of different sorts and respect each other's muscles, if nothing else. But I am sorry if she was too insistent on coming to Oxford. Still, you forgave her, with all your usual sweetness of spirit.' Evidently, my defences were well up: like Arthur Balfour, where women were concerned, I 'fancied a career for myself'.

'How charming of you to think that my nephew has charm. Yes, I think that in the kingdom of heaven everybody will fall for everybody all round. And how lovely it will be, with those enfolding wings, so much better than what Leda got, which I have thought must have been technically so unmanageable.' I fear that I was unresponsive to Rebecca's bawdy streak – all very well for H.G., not for H.J.

At this point came the letter giving her version of why she had 'gone off with' H.G. And later I was to receive an invitation to meet Gordon Ray of the Guggenheim – whom I already knew – who was writing up her account of the affair. She would, if only I would come, put me up for the night: 'No strings.' Nor did another invitation to meet Violet Trefusis lure me out of my defences: 'Violet was so disappointed.' I was more pleased to learn that Rebecca had always adored Hawker of Morwenstow, when I sent her my essay on him. 'I had overlooked the delightful incident when he read the Exorcistic Service over the five farmers. This is not only endearing but really useful information, for I fly to South Africa on January

6th, and I shall now know what to do at any awkward moment. I shall be back in two months and hope to see you if greedy America hasn't snatched you from us.' It had – after various disappointments I wasn't the one to put up with (always from the second- and third-rate, never the first-rate), I was spending half my time there now: a new phase to my life, an altogether new experience, after claustrophobic Oxford (which I had loved), a new world to explore.

Through all these years Rebecca had kept up her journalism. Now she was one of a cloud of vultures from all over the world who settled on South Africa to report the consequences of the Soweto shooting, when the Africaners, who now had their own way in what they regarded as their own country, fulfilled Milner's pessimistic forecast of what would happen when they had. The world's journalists were all of one liberal mind, quite sure that such a state of affairs, the Africaner ascendancy, could not last more than two or three years. Rebecca, always a liberal, subscribed to this illusion like the rest of them. I thought at the time what fools they were. Had they no judgment? Didn't they know how tough the Boers were? They hadn't fought the whole British Empire to see their country become another Nigeria, or Uganda. The liberal illusions of those who suppose themselves to be so intelligent – and sometimes are – are ludicrous to a historian. Dear Rebecca was no exception; but then she was no historian. H.G. had ended in utter despair, with *Mankind at the End of its Tether*. He should never have entertained such superficial hopes of mankind earlier. And how the world's prospects have worsened even in the years since then!

With Henry Andrews I had good relations. A nice but uninteresting rich man, he worshipped Rebecca and made it his prime business to look after her, which was what she needed. When she wrote her book, *The Court and the Castle*, an interpretation of *Hamlet*, he wrote to me privately to vet the typescript: he was afraid for her that she might put a foot wrong. I dutifully read it, but remember nothing of it. I didn't see why she had to write her interpretation of *Hamlet*. There are hundreds of superfluous works on Shakespeare's plays, practically all of them of little value. The play itself is the thing: let it speak for itself. Beyond that, one needs to know its place in Shakespeare's work, when it was written, the circumstances of the time, the personal and topical experience that went into its making. This is precisely what the critics are incapable of providing, and cannot see the significance of when it is provided for them. As the leading Canadian novelist today, though a professor – Hugh MacLennan – writes to me: 'They simply don't understand how plays and novels are written.'

Instead of wasting her time on a critical 'interpretation', Rebecca might have re-written *Hamlet* as a novel – she did know how to write a novel – as Tom Stoppard re-worked the theme of Rosencrantz and Guildenstern in an exciting play. (Louis Auchincloss, with whom I saw the play in New York, missed the point of it – as with my own Shakespeare discoveries.)

On my summer return to All Souls I regularly had lunch parties in that *décor* to mingle my American and British friends, new and old. I find a letter from Henry to tell me how impressed he was by a party for Rouben Mamoulian, the film producer, who had first brought Greta Garbo to the fore in *Queen Christina* (Stalin's favourite film). He was the first too to produce a modern acting version of *Hamlet*. He made the point that, when he was young in Russia, he could always understand Shakespeare in Russian. When he became American, though he had a remarkable command of English, he could not always understand Shakespeare's archaic language. This put an idea into my head.

When Henry died Rebecca gave up the country house near Oxford, and moved back to an entirely London life at Prince's Gate in Kensington. Without Henry she was once more at a loss. In June 1967, 'I am in a welter of distress and incompetence. I do not really suffer from the loss of Henry because the last two years made it a cruelty to wish anything for him but release, it was like an animal caught in a trap. Now what is left for me demands adaptations I find so difficult to make. I should be at home in this place [Kingston House North, where she had a large flat], with which I have long and mystical ties – really strange ones. It was built on the site of the house where the bigamous Duchess of Kingston died – a lovely house – my mother and I used to go on the top of a bus to visit a cousin, who had one of those Regency houses near Chiswick House. I used to point to Kingston House and say, "I will live there when I am grown up" – and it has come about, but *not* as I hoped!

'I could be reasonably happy here if I had not had to break up my library. I could not bring even half of it here, and I have almost no hope of ever arranging it in a usable way. The use I made of it didn't come out so much in my work as in my own personal life. . . . I am speaking on McLuhan to the English Association, and I wanted to illustrate a point by a reference to an odd essay of Valéry on Le Prince et la Jeune Parque (a German prince who was in love with Rachel, do you remember).' She couldn't recall the name of the volume, and so couldn't get it from the library; when she panicked – one knows the feeling – it turned up by miracle.

She wanted to read my 'Cornish Oxford' book, I suppose *A Cornishman Abroad*, for 'I would like to talk to you about Adam von Trott.' She knew what odious German characteristics are, for they are portrayed to the life in her *Black Lamb and Grey Falcon*, a big two-tiered best-seller which must have made her a small fortune. 'I went to Oxford the other day . . . and walked about all Sunday morning, and envied everybody who had been a (male) student there. What is it Oxford does to girls? They all look Kardomah, except the ones I meet with you. Tell me when you are in London and want lunch – I will be [Scotch-Irish usage for 'shall'] fit for receiving the great in about a fortnight. Love from your faithful Rebecca.'

Next summer I came back from the USA to find that Rebecca had returned from Mexico to deal with business concerning Henry's estate, and 'to find my house had been *stripped* by a wicked charwoman during my absence, and as she has elected to be tried by jury this goes on and on. I am so appalled to find that the courts are simply choked by the crime wave. This woman was arrested on February 17, she has not been tried yet [June]. This social crisis is a great deal worse than people realise.' But, of course: I had realised it all along, belonging to the people I know what they are – it was middle-class people, like Rebecca, with their liberal illusions, who hadn't realised. She wanted me to come and comfort her, 'for you are one of the few people I dearly love.' Dear Rebecca, she was full of love; sad that I could not respond more, I see now. However, I did respond to her invitation 'to meet someone whose ancestors you know very well – my cousin, Anthony Denny.'

Next spring she took the chair for me at a lecture at the Royal Society of Literature on Simon Forman; but I could not recognise myself in the description she gave of me. I suppose we think of other people's view of us as subjective, and our own as objective; and men regard themselves as more objective. Virginia Woolf – what did Rebecca think of her? – made a case for feminine subjectiveness as equipment for the novelist: but not for a historian, and Rebecca was given to fantasies. She wrote me after: 'It was such a lovely lecture and you gave it so well and looked so entrancing. (My niece said, "Nothing prepared me for such an absolute *beauty*.")' Well, really: what nonsense! She made me an offer of two whole albums of photographs of astrological material which Henry had had made for the Yale Library. I wasn't interested in astrological nonsense – like Frances Yates who wasted her scholarship on it, Hermeticism, Rosicrucianism and such. As a historian I was concerned with facts, the intimate facts of Elizabethan social and sexual life revealed by Forman. Academic historians, except for Lawrence Stone, have not caught up with it yet. Rebecca's bawdy side was tickled by Forman's code-word for copulation: *halek*. One still doesn't know its derivation, but a musical was devoted to Forman in California under that title. 'What a lovely phrase it sounds now: "The March of the men of Halek." Much affection and admiration, Your devoted Rebecca.'

At last, in 1971, she visited Ireland, and wrote me yards about it; the novelist took charge, and I must contract its exuberance. 'My Anglo-Irish father was elderly when I was born and we had no family to go to there, and so we stayed among our Scottish relatives. My sister Letitia, now 86, and I did a pilgrimage to the homes and tombs of our ancestors in County Cork and County Kerry, and I was staggered by the collision there between the lushness of County Cork and

South Kerry – with its hedges of fuchsias and hydrangeas and wild montbretias – and the mountain wildness of North Kerry. We went to Youghal . . . to see the tombs of our remote ancestors, the Ormondes, in the old Protestant church, and to visit Ralegh's house. We asked the owner, Commander Arbuthnot if we might see the house, as Ralegh was a collateral ancestor of ours.

'We turned up in a car driven by one of the many out-of-work, white-collar Irishmen, very sad and very sensitive and sick at heart over the Ulster business.' (He might well be – much worsened since.) Ralegh's house is 'a long low building, quite small, and it has a gravel sweep in front of it. Round and round the gravel sweep were walking the Commander, his wife and his schoolgirl daughter, not together but isolated, all looking down on the gravel. When we went across they greeted us with the abandonment of ordinary custom one would expect from ghosts. They were not uncivil, they were just hardly there. They all spoke very softly, and never volunteered a remark, or answered one except in monosyllables. They were really extraordinarily like ghosts.'

The novelist describes the interior, the staircase 'ornamented with the most beautiful Victorian flower-paintings from some relative whose husband had been stationed abroad. What acres of flower-paintings the British Empire produced. He told us that this had been the home of Sir John Pope Hennessy's father; and that his sister-in-law was the sister of Claud Cockburn' – famous in the Thirties as creator of *The Week*. (He retired to Ireland, whence I have letters from him: we were Anti-Appeasers together.)

Rebecca noticed the Commander's resemblance to Wellington's delightful Mrs Arbuthnot of the Diary, and a portrait of her was fetched which corroborated it. Rebecca felt the whole atmosphere to smack of the supernatural (but couldn't it have been fear?). At the church the sexton was astonished to hear that they had been inside: 'Nobody went to the house. The incident seemed to me typical of Ireland. It was as if there was a chemical process going on which drained everything off the country and left a precipitate of fear.

'I was so horrified by what had happened to the house in Tralee where my father was born, in Day Place, an exquisite

Georgian terrace. It belongs to a prosperous dentist, and he has gutted the interior.' But of course. 'It looks like a Council-house, while his wife potters about, holding up china cherubs out of no known ceramic stable, and Woolworth pink glass vases and says how she loves anteeks. (Spondee.) How horrible it is to know that the same thing has happened to Ibstone House, which has been mutilated; the present owner runs a chain of dress-shops in the Thames Valley and is a Christian Science practitioner.

'In Tralee we met quite an interesting character, a young man who was risking much by saying that Ireland was a product of Celt plus Englishman; his great-grandfather having come from Cornwall to join the R.I.C. [Royal Irish Constabulary], and his grandfather having followed suit; and his father also, having passed into the service of the municipality, as R.I.C. personnel did when the body was broken up. What an odd situation, how like what must have happened on the fringes of the Roman Empire at a certain time. And how the Catholic middle-class can allure one by its innocence and its sweetness. There was a family we visited in Listowel who had the ideal Quaker sweetness about them.

'But in Dublin I sat next – at a party I got roped into in the Kildare Street Club (which used to be a Protestant stronghold) Erskine Childers, who has, I think, no drop of Irish blood in him, English and American [Irish American and a bit of Scotch, Rebecca], and is a Cabinet Minister. Looking exactly like Beaverbrook, he sat beside me and hissed in my ear denunciations of the wickedness of – who do you think? – who could be most irrelevant to the tragedy of North Ireland? Believe it or not – the Duke of Windsor.' Erskine Childers, whose Republican father was shot as a rebel by the Free State, became President of the Republic. He was a reader of my Elizabethan books, and invited me, when in Dublin, to the former Vice-Regal Lodge I should like to have seen. Next thing he was dead.

'How smartly your familiar goes for the seat of Trevor-Roper's trousers. Your familiar is a very engaging animal. I shall be happy with your book for the next week or two. Longer, of course, but my happiness will be intense during that period. And do see me when you come back. It is such a

long time since you came and nearly haleked the debs in my
kitchen.' Not so, dear Rebecca: merely polite flirtation.

She followed up with a 'Supplementary' to correct my
saying that Belloc's sister had been worldly enough to marry
her daughters off very well. 'But she didn't. She let both her
daughters, without a protest, marry husbands quite
unsatisfactory from a worldly point of view. Elizabeth married Lord Iddesleigh, who had no money at all and gave her no
other distinction than that which belongs to the wife of the
only known Albino Peer. [However, an earl is an earl is an
earl, and a Catholic earl rarer still.] Her other daughter
married a Portuguese journalist and – believe me, Leslie, as
only your adopted mother – I should be bitterly disappointed
if you made such an alliance. It would be as if I had heard you
had married Helen Gardner.'

In February 1972, 'I think of you so often now, for I am
writing my memoirs and in 100 pages have not got past the
year 1800 – my family history has so much affected me. It
grieves me very much to pass from the Denny who was a
cousin of Swiss[3] Sir Walter and the Gilberts to the Dennys (my
great-great grandfather and my grandmother), who handed
over all the family fortune to the Plymouth Brethren.' That
bespeaks a crazy streak in the family line. She goes over again
her visit to the homes of her ancestors and how she so loved
the place – 'those hedges of crimson fuchsias and the ancient
high crosses, the spitting images of the ones in Macedonia, and
Dingle Peninsula which is so like a grey Greece. But oh the
JOIN THE IЯA painted across the railway bridges and the
children playing with pistols in the market-place, and the
grinning woman who said to me, "Aar, they're playin' theyre

---

[3] This is a reference to John Aubrey's bawdy story, how Ralegh 'one time
getting up one of the Maids of Honour against a tree in a wood, who seemed
at first boarding to be something fearful of her honour – she cried, "Sweet
Sir Walter, what do you me ask? Will you undo me? Nay, sweet Sir Walter!
Sweet Sir Walter." At last, as the danger and the pleasure at the same time
grew higher, she cried in the ecstasy, "Swisser Swatter! Switter Swatter!"
She proved with child. . . .' And hence Ralegh's trouble with the Queen.
The prig of an editor of the otherwise standard edition of Aubrey's *Brief
Lives* – Andrew Clark – omitted this, along with a good deal more fun. One
has to look elsewhere.

in Bélfâst!" How I hate the thought of the young soldiers being killed. Denny wrote that queer phrase about Ireland being fitter for mastiffs than for men. I wonder why mastiffs.' I suppose because they were fierce dogs. Swift regarded the Irish as mad.

'My dear Leslie, I hope we meet sometime soon. You have become very retiring – do consider that in these hard times you should shed your light around.' To what point, in such a filthy society? I was more and more determined on withdrawal from it.

At the end of that year, 'Were you in England at Christmas time, would you come to my birthday and watch me gracefully becoming eighty during either lunch or dinner? I should so love to have you there – think of me as your little Champernowne, you don't know many people as thoroughly Tudor as me.' However, I was in Cornwall at Christmas time, so I asked if my celebration might take the form of dedicating a book to her. She replied, 'I can't quite believe it about the dedication – are you not just "leading me in" like a Victorian seducer – will you not turn to me and break my heart with your mocking laughter? – I am still enchanted by your book, in spite of its revelation about my collateral ancestor, Richard Champernowne.' This was merely a rumour at Court, reported by fellow-Devonian Drake, that he was 'a gelder of boys' to preserve their voices. He had a choir at Dartington, and Robert Cecil wanted one of his boys with a fine voice for his choir. This came into *The Elizabethan Renaissance: the Cultural Achievement.* 'What an odd world you suddenly reveal in those pages. I was thinking the other day that the person I would most desire to meet of them all would be Thomas Hariot – but by preference with Walter Ralegh. What a bright vision you give of it all.' Her choice showed her judgment: Hariot was the most brilliant scientific intellect of the time, the most hidden and mysterious.

Simon Forman: Sex and Society in Shakespeare's Age was duly dedicated to her, as 'admirable writer, constant friend', not without a naughty suggestion of the propriety of dedicating so sexy a book to her.

'The wording of your dedication gives me such pleasure. That is the way one would like to be described by someone whom one loves and honours, and, dear, how lovely it is that honour is the word, though you are such fun.' She would pass over more of her 'peculiarly eerie family trouble' – I never entered into that, regarding families (my own especially) as such a bore.

'My egotism gloats over the knowledge that the Dark Lady was kept by an ancestor, but I don't know if direct or collateral, Lord Hunsdon. . . . There was evidently something in Simon Forman's claims to magic powers.' And she told me yet another story of coincidence regarding a book. Her secretary had fetched her a *Who's Who*, to look up an Elton, but her thumb had rested on the only Forman in the book. She wondered whether Simon went as far as a soothsayer, for 'he cannot have been able to concentrate with all that haleking. How beautifully, by the way, do you discern who it was that was Forman's true love.'

This identification, Avice Allen, wife of a London grocer, gave me far more trouble than the obvious identity of Shakespeare's Dark Lady, with the patron of his Company, the Lord Chamberlain, as her protector – so close, along with complete corroboration as to circumstances, characteristics and definite dating. When Avice Allen died, my research helper and I looked through all the London parish registers in print for her burial. In vain: no luck. Then it occurred to me that the reason for her not being there was that she might have been a Catholic. I looked up the Roll of Middlesex Catholic Recusants – and there she was.

'I wish you hadn't told me that Emilia had been converted to her really very touching Christianity – Christ wasn't, she's obviously saying, a bit like all those rude boys that haleked her with their boots on – at Cookham, where later St Spencer painted all those screaming religious paintings – it suggests that places determinate.' She then goes into various odd events and happenings at Cookham. 'Your writing of this book is tighter than some of your other work – and must have been written with great care, and I suppose that's why it has such an effect.' Not much effect on the numb, and dumb, I fear. 'I liked the Life, with its picture of a man in the difficult situation of having a burning passion to practice a science that had not yet been truly invented.'

My sympathy for Forman was for the poor boy who was desperately keen to educate himself, when others who had all the chances gave themselves no trouble. We have reason to be grateful too to the old *roué* for the information that directed me to the Dark Lady, with whom his experience exactly corroborated that of William Shakespeare four and five years before. 'This is indeed my book. Somehow your dedication has given it to me in a special sense. I was so moved by Forman's account of his father's death. And surely it is an extraordinary piece of writing, as well as of feeling.' No one else noticed it, except this woman of genius. Perhaps this is to be expected; but ordinary people need to be, and should have been, told. Simon Forman was a very interesting character, an addition to the gallery of remarkable Elizabethans.

I followed this up by publishing the Dark Lady's long religious poem, *Salve Deus, Rex Judaeorum,* for which we had a celebration thoughtfully laid on by the learned librarian at All Souls, John Simmons. What fun we had in those days, one way and another: he sprang surprise quotations for us under our plates at lunch. Rebecca: 'The Rivers-Scotts are bringing me down to your Dark Lady festival, and we will present ourselves in a state of delight, because we are to be with you, the great Illuminator, the power Exorciser.' One Nigel Dennis had crabbed a book of mine in her paper, and I inquired who he was. 'No, Nigel Dennis is not a Catholic. If he dies and finds there is a God he will sue. He is a gloom-browed congenital sourpuss and is worse now because he is living in Malta.'

In 1975 I was asking her about Mary Renault, whose books I admired, and Rebecca had lived so much in London that she knew, or knew about, everybody. 'She is an ex-hospital nurse of quite a high standing. I think she was a theatre sister at one of the teaching hospitals. She then went to South Africa and lived with another nurse in a most revolting shanty on the edge of the Indian ocean. The breakers pounded down on the rocks only a few yards away from you. It was most alarming. I think she is an extremely good writer and she was also very good-looking in a severe way. I agree with you about Elizabeth Jenkins' – another admiration of mine, who wrote the best letters I have ever received. I have kept them all (she did not keep mine). 'I am being as happy as the world allows me, following your injunction' – this was not to fuss about family troubles, 'a predicament I should have got used to.'

A couple of years later, why had I not let her know beforehand about my *Homosexuals in History*? – she would have reviewed it and 'cheered on the cause'. Now she longed to read it. 'E.M. Forster was simply the largest marshmallow ever created, what a SILLY book *Howard's End* is, and as mascot of King's he was hardly worthy to be in the company of mascots like the Welsh Guards' goat.' We agreed about him, altogether made too much of by the claque, really rather comic; I enjoyed his essays and occasional writings, his novels too namby-pamby, for an obvious reason, a *castrato*.[4] On the other hand, 'I like Oscar Wilde's grandson too much to concede that Oscar was just an Irish Exhibitionist, but loving you too I am also prone to think that I must be wrong.' Of course I did not think that Wilde was 'just' an Irish Exhibitionist, but another writer made too much of by *his* claque. And his exhibitionism brought untold misery and sufferings upon hundreds of people, humans being the idiots they are. He of all people should have known that, and kept his tastes to himself, or to the intelligent. Dear Rebecca, being highly intelligent, had no prejudices regarding those.

Her letters as usual were full of her troubles; she was a regular complainer. Now her 'sister of 91 has had a stroke and had to be found a hospital, and how strange that is; she now looks beautiful as she was when she was young, but as if she were young and made up for the stage.' (Rebecca had fancied herself for the stage when young; but was rejected by a fool who thought she had not enough personality, when her trouble was that she had too much. In fact I think she was given to 'acting up' all through her life; one sees this in her relations with Wells – very Irish of her, and he after all was very English: it must have bored him. It did not bore me, for I kept a safe distance and observed, as Henry James would have done.)

In spite of constant complaints about health, Rebecca was as

---

[4] cf. my essay, 'A Great Writer? – The Case of E. M. Forster', in *Portraits and Views*.

vital and active as ever in her eighties, and as observant. Her sister's paralysis had a 'Byzantine effect' – who would have thought of that? And 'how odd it is that royalty all over the world and all through time imitate the paralysed.' Meanwhile, she had had 'a curious upheaval of my life, of which I will tell you someday'. This did not prevent her from a visit to Rouen, 'which is magnificently rebuilt, and the poorer quarters are no longer poor, everyone looks healthy and is well dressed, and the students look ravishing. But it is hell because of a maze of one-way streets, and coming down from Calais through Picardy I marked a terrible loss – not a Percherin to be seen, and surely they were among the world's most beautiful inhabitants, just scruffy tractors. . . . Did you know what I learned from a votive tablet in the *église abbatiale* of St George in St Martin de Boisselle that Linley Sambourne, the *Punch* cartoonist who succeeded Tenniel, was saved from drowning in the Seine by appealing to the Virgin Mary as represented in that church? – on August 19, 1873.' I was always surprised at how much Rebecca *knew*, if discursively. She was a great reader.

When my book, *Memories of Men and Women*, arrived, 'I have been reading *it* instead of finishing my book on 1900, and I doubt if I shall be able to pick up my Biro again. *Your* book is so charming. I don't agree with you in your estimate of the people you write about in some cases.' I only hope the historian was more objective. 'I was specially amused at your paper on Beaverbrook whom I knew well. The curious thing about him was that he never got a story right, and as he chose as his biographer A. J. P. Taylor, who had the same character-istic, their cooperation must have made a huge rent in reality! I have been writing about Milner and was amused to see Beaverbrook's account of his ancestry on p. 221 of your book. Milner, that detestable man, cannot be laid at the door of the Germans: his soundly English grandfather lived in Germany and married a German lady called Sophie von Rapport.[5] But his mother was English. . . . It's perfectly true he was spiritually German, but not because of Bismarck, because of Treitschke. But all that of course you know.

[5] I do not agree that Milner was 'a detestable man', and his grandmother *was* German, a von Rappard, not Rapport, by the way.

'I was amused to find that Taylor had included in his biography Beaverbrook's story of how, when he was a young MP staying at a hotel in Cannes, he found that Dilke was staying in the same hotel . . . and that they spent hours walking along the Promenade at Cannes talking about politics and the Empire. In fact the year this was supposed to have happened Dilke *did* go to the Riviera, but to Hyères, in an invalid carriage, where he had a house, and he hadn't for some time been able to walk along promenades.' Nothing surprising in this: Taylor admits that Beaverbrook regularly embellished a story or improved on the facts. What is surprising is then to praise Beaverbrook as a brilliant historian. No historian worthy of the name should tamper with the facts.

'Regarding Milner', she continues, 'it irks me how his Kindergarten lived on to be Appeasers from the word go, such as lived long enough. The odious editor of *The Times* for one, who liked Hitler so much.' Of the Kindergarten, Geoffrey Dawson of *The Times* and Philip Lothian were arrant (and errant) Appeasers; Bob Brand and Leo Amery were not; Lionel Curtis lay low. Those are the objective facts.

As for the feminine subjectivism of Rebecca's judgments, I registered a couple of cases from her lively *Sunday Telegraph* reviews. She gave a severe wigging to the celebrated Lady Salisbury, wife of the Prime Minister. Rebecca thought her simply appalling. She was a bit of a dragon, but anyone who knows the history of the family knows how much the great Lord Salisbury owed to his rather middle-class wife. As a young man he had been highly nervous, something of a neurotic; she built him up steadfastly into the steady, monumental statesman he became.

Another case was that of Edith Wharton's lover, Morton Fullerton, whom Rebecca slated the length of a review as an appalling blackmailer. He gave Edith Wharton the satisfaction she did not get from the man she loved, Walter Berry, who was not responsive. Fullerton gave her what she wanted. Ambivalent and not at all well off, he accepted some cash when needed. Not very dignified, but women do for services rendered. I do not call it blackmail.

Incidentally, I several times urged Rebecca to collect some of these amusing later pieces. Her earlier journalism has been admirably collected in *The Young Rebecca*.[6]

'I have not seen you for a long time, but I dearly love you. I have been ill and have had other forms of hell in the last years. My family have been smitten in various ways' – then she goes into detail. (I wasn't interested in people's families: the joys of family life were not for me.) 'The relatives I love – not that I don't love my grand-daughter and my strange son – live in Edinburgh, which is sad. I know you are happy because you are in Cornwall.'

This penultimate letter was typed by a secretary, who gave Rebecca her title: 'Dame Rebecca West, D.B.E.' – a pseudonym after all, and Dame of the no longer existing British Empire. Indeed it was an end. Rebecca was a lady, but not lady-like – she was above all that. Now that she was a Dame, she had become – after those earlier embarrassing years (and she had had a good many embarrassments to put up with) – rather a *grande dame*. It was ironical that by the end she had become, like Mrs Humphry Ward in her day, the *grande dame* of English letters.

She had always been generous about my poetry, buried under – and overlooked on account of – the history. Rebecca was not so compartmented, unimaginatively specialised – she was more Elizabethan. When I sent her my *A Life: Collected Poems* – my life's work in poetry (more important to me than the history, my inner life as opposed to the outer, my secret life) – she was responsive as ever. 'Beautiful affectionate poems, affectionate towards all the right things. Shall I never see you again?'[7]

Alas, we never did meet again. In spite of illness her interest in life remained inexhaustible. 'I am distressed by the Brixton riots beyond measure.' I wasn't – just what one should have

[6] *The Young Rebecca: Writings of Rebecca West 1911–1917*. Selected by Jane Marcus.

[7] My verses about the cult of the suicidal Sylvia Plath, making a plain straightforward statement, aroused the ire of a third-rate poetry-resident at a provincial university – typical humbug-job created in our cultivated society – to whom the *Times Literary Supplement* fobbed it off for review, instead of someone qualified to write about it. Rebecca responded with comic verses about the Plath cult. Once before a volume of my verse had been disparaged, by a Miss Phoebe Pool, feeble little fool. Who now remembers who the creature was?

expected from the Macmillan government's leaving the door to immigration irresponsibly open. As with Appeasement, anybody of sense could have seen that it would mount up until it became an almighty problem. And in a small, heavily overpopulated island, at the apogee of power and prosperity at the beginning of the century with a population of 40 million – now towards the end approaching 60 million! What are politicians *for*, if not to think of the long-term interests of their country?

Rebecca's attitude was more subjective. 'I have in recent years constantly passed through Brixton. I had some ties there, with a most charming Negro accountant. He was utterly happy there with his family, till the Left Wing Council on the one hand, and the crime, gave him a nervous breakdown. These riots mean the end of bourgeois happiness for a lot of very nice black people. . . . What horrible times we have lived to see.

'I spent some years of my childhood in the last house we owned, in Streatham – a very pretty little Regency house finally bombed to the ground. My great-great plus grandmother . . . came to live in those parts when she married Richard Fairfield on his return from India in mid-18th century and is buried at Lewisham. And her sister, the mother-in-law of Sydney Smith lived at Cheam.' That seems an appropriate ghost for Rebecca at the end. 'I am full of serious, sad troubles, but thoughts of the people I love such as you bear me up.'

With the end approaching I had asked if she kept my letters, as I kept hers. I hope that I did not hurt her feelings, but that she was only teasing me when she replied: 'I am sending back your letters, but I am heartbroken by the implied lack of trust – of course I would *never* have sued you for breach of promise. But here they are, with all my love.'[8]

Dear, generous, warm-hearted, *great* woman: she was all for love – made for love, as H.G. had well realised. I feel now, reading through her letters again, how somehow inadequate I had been.

---

[8] In the event she decided to keep the originals, and sent me photo-copies, largely illegible.

8

Elizabeth Bowen; Goronwy Rees

What is curious about my relations with Elizabeth Bowen is
that for a considerable time I got her quite wrong. Perhaps that
was understandable since, during the early years of a long
acquaintance, I did not know her well; later on I came to know
her much better. Earlier, I had been wrong on two counts. I
thought her a more remarkable woman than she was a writer –
the development of her writing, her fulfilment as novelist, in
time put that right. Secondly, I thought her too cerebral for a
novelist; I put this down to her deracination as Anglo-Irish,
that she was somehow cut off from the sources of life, and was
perhaps rather sexless.

How wrong I turned out to be! But there was something to
be said for my assumptions before I came to know her. My
close friend Elizabeth Jenkins, who knew her well, thought
that she was 'a writer before she was a woman.' She herself
gave a clue, I thought, in a tell-tale phrase, 'her sex is all in her
head' (just what I thought); and another clue in her description
of Le Fanu, a fellow Anglo-Irish writer, as having Irish
infantilism and sexlessness. This became corroborated in her
own case in that her sexual interest was rather belated, and,
when aroused, was regularly directed to young men years
younger than herself.

Her marriage to Alan Cameron – part Scotch, part Cornish
(a Lanyon) – was odd, and appeared to be sexless; he was
rather ambivalent, and they had no children. She was the
closest friend of my oldest Oxford friend, David Cecil and,
though that was an emotional relationship, a love affair, it was
platonic, apparently non-sexual. Above all, Elizabeth was an
aristocrat, with an aristocratic reticence – that would have

made a bond between them. Though I had a close friendship with him, neither of them betrayed anything to me, though I was a bit curious. Elizabeth never had the slightest interest of that sort in me (nor I in her): David would have let her know what the score was.

So altogether circumstances conspired to put me wrong. Young, I thought she was a cold woman. I still do not think she was a warm one, though it transpired that she was capable of passion – a different matter. Eventually, she became friendly, well-disposed, appreciative of my own writing, always loyal, never crabbing or malicious – she was above all that. She was a great woman – I always thought that – but not easy to know.

To my mind she was, in those early years, a strange woman. I did not know that her father had been mad, or that she had had an earlier breakdown. She was excessively sensitive; an unfavourable review would send her to bed for a couple of days. Once, when I might have called on her at the tiny cottage where she and Alan then lived up at Headington (he was Director of Education down in Oxford), she was laid up in bed: she had had a bad review. Really! Later on, with success – or, better, fulfilment in her work – she became more normal. I thought of her, perhaps not altogether wrongly, as an over-intellectualised woman, like Virginia Woolf: hence the mental strain.

Her appearance was sufficiently striking, not exactly welcoming. I thought her very handsome: a magnificent head and profile, rather masculine, with beautiful fine red-gold hair; large, unfeminine hands and feet, and what she herself described as an 'androgynous' figure. Then there was her stammer, which in itself put a distance between her and the outside world. The odd thing was that her stammer was very attractive (I don't know if she knew that): it added distinction to everything she said, for it was clearly due to her having so many thoughts in that quick brilliant brain which she could not bring out all at once. But I did not know, another clue, that it started at the time of her father's madness.

Altogether someone very exceptional, most uncommon, not to be familiar with; as time went on, and, in spite of the burden (and danger) of excessive sensibility and intellectuality, she fulfilled herself in her work by sticking to her last, with underlying strength of character. It became evident that she was a woman of genius.

Again, I was not particularly impressed by her early novels. David Cecil thought best of *The Last September*. The historian recognised her obsession that her home in County Cork, Bowen's Court, was in danger of being burned down; three neighbouring country houses were burned by the mad Irish, outposts of civilisation amid mountain and bog – if civilisation of a Somerville-and-Ross character. I was myself critical of *The House in Paris,* with its middle section given up to the unconvincingly clever conversation of children – almost a transcript (did anyone else notice?) from Cocteau's *Les Enfants Terribles*. Agatha Christie, unappreciated by intellectuals, was far better at children's talk.

Elizabeth herself said that she never expected to write novels, but short stories; and in her early work I appreciated those most – she was always a fine short-story writer. *Death of the Heart,* longest of the earlier novels, she condemned as an inflated short story; the kernel of it is an autobiographical episode which gave her a theme – which I happened to be very close to, at the time it was written. I thought that book artistically unintegrated, it did not altogether come together; and she had another reason for liking it least of all her work. The essence of the book went back to a now celebrated house-party at Bowen's Court in 1936, and her relationship with Goronwy Rees, by whom she felt herself betrayed; she had not yet distanced herself from that awkward experience when she wrote the book.

When I read it I recognised his personality – which I knew only too well – at once: a speaking likeness. Various clues are there: he is lower-class for one thing. That made for difficulty in the relationship with Elizabeth, who was not only a lady, but a great lady – difficulties on both sides. I realised these so well, as working-class myself, that I wondered that people should be willing to risk the inevitable misunderstandings in mixing classes, crossing bounds, fences, ditches. True, one can see that there is an element of challenge, and some people are impelled – chiefly by sex – to take risks. But it doesn't come off well in literature, let alone life: Henry James's *The Princess Casamassima* is a failure on this count; so is *Lady Chatterley's Lover*; and Hardy is unconvincing when he tries to portray aristocrats.

I knew the people present at that crucial house party pretty well: Isaiah Berlin from the time he was an undergraduate, Goronwy Rees from the time he became a Fellow of All Souls, Elizabeth less well, Rosamond Lehmann not at all. As usual I observed from the side-lines, not giving myself away. Isaiah and Goronwy had every reason to know me well enough, since I lived with them in College – though Goronwy later gave as reason for his younger generation not wanting me as their Warden that they felt that they did not know me. (I dare say they were right to reject me: I would have seen to it that they did their research – as he had not done his.)

Since I formed an unfavourable, and perhaps prejudiced, view of Goronwy Rees's character, I must in justice say what was in his favour. It goes without saying that he was highly intelligent, or he would never have been elected as a Prize Fellow on the examination; he was cultivated and amusing; he was warm-hearted and spirited; he had courage and a good war record. He was a natural writer and should have stuck to his last. He was very handsome, with an irresistible combination of beautiful curly raven-black hair and blue eyes; well-made and masculine figure, a good footballer. In sum, one of Connolly's 'deadly irresistibles': several people fell for him, and in both sexes (I was not one). Geoffrey Faber was in love with him, and eventually wished him on the College as his successor as Estates Bursar. I had no confidence in his running the business, estates and finance, of the College. When Warden Sumner asked me if I, as Sub-Warden, minded his appointment (I could have stopped it), I said, 'Well, it's your funeral.' It turned out to be so.

For, the fundamental thing lacking in Goronwy, was, quite simply: character. He admits this in his well-written, *A Bundle of Sensations*. 'It has always surprised, and slightly bewildered me', he writes, 'that other people should take it so much for granted that they each possess what is usually called "a character". That is to say, a personality with its own continuous history. . . . I have never been able to find anything of that sort in myself; and in the course of my life this has been the source of many misunderstandings, since other people persist in expecting of one a kind of consistency – which they really have no right to demand.'

Perhaps they have no right to 'demand', but it is only reasonable that they should expect some consistency of conduct and also in the treatment they receive from others. I take it that it is a good thing that we should aim at achieving some consistency, even if we are not very good at it – all the more reason then to try. Goronwy never tried; he is here making a plausible case for his own weakness of character – he was always only 'a bundle of sensations', and himself in the event a chief sufferer from this. A natural writer, he had not the character to stick to his gift and make something of it. (Elizabeth had, and did.) A writer needs not only his original gift of nature but also the strength of character to abide by it, tie himself to his desk and endure the burden and the drudgery.

Goronwy couldn't, or wouldn't; he tried everything else, for he was of an adventurous spirit, a good deal of an adventurer. He wrote two early novels, really long short-stories, which showed some promise, but did not press on to anything better. He fell back on College research – would the College support him in a research project? He hadn't thought of a subject: I thought of a suitable one for him. Our Leftist group was much interested in Marxism and its German affiliations; Lassalle was a significant figure, a fascinating adventurer, a suitable subject for Goronwy. He was keen on going to Germany – they all were, Auden, Isherwood, Spender – and Goronwy was glad of the opportunity. He took it, enjoyed himself there like the rest of them, did no research whatever; then came back and handed in his cards.

That was the end of him as a researcher: he would never have made a historian. However, John Sparrow and I got him a job as assistant literary editor on the *Spectator*. This at least gave him a *stellung* in London, and enabled him to lead a London life, occasional week-ends at All Souls. Then came the *fracas* with Elizabeth Bowen and the fuss over *Death of the Heart*. Elizabeth had already had an affair with a much

younger married man at Oxford – small blame to her, she
needed sexual experience for her writing.

She then fell in love with Goronwy, a lower-class irresistible some eight or ten years younger – apt to be an humiliating
situation, as it turned out to be. His character, or lack of it, is
recognisably rendered in the novel, where the young man
complains that women 'have a lunatic instinct for picking on
another person who doesn't know where he is. How can I
keep on feeling something I once felt, when there are so many
things one can feel? . . . I may be a crook, but I'm not a fake.'
Goronwy was neither a crook nor a fake, but I thought he was
something of a cad, and would never trust him after being let
down over his research assignment. After all, he had the
ability to write a life of Lassalle – why not stick to it and do it?
The novelist's comment on the young man in the novel is that
he tries to get off with people because he could not get on with
them.

He could never have got on with me, though we were both,
after all, Celts. I once teased Geoffrey Faber about this, who
was publishing us both, but with an emotional fixation on
Goronwy; Geoffrey remarked what very different characters
we were. I don't think he got much change out of the
relationship, Goronwy was so keen on getting off with the
other sex. He made this clear at the beginning of his long and
close relationship with Guy Burgess. Then what was the basis
of this peculiar intimacy? Goronwy was neither a Communist, nor a spy: I think it was just that they were both
adventurers, with a very flexible, fluent, free-wheeling and
-dealing attitude to life, both cads.

It was utterly contrary to my own view of life. The only
time I ever saw Guy Burgess was when Goronwy brought
him into our smoking-room after dinner one night. Burgess
hadn't been there twenty minutes before the Junior Fellow
came up to complain to me that Burgess had made a pass at
him. I happened to be the Senior Fellow present: but what was
I supposed to do about that? I said sympathetically, 'Well, you
can keep away from him' (Burgess remained away at the end
of the room). What was the basis of Goronwy's friendship
with Anthony Blunt? I suppose, intellectual rather than sexual
ambivalence; they belonged to the same circle, and in fact

Goronwy was all over the place.

The affair with Elizabeth received its *coup-de-grace* at that disastrous summer house-party at Bowen's Court. Goronwy and the younger woman not only fell for each other but 'carried on' under the eyes of the *châtelaine*. Reproaches ensued, with Goronwy being hysterical on the drawing-room carpet. Really, one didn't behave like that in a country-house, in front of one's hostess, whatever one's emotions or private relations: Elizabeth was one for upper-class standards, a proper *tenue*. I'll bet she maintained them throughout, though mortally offended; indeed, she felt betrayed – betrayal is the theme of *Death of the Heart*. Apparently she said something frightening to Goronwy at the time: 'My father went mad in this house. Will we?' When I stayed at Bowen's Court later, I felt that the house was overwhelmingly melancholy, even something sinister.

I had made a mistake about Goronwy. With our joint Leftist views I assumed that he was working-class, like myself. He was not: he was Welsh middle-class, his father a well-known Calvinist minister. In College I assumed a leadership of our Leftist group, as a born proletarian and, a few years senior, having helped to elect Goronwy, I may have seemed patronising – though one couldn't very well patronise a chameleon.

When *Death of the Heart* came out, he was at first delighted and told Rosamond how brilliant it was. He then changed his mind completely, wrote Elizabeth bitterly, threatening libel. Again, one doesn't do that between friends – and it was Geoffrey Faber who persuaded him against such caddishness. When Goronwy told me all about it I took very much a senior prefect's line, and said, 'If you give yourself away to the upper classes, this is what you must expect. Why don't you give it up, and devote yourself for five or ten years to a wonderful subject – Tudor Wales?' I was then researching away at what was to become *Tudor Cornwall*. Tudor Wales is a much bigger, richer and more variegated subject – no Welsh historian has yet got round to giving us a picture of it as a whole. I think that Goronwy knew Welsh, and he had the writing ability; what he had not got was the character, the stability or persistency. He was quite candid about it, and gave me the answer: 'My dear Leslie, I couldn't do it.'

As for Elizabeth, her last word on the affair came in a short story: 'Before you came, I was walled in alive. I didn't know where to turn. I was burning myself out.'

Then the war came down on us – in which Goronwy acquitted himself well, and in which Elizabeth reached her apogee as a writer. The war released something in her as it did for all of us – the sense of excitement, the ever-present danger, the leave-takings and homecomings, the heart-breaks, the grief for those who never returned, the joy for those who did, the camaraderie and good fellowship: those were unforgettable years in which Britain's glorious past came to an end in flames. Elizabeth sensed what happened to herself, and expressed it in her own oblique, too clever way: 'It seems to me that during the war in England the overcharged subconsciousness of everybody overflowed and merged.' It seems an odd way of putting it; more directly, love and sex were a free-for-all. Her own phrase 'life with the lid on' was over, and that released her into her finest work.

To my mind *The Heat of the Day* is not only her best novel, but gives the truest picture of wartime London – along with James Lees-Milne's factual Diaries: the bombings, fires, crumps, houses crashing, whole blocks falling, splintered glass everywhere; the glow and glory, the casualties, pain and squalor; the fun and jokes amid the misery; the unspoken bravery. She worked as an air-raid warden, and on her patrols met all kinds of people she would never have met before. Once more she met a much younger man with whom she fell in love – one recognises him, yet another Oxford man, but a Canadian, in the novel; his height, 'the long elegant hands and head', the way he lies on a sofa, 'extended at full length, narrow and Byzantine in a dressing gown.'

Elizabeth was now a famous author, success put her in full control and made money for her; everybody has the phrase that she could 'use' a lot of money, I should regard her as rather extravagant, with Irish notions of hospitality. I was bidden to stay at Bowen's Court, which I was the more glad to do because it gave me a chance to see Spenser's Kilcolman Castle not far away. I had read her book about the house and the history of her family, Cromwellian Welsh by origin – she was a better historian than Goronwy, though he had been trained to it at Oxford. Here was something Elizabeth Bowen and Rebecca West had in common, an absorbing interest in their Anglo-Irish family. Elizabeth's description of her family home was so vivid that I was pleased to discover that I could find my way round that overtall, gawky mansion almost blindfold – and there was a trap in it: the top story, where my bedroom was, did not communicate direct with the main staircase, one had to go round behind. Was that architectural solecism, something unfinished, peculiarly Irish?

The rest of the house was in keeping, rather down-at-heel, a lot of it unfurnished. The big western drawing-room was very sparse; it did not seem that Elizabeth spent anything on furniture. I remember her irritation when a castor came off an old armchair – 'so like everything in Ireland', she said. With a big, semi-vacant Georgian house at hand, I amused myself fantasying how I would furnish it if it were mine – all those sales with lovely eighteenth-century furniture going cheap from emptied houses! The dining room was kept up; one can see what life was like there, now all has gone, from the photographs. Elizabeth sits there again at the head of her hospitable dinner table, extremely *décolletée*, face like a noble thoroughbred; silver candlesticks, flowers, grand guests, family portraits looking down on the improbably intellectual converse.

My fellow-guest was another friend of David Cecil's, Cynthia Asquith, who had won a huge BBC prize by answering all sixty-four questions about Jane Austen correctly. I did not feel altogether at ease in such highly geared society, with two such hypersensitive women, electric as eels. When my heavy-soled country shoes scraped once on the drawing-room floor, Cynthia shuddered from head to foot. (Could one have lived cheek by jowl with that? I would never have made the mistake of trying.)

However, I took the ladies off to dinner at a hotel in Cork, where I had to give a lecture. Elizabeth was convulsed by being led into a room entirely populated by ladies' hats. There must have been some convention or meeting afoot, but she kept referring to the oddity of it – the kind of thing that appealed to her imagination. I remembered her queer short-story of the unruly children, who were inexplicably kept under control – though their complexions suffered – by a governess in charge in the absence of their parents. They were quietened all right, reduced to silence, but debauched. The explanation appeared when the parents returned, to find a cubby-hole stuffed with scores of empty boxes of chocolates.

She made it all sound convincing, but queer; indeed she had a lively sense of the strange and untoward, a distinct gift for rendering fear and the supernatural. (Apparently she did *believe*, as Flannery O'Connor did.) I wonder that she was not frightened to live alone in that big house full of ghosts. While Alan Cameron lived he looked after the place; but he can have done nothing about the rooks. They came back at evening in clouds, overcasting the sky. I said to Elizabeth, 'Don't you shoot them?' Oh no, she loved them, and the sound they made. I said, but surely they ate up the place, the corn in the fields; and, firmly, that they needed keeping down.

I find that we both attended the Coronation, though I did not see her there; she was reporting the event for *Vogue*, I for *The Western Morning News* and a Canadian paper. Nor did I know that she always had a desire to write about Swift – an obsessive figure, one can hardly say patron-saint – to all Anglo-Irish. I too had always wanted to write about him, and eventually did, though we never discussed him. Nor did we exchange many letters (I cannot find hers to me), though she was always characteristically generous in her reviews of my books, and noticed things that others didn't – effects of light on landscape, for one thing.

After the war she took to going to the United States, where she became a distinguished figure in the literary landscape: all quite convenient, a motor drive to Shannon Airport, and next thing she was in New York, where she had publishers to look after her and literary parties to be lionised at. For me things were more difficult. For years I had been ill, endless ulceration deflected by a series of dangerous operations. (I suppose only a sound proletarian constitution underneath pulled me through – to become a reformed character in old age.)

I loved All Souls, and the College constituted my chief sustaining happiness in life. Goronwy Rees played a part in weaning me from it. During the mortal illness of two Wardens in succession I had the burden of running the College as Sub-Warden, responsibility without authority. It was agonising: the group of young men who were elected from and after the war – Isaiah Berlin called them the *sans-culottes* – had got out of hand under Humphry Sumner, who was a dying man (another duodenal) and afraid of them.

I was not in the least afraid of these young men, some of whom owed their election to me (dear Cyril Falls thought that I would always remain 'influential' in the College), but they had me framed as Authority and thought that I wanted to run the place. So far from that, during the agitating nine months when I was left alone in charge, and two elections to the Wardenship to conduct, I never wrote a single sentence of a book of mine. Writing was all in all to me, not endless committees to decide who should cook, or cook up, what. All the College officers, except one, wanted me to go on to become Warden. Privately, I did not want this, but could hardly say so to such loyal supporters and a varied following, from Lionel Curtis to G. D. H. Cole.

The chief exception was Goronwy Rees who, returned like the whole of the younger generation from the war, behaved like a *Partei-Führer* and organised them to a man against the Sub-Warden, simply engaged in doing his duty for the place he loved beyond anything. Rees's partisanship was precisely in keeping with the way he behaved subsequently as Principal of Aberystwyth, which brought him down.

He came to consult me as Sub-Warden whether he should accept the offer (he was Tom Jones's candidate, and he put Goronwy into the job). Though I was longing to get rid of him as our Estates Bursar, I gave him honest advice. He gave every secondary reason for accepting: good salary, healthy climate for the family, cheap schooling for the children (Margie was a wonderful wife, who gave him what stability he had). He gave every reason, except the fundamental question I conscientiously put to him: Could he stand it? He never answered that one, and the event showed that he could never stand it, or they him.

Meanwhile, his candidate for the Wardenship at All Souls won the election by a considerable majority: every single member of the younger generation he had organised, with a

sufficient number of seniors, like his old patron Geoffrey
Faber, and the Wykehamists – who were almost a majority in
themselves – to elect a young Wykehamist. For me it was an
almighty deliverance, for which I was not at all grateful. I was
incensed that these young people – several of whom owed
their Fellowships to me, and a few had been pupils or protégés
– should follow the lead of a light-weight irresponsible like
Rees, as against mine. Though I did not want the job, I have
never put up with being turned down by the second- or third-
rate: one does not have to put up with that sort of thing from
the first-rate. And, a good Celt, I never forgave it or them.

When the historian Grant Robertson, who should have
succeeded the fine Warden Anson who had wished it, was
turned down for a classical lawyer from London whom the
kindly Oman described as 'a returned empty', Robertson
hived off to Birmingham to become an eminent and constructive Vice-Chancellor. I remained a Fellow, but turned my face
to America, where I had been invited to become a Research
Associate at the Huntington Library. Ambivalent as always, I
elected to keep a foot in each camp, free of either and to pursue
my own course, with no further obligations to anyone except
myself, to research and write. My solipsism was confirmed.

It was typical of Rees's light-headedness and warmth of
nature that, the next thing, he should invite me to give a few
well-paid lectures at Aberystwyth. This fitted in with my
work: I wanted to meet the Welsh historians and gain their
help for my chapter on Wales, one of the best, for the next
volume of my planned trilogy on the Elizabethan Age, *The
Expansion of Elizabethan England*. So I accepted. Goronwy was
friendly and hospitable. It did not make any difference to my
well-formed and long-tested opinion of him.

In New York I met up with Elizabeth, whom I was glad to see,
for I was not yet at home in the brave New World. I came to
stay regularly at a cheap hotel on Seventh Avenue, convenient
to Central Park and the Carnegie Hall for concerts. I had
originally been recommended to it by the Rockefeller Foundation, when it was quite pleasant; over the years I saw it go
down and down – little did I care about appearances, so long as

I had a clean bedroom and bathroom to myself. Elizabeth stayed a long way down town, at the Gladstone Hotel, near Henry James's Washington Square – very appropriate for her, I thought. I arranged to go down and take her out to lunch.

In those days after the war British people were very hard up for dollars. All the same, I was a little taken aback when Elizabeth suddenly said, 'Leslie, *could* you lend me ten dollars?' I was just back from a lecture tour, so I could; but said, 'Ten dollars – that's no good; what about thirty?' Then, as an after-thought, 'What about a hundred?' 'O darling, could you? I'll write you a cheque in pounds.'

It was the only time in my life that Elizabeth called me 'darling', and I shortly saw why. She immediately rushed to the machine to get a packet of cigarettes: she was an utter addict, hipped on smoking. As her biographer says, for years she had a smokers' cough, and lung cancer got her in the end. It doesn't so much matter that ordinary folk kill themselves with smoking: they are all too easily replaceable. But I resent it when intelligent people, especially friends of mine, unnecess-arily kill themselves this way. One sees a typical photograph of Elizabeth, out for a walk at Bowen's Court, clutching the inevitable packet of fags in hand.

We went out and up the street to find a restaurant. I thought it characteristic of what a lady Elizabeth was that she led the way into, and would have settled for, a cheap little place which one glance told me wouldn't do at all. I wouldn't have it; we went on to find a place which was, though not expensive, decent and good: more my style.

At Aberystwyth Goronwy went racketing on to his downfall. For one thing, he behaved as he had done at All Souls and became the *Partei-Führer* of the younger generation, the students with whom he was, I believe, popular and who imitated their leader's style in white socks. Imagine the silli-ness of a Principal, who should by definition be the head of the whole institution, becoming the leader of a party! He gave his opponents their opportunity to get rid of him by the bad mistake he made of publishing a couple of notorious articles in a popular newspaper at the time of Burgess and Maclean's escape to Soviet Russia.

There had been much discussion as to Rees's motives in this, whether to clear himself of suspicion, or to forestall charges against him. I am not concerned with any of the *bas-fonds*. It is enough for me that the Principal, who always lived light-heartedly and denied himself nothing, was considerably indebted and that the not inconsiderable sum he raised paid his debts.

The articles, with their revelation of his contacts, finished him at Aberystwyth and in the eyes of his Oxford friends – I don't know about London. Maurice Bowra wrote to him that Judas-trees should be planted around the campus at Aberystwyth, and cut off communications. I was not surprised, I merely felt corroborated; nor did I come forward to take any line, for I had already written him off. In these articles he had spilled a good many beans about that circle of his close friends, ambivalent both politically and sexually. He said nothing about its most eminent member, Sir Anthony Blunt – he may have guessed, if not known, that he was a spy; but he gave the name of a working-class lad in this ambivalent circle. I thought that caddish.

In the first half of his career Goronwy had always fallen on his feet; we were there to help, and he had more than his share of good luck – he was a spoiled child of fortune. In the latter half of his life he had less than his share – fortune turned against him. He relates some of this in a second volume of autobiography, *A Chapter of Accidents*, again well-written, and true so far as it goes. But it is only one side of the story; he omits the other side – as to which I am quite sufficiently informed – and the effect therefore is decidedly disingenuous.

He did indeed have more than his share of accidents; ill luck caught up with him; old friends fell away. It was some years before he dared to show his face again at All Souls and, when he did, I did not speak to him. Not until towards the end, after Margie died – who was his good angel; I felt sorry for that, she was a fine woman, who must have had a difficult job keeping him on the rails. After she died, he went off them, and took to drink, as such people are apt to do.

I don't know whether Elizabeth kept any contact with Goronwy after *The Death of the Heart*. She at any rate went on to fulfil herself in her work, as he never did. I think he mistook himself, as I have seen other gifted young Fellows do at All Souls – as I nearly did myself with my anguished pre-occupation with politics all through the Thirties. Even so, I never let go of my writing, and Providence stepped in to bar the way from deviating from my real vocation – which was, from my boyhood on, to write *und sonst nichts*. Goronwy, with his talents, should have been a writer; what he left are fragments of what he might have accomplished.

Elizabeth was a woman of genius, and that means obsession with one's work. In her last years she moved to Hythe – she wrote to me from there; I fancy that it was partly out of devotion to Henry James, but it was a mistake and she came back to London. She had no illusions about the world, the society, she had lived into – the end of civilisation – for there was Ireland as well as ruined London to remind her. A sympathetic study of her work summed it up. 'The earlier books dealt with a world that has, for all practical purposes, ceased to exist: the crust of civilised life has been cracked in too many places, the abyss beneath our feet can no longer be ignored. What will be her approach as a novelist to the squalid, standardised, and unhopeful world in which we are now living?'

The answer to that, in my view, is – Turn back to the better past, and live in that, if you can. Elizabeth had turned back to it with her book on her family, *Bowen's Court*. After all, Anglo-Irish society had been a civilisation, with standards of culture – something better than the lower middle-class *régime* of the 'gombeen man' which took its place. Myles Dillon described it thus to me, son of the Nationalist leader, John Dillon, who died a bitterly disillusioned man, saying that English rule after all had been better than the outcome he had fought for. George Russell, that statesman-like man – known as a writer as AE – left the country in disgust; Joyce lived in exile; Shaw and Wilde had lived in London when the going was good; Yeats died at Rapallo; I met other members of the diaspora, like James Stephens, in America.

Elizabeth could no longer keep Bowen's Court going. She sold it to a neighbouring farmer, thinking that his handsome children would be running about the vacant rooms, bringing back life to it. Not a bit of it: he pulled it all down – one more country house, island of civilisation, gone. 'The shallow hollow of land, under the mountains, on which Bowen's Court stood', she wrote in her farewell to it, 'is again empty. Not one hewn stone left on another on the fresh-growing grass. Green covers all traces of the foundations. Today, as far as the eye can see, there might never have been a house there.'

Since Elizabeth had lived the life of the mind, it was still there in hers, as it is in mine. 'When I think of Bowen's Court, there it is. And when others who knew it think of it, there it is, also' – illumined by the presence of this woman of genius.

9

How Good Was Connolly?

Cyril Connolly and I were exact contemporaries at Oxford. We came up in the Michaelmas term of 1922; he, with a brilliant reputation from Eton, as Brackenbury Scholar at Balliol; I, an unknown quantity from working-class Cornwall, as Douglas Jerrold Scholar at Christ Church. It may surprise the reader, considering our subsequent careers, that Connolly's scholarship was in Modern History, mine in English Literature. The Eng. Lit. School was regarded as a soft option, mainly for women, and Christ Church, not having an Eng. Lit. don, directed me into the History School, which had a higher standing, second only to Greats (ancient history and philosophy, Greek and Latin).

Having brought myself up in remote Cornwall largely on literature and the poets, I found the History School uphill work.[1] However, I was too poor to have distractions, so at home in vacations I worked (in term time diverting myself with politics and contributing, mostly verse, to *Oxford Poetry, The Oxford Outlook*, etc, along with Graham Greene and Harold Acton. I don't think Connolly did – too idle). In the event I emerged, to my immense relief, with an unquestioned First, Connolly with a Third. He should never have taken the History School; he found it boring and had not the mind for an historian: *he* should have taken Eng. Lit. After all, he had a passion for literature, and was very well read. He came up from Eton with some knowledge of the literatures of five civilisations.

As a Colleger, living in daily contact with other clever boys

[1] cf. *A Cornishman at Oxford,* for the ways and means of self-education.

– they all appear in *Enemies of Promise* – he was years ahead in sophistication. One sees that in the brilliant letters he and Noel Blakiston exchanged as schoolboys and undergraduates. I can only compare those letters with the extraordinary sophistication of the young Flaubert's correspondence with his friend, Alfred Le Poittevin, or the Home Letters of T. E. Lawrence.

Nothing of this in my simple correspondence with my uneducated home, where my parents could barely read or write. (I have rather over-compensated there, in both fields.) All my life I have been competing with these brilliant begonias in literary life, and – when it hasn't been Etonians – it has been sharp-witted Wykehamists at All Souls. And how they looked after each other in the literary papers, pushed one another and wrote each other up! Connolly and Eric Blair, i.e. George Orwell, were at Prep. School together as well as at Eton, and a good deal of the over-estimation of Orwell, writing him up into a veritable cult, came from that. As if Orwell's knowledge of the working-class is to be compared with D. H. Lawrence's or mine! *We* come from the people: he was merely slumming in Wigan, as people there realised quite well, and rather resented it.

Connolly tells us, 'my Oxford generation were all highly successful social climbers. They had no political awareness (I am speaking of the writers): Acton liked the Prince of Wales, Waugh the Lygons, Betjeman Irish peers. How different to [*sc.* from] the political thrusters of the Thirties do these delicate aesthetes seem. Clothes were an intoxication. Waisted suits by Lesley and Roberts, white waistcoats from Hawes and Curtis, monogrammed silk shirts arrived in cardboard boxes, top hats, opera hats, Oxford bags. Credit seemed unlimited, fathers had no idea of what they were in for. Lobster Neuberg, foie gras sandwiches, Yquem daily crossed the quad.' – Not to my rooms, where I daily lunched off bread and jam. 'It appears that those afternoons which I spent under some hot towels in Germers were full of goings-on, lectures, tutorials, Heaven knows what.' Germers was then the fashionable hairdressers where these pimpled youths had their complexions improved under hot towels. I had my hair cut cheaply at home in Cornwall.

Then, Connolly writes, 'I went down. London at last. The

Twenties. Parties, Parties, Parties. And behind them all an aching feeling – Was it worth it?' To my mind it wasn't. But they all had somebody to look after them when they went down with their Thirds. Connolly had Logan Pearsall Smith to put him up – he was always an arch-scrounger – while his fellow Anglo-Irishman, Desmond MacCarthy, got him on to the *New Statesman.*

MacCarthy and Connolly had much in common. In 1927 Connolly notes, 'Asked Desmond about himself, and he spoke of his life at twenty-three. He told me he was as idle as I was, and eventually it made him ill. I said I knew the feeling.' Then why didn't these two Irish Etonians get down to some solid work? – Weakness of character, not want of talent. They talked it away – brilliant conversationists – in smoke. MacCarthy was one of the first to get on to the new appreciation of Donne, and was to have written *the* book on it – he never did. He was early in on the modern interpretation of Coleridge, and was going to write *the* book on that; he never did, that book was written by Hugh Ianson Fausset. MacCarthy, for all his talent and feeling for literature, merely wrote hundreds of reviews. Connolly similarly, though that was not quite all – he did rather better.

Why didn't Connolly do better with his precocious talent and his evident love of literature? He wrote a book to explain that away, *Enemies of Promise,* largely self-defence under the technique of self-accusation. We need not be taken in by that – Connolly played that card from the beginning to the end of his career. Depreciating oneself is a well known ploy to flatter others' self-esteem – La Rochefoucauld understood that. Only fools are taken in by it, but since most people are such, it is highly successful. 'Trying to be funny', turning the laugh against himself, was the way this Irishman sucked up to the English, and got into Pop – otherwise inaccessible to him – at Eton.

It is the chief theme of *The Unquiet Grave*, his one success: 'I am one of those whom suffering has made empty and frivolous: each night in my dreams I pull the scab off a wound; each day, vacuous and habit-ridden, I let it re-form.' What did he suffer from? So far as I can see, the effects of over-indulgence. The books are full of eating and drinking, the cult of the best food and wine, the grandest restaurants. The last time I saw him he was being lunched at the Ritz by a publisher with an eye, no doubt, to a review of a forthcoming book in the *Sunday Times*.

Since *Enemies of Promise* gives us his views we need not go in detail into what he considered holds writers up. Success, for one – we see the sour grapes in that; but Shakespeare, Balzac, Tolstoy? The book begins with lunch on the French Riviera – omelette, vichy, peaches, and 'I always try to write in the afternoons for I have enough Irish blood to be afraid of the Irish temperament.' (The fact was that he did not get up in the mornings.) A main theme of the book is the obsession with Money: one cannot write unless one has an income of several hundred a year. Well, after being kept a year or two by Logan Pearsall Smith[2] as his secretary – I don't know what secretarial duties were involved, but it was good for Cyril's knowledge of literature (one sees Logan's influence in the book, for he was a scholar) – Cyril married money. This freed him for a bit – I do not know that he wrote any the more for it, except an unmemorable novella, *The Rock Pool*. Then the marriage broke up, as they say, with a good deal of inconsiderateness on his part, and back he came to the drudgery of reviewing.

'Ninety Years of Novel-Reviewing', he put it in an essay of 1929, getting amusement out of despair. 'The reviewing of novels is the white man's grave of journalism. . . . The early expectations of discovering a new writer are perhaps less keen a pleasure than one's later hopes of being able to discredit an old one. . . . Remember that the object of the critic is to revenge himself on the creator, and his method must depend on whether the book is good or bad, whether he dare condemn it himself or must lie quiet and let it blow over. Every good reviewer specialized in that subject on which he has not been able to write a book, and his aim is to see that no-one else does.' *Verb. sap.*

So we need not take seriously the portentous opening of *The Unquiet Grave,* so often quoted and to which too much attention has been unnecessarily paid. 'The true function of a writer is to produce a masterpiece and no other task is of any

---

[2] First in Bertrand Russell's varied collection of brothers-in-law.

consequence.' Silly. William Shakespeare did not think like that; he produced a number of plays that are not masterpieces, and in consequence eventually wrote others that were. It is only one more example of Connolly's sleight-of-hand defence for not tackling a solid piece of work himself. Like other Anglo-Irish writers, when young he hoped to write a brave book on Swift. He never got round to doing it.

It was an odd and unsatisfactory notion to write *Enemies of Promise* in two halves, the first literary criticism, the second autobiography. Connolly could be interesting even when writing criticism, as few can, but much the more interesting is the second half about Eton. That was the seminal and happiest period of his life, the most blissful, the cleverest boys in England (besides those at Winchester, of course) living together in College in that lovely place – the river, the bridges, Lupton's Tower, afternoon sunlight falling like honey on the Chapel walls, looking up to the towers and battlements of Windsor Castle, the history of England in mellow brick and stone.

Lucky boys! How I wish I could have been one of them – the camaraderie, the Library, the music, the Chapel! I mustn't be disloyal to my own background, the little Cornish grammar school where I was happy; but that was a rather lonely affair, where there was no-one of comparable intelligence to those Collegers to keep one company. Edward Marjoribanks, Denis Dannreuther, Roger Mynors, Bobby Longden, Victor Cazalet, Connolly himself (it took me a long time to catch up with them). The cruel disadvantage was that everything that came after that Paradise (as Horace Walpole, Gray and West had found it too) was decline – even Oxford. Connolly writes nostalgically, 'Early laurels weigh like lead and of many of the boys whom I knew at Eton, I can say that their lives are over. Those who knew them then knew them at their best and fullest; now, in their early thirties, they are haunted ruins. When we meet we look at each other, there is a pause of recognition, then a subsequent moment of guilt and fear.'

Exaggeration – typical Connolly: the usual ploy of self accusation to excuse non-fulfilment of promise. Guilt-complex is rather a fashionable mode, too prevalent, partly assumed. But there are worse things than guilt: of those six boys, one committed suicide, one was killed in action in the Second German War, another by a German bomb, a fourth (Denis Dannreuther, with all his promise) died as a young Fellow of All Souls. There remained only two to fulfil that promise.

Myself, I could never understand the cult of misery with which the intellectuals wrote up their time at their Public Schools[3] – Raymond Mortimer, for example, a fellow Etonian promoted with Connolly from the *New Statesman* to the literary pages of the *Sunday Times*. Desmond MacCarthy, who preceded and promoted them, always said that he was 'bird-happy' at Eton. Dick Crossman, who had no reason whatever to be unhappy at Winchester where he was top-dog, used to give as a reason for being in politics the aim of ending the Public Schools (and All Souls, of which he was not a Fellow). I noticed that the declared enemies of the Public Schools were always Public Schoolboys, rebels or misfits, never working-class fellows like Bevin or Morrison or me. The Public Schools provide the best education in the country – I only wish I had been at one (preferably Eton or Winchester). The people who attack them are not interested in education, let alone educational standards, only in levelling down.

I didn't know Connolly when we were undergraduates, but I came to know some of his close friends at Balliol – the favourites of 'Sligger' (Urquhart), whom I did not like, with his lascivious blue lips and hooded erotic eyes (repressed of course). It was not until some years later, when I was in turn contributing to the *New Statesman* that, first, Raymond Mortimer, then Cyril Connolly, tracked me down to my lair at All Souls.

I well remember Cyril's first visit: my dark-panelled rooms in the front Quad, small shuttered windows looking out on the Warden's garden on one side, the spire of St Mary's, Newman's St Mary's, on the other. When Cyril glimpsed *Enemies of Promise* on my table I got no further word out of him. With the usual writer's egoism he was fascinated by the marginalia, the running commentary with which I had accompanied him all through his book, mostly favourable,

---

[3] cf. *The Old School. Essays by Divers Hands.* Edited by Graham Greene.

sometimes critical.

The year was 1938 or 1939, the time of Munich, the German danger threatening all Europe, the war inevitable. Cyril had the usual flavouring of the intellectuals, lenient to the Germans, not unsympathetic – his London associates were the Berlin boys, Spender, Auden, Isherwood. He was not a pro-German, but intellectually confused on the German Question. He was not a historian, and did not know the German record historically in the past century: the three wars of aggression against Denmark, then Austria, then France; the prime responsibility for 1914–18; the renewal of the attempt. Nor was he a thinker; so he did not know the German intellectual disease, from Fichte onwards to Hegel, which had such a disastrous hold on Germany, and a distasteful influence all over Europe (including Oxford, with Green and Bosanquet; Cambridge, with McTaggart).

When Cyril had finished checking up on himself, I sat him down to a tutorial on the German mind and mentality; concluding by reading to him that marvellously penetrating passage, in Santayana's *Egotism and German Philosophy*, in which he diagnosed and precisely pin-pointed the disease during the First War, long before it became so brutally self-evident in Nazism, the full flowering of it in the popular low standards appropriate to a demotic age.

'The transcendental theory of a world merely imagined by the ego, and the will that deems itself absolute, are certainly desperate delusions. . . . The thing bears all the marks of a new religion. The fact that the established religions of Germany are still forms of Christianity may obscure the explicit and heathen character of the new faith: it passes for the faith of a few extremists, when in reality it dominates the judgment and conduct of the nation. No religious tyranny could be more complete. It has its prophets in the great philosophers and historians of the last century: its high priests and pharisees in the Government and the professors; its faithful flock in the disciplined mass of the nation; its heretics in the Socialists; its dupes in the Catholics and the Liberals, to both of whom the national creed – if they understood it – would be an abomination. It has its martyrs now by the million, and its victims among unbelievers are even more numerous, for its victims, in some degree, are all men.'

That was written in the first years of the 1914–18 war, decades before the German mania had devastated all Europe. At the time Santayana so exactly diagnosed the disease, writing in Oxford, thousands of young fellows were sacrificing their lives to counter it – while Russell, Keynes, and Bloomsbury (but not Eliot: he knew better) were 'conscientious objectors' to fighting it. If those in charge of the nation's affairs between the two German wars had been capable of reading and understanding Santayana, they would have known what they were up against.

Connolly was an intellectual, but not a second-rate one: he immediately got the message, and was visibly impressed. After that exercise he was not taken in by the pro-German intellectuals any more – the insufferable Kingsley Martin, H. N. Brailsford with his German wife, the Headlam-Morleys with their German mother; I never heard Connolly expressing pro-German sentiments thereafter. I will say for him that he was teachable: he learned. The second- and third-rate, of course, not; with them I had the utmost trouble in getting the message across. Perhaps one could not expect them to understand Santayana – and he never seems to have penetrated minds at Cambridge. They would have done far better to listen to him than to a Russell – whom Santayana knew intimately and saw through perfectly.

Connolly made a brilliant periodical of *Horizon* and several times asked me to write a political article for it – I think once I did. Just like Eliot with the *New Criterion*, it was politics that they pressed me to write about – when I was already writing enough about politics for Leonard Woolf's *Political Quarterly*. Raymond Mortimer in the *New Statesman* at least published my poems; so did Joe Ackerley, best of literary editors, in the *Listener*. When it came to the most important of my earlier poems, 'The Old Cemetery at St Austell', I sent it to Connolly with a defensive note to say that the metre was that of Valéry's 'Cimetière Marin', the poem influenced by Yeats. These were admirations of mine, though the poem was not a bit like either of them: it turned out much more after Gray's 'Elegy in a Country Churchyard', similar melancholy tone, same sad concern for and sense of the past. Connolly used my very words to reject the poem – as it if were a pastiche of Yeats and Valéry, of which I was quite incapable.

For long I held this against him. Can he have read it? He certainly had not considered it – and would have been incapable of writing it himself. Actually Gray was a good deal of a historian and scholar, but poet first. Connolly, like all the pure *littérateurs,* had me categorised as historian; and it is a curious thing that, though one may be novelist and poet (Hardy, Meredith), or critic and poet (Arnold, Eliot), one is not allowed to be historian and poet. It is true that it is a very rare combination: I can think only of Macaulay, whose poetry should not be overlooked, and in the Elizabethan age Samuel Daniel, who was poet first, historian second. Actually I was writing poetry from my schooldays, long before I dared to write history. Connolly should have known better – he could have remembered that at Oxford I had been the Eng. Lit. scholar when he was the History scholar (not a very good one). It was Eliot who took my poetry under his wing and published it, and if it was good enough for him, it should certainly have been good enough for Cyril, still more the third-rate reviewers of the *T.L.S.* and the media.

Cyril himself was a poet *manqué.* It is odd that he should not have realised this: he had the eye, and the ear, and the heart. What was missing? It was not that he was too intellectually indolent, that was merely an exterior element in the non-fulfilment creatively; it was something deeper. Sophistication is a dangerous enemy of poetry; in one way, one has to become like a child again, trust to the inner springs, not let self-consciousness get in the way and stop the flow; poetry is written from a deeper level than the cerebellum, from the whole heart and mind, what D. H. Lawrence would call the bloodstream. Hardy was deeply right – and Philip Larkin is right to call attention to it – in saying that poetry is what moves the heart expressed in a way that moves other hearts. That is all: it needs no lit. crit. Neither Hardy nor Larkin, Betjeman nor I, write lit. crit. Self-consciousness stops this most delicate and subtle flow. It is the rarest thing for poetry to be created intellectually, as with Eliot and Valéry; no wonder so much of the verse poured out by inferior intellects today, under that misconception, is not poetry at all.

Cyril wrote a generous obituary tribute to Maurice Bowra: that 'massive head replete with value judgments, innumerable lines of poetry in many languages, seventy-four years of discrimination, affection, love, memories of old battles, all rendered in his unforgettable voice with its fastidious rasping musical glow, an epigram whistling over like an untakeable service, a qualification or a pun woven into the verdict.' Cyril goes on, 'I am convinced that his tragedy, since every man has a tragedy, is that he was not a poet. Such a lifetime's devotion to the critique of poetry must have been the sign of the poet manqué.'

That does not follow; and the Connolly signature-tune, 'since every man has a tragedy', betrays that Cyril was thinking of himself. Everyone who reads or knew Bowra realised that his genius, if genius it was, was a prose genius. I knew Maurice better than his followers, his claque, did: they knew the outer, public man, the noisy, rhetorical Bowra, the natural wit, dominating the company with his cracks, setting the table on a roar, shouting people down. That was not the Maurice I cared for. Cyril had an image which became notorious, that inside every fat man there was a thin one longing to get out (referring to himself as usual). Inside the extrovert Maurice was a sensitive shy man, extremely afraid of ridicule (he had a short, comic figure), and he had been deeply wounded by the 1914–18 war into which he had been thrown as a boy. Beneath the bluster and aggressiveness – it is a familiar enough psychological pattern – Maurice was *afraid*, especially of ridicule. So was Cyril, who took refuge in self-parody. Fancy being afraid of anything the third-rate may say or think! One should be above that: I suspect that this came from their early Prep.-and-Public School exposure to self-consciousness.

Something of Cyril's suppressed poetry comes out in his vocabulary, his love of rare words, his verbal (and visual) intoxication, his images and metaphors, the unexpected or striking connotations that occurred to him as he went along. One of them occurs above, where he compares a Bowra 'epigram whistling over like an untakeable service.' On another visit to All Souls Cyril was sitting with me in our little

Common-room garden, where the fig-trees are trained up the crumbling grey walls. They were leafless, and Cyril at once saw that their intricate bare branches and stems were like the mechanical pipes of an engine-room on board a ship.

One sees this gift again and again. Even when hardly more than a schoolboy, in Switzerland 'the big mountains look as if they had skins like elephants.' On the Piazza in Venice: 'those pigeons! Strutting banality, flying sewers.' In Africa, the elephants – 'their ears flap like canvas on a dinghy, their droppings are like enormous vol-au-vents.' The giraffes have 'creamy suède scrotums, the hyenas faces like sex-tormented scoutmasters.' 'Monotonous as the tap of a lecturer's pole'; or 'a strained voice emerged from his tortured face like a cobra from a snake-charmer's basket.' There are innumerable memorable phrases. Myself a devout lover of cats (and secondarily dogs and donkeys), I never forget that 'affection for animals is the honey of misanthropy.' *Touché.* And the rare words: pericope and pangolin; native fruits such as corassol and darkassou; amniotic, satyriasis – to rival my own addiction to banausic or apolaustic, borborygmic or steatopygous. Cyril had the advantage of a knowledge of botany, and doesn't he display it – as no doubt he did as a member of Pop. Did he collect these words like a conscientious artist, as Pater did adjectives to go with his nouns for future use? Or as Eliot did definitions: a Fellow of All Souls once watched him at work on the dictionary, in the train between Oxford and London. Hence those hair-splitting distinctions in both prose and verse, the refinements of meaning until one reaches the (sometimes) meaningless, so well caught in Henry Reed's parody:

> As we get older we do not get any younger . . .
> 　　　　　. . . *vento dei venti*
> The wind within a wind, unable to speak for wind.
> 　　　　　I think you will find this put,
> Far better than I could hope to express it,
> In the words of Kharma . . .

All this equipped Connolly to be a brilliant parodist, and he evidently regarded his masterly parodies of the Thirties as the top of his achievement. Here you have Connolly playing the funny man for the benefit of Pop again. Aldous Huxley was an obvious target: he meant so much to the intellectuals of the Twenties and Thirties, especially if they were Balliol men. He did not speak for me, any more than Wells did, in spite of my knowing Garsington and its denizens, the *décor* and creatures of *Crome Yellow*.

As a schoolboy Cyril was a devotee. 'I bought *Crome Yellow* out of some prize money. After that his novels and stories continued to dominate my horizon, so enormously competent, so clever, sympathetic, on the spot.' I was never on that spot. 'Now that I have been free for a few years I see *Crome Yellow* as his best book, backed up by *Limbo, Antic Hay,* and his short stories.' That was written in 1936. I tried *Crome Yellow* again recently and, in spite of the nostalgic appeal of its rendering of Garsington and Ottoline, I do not think it a good book: not only faded – it does not live, and to me Huxley is a dead writer. He never did appeal to me; Lawrence did: a most uncertain and fallible artist, who wrote a lot of nonsense, he yet *lives*.

Connolly condemned Huxley for over-production, 'for which the present economic system is to blame' – a Leftist sentiment popular at the time. In this guide we have yet another excuse for Connolly's own under-production – one not very good novella. Really great writers have a way of over-producing, evidence of their prolific creative energy, witness Shakespeare, Walter Scott, Balzac, Victor Hugo. Connolly's ideal was a Flaubert, or Gérard de Nerval, Baudelaire. 'As for Lawrence, I really believe he is asleep at last, and I think nothing should be done to disturb him.' That sentence shows how fallible Connolly's literary criticism was. He thought that Evelyn Waugh would find it difficult to continue after *A Handful of Dust*, 'since Tory satire, directed at people on a moving staircase from a stationary one, is doomed to ultimate peevishness.' A wrong judgment again: the finest satire in the language is the Tory satire of 'Hudibras' Butler, Dryden and Swift.

Far better is Cyril 'being funny' at the expense of his own admirations. Even the names in 'Told in Gath' are perfect Huxley: 'Giles Pentateuch, scatologist and eschatologist, as he dubbed himself.' Then there are Luke Snarthes, 'with that splayed ascetic face of his, consulting his guru, Chandra Nandra'; Reggie Ringworm and Mr Encolpius, Roland Narthex and Mary Pippin, 'whose arm had been eaten away by termites in Tehuantepec'; 'Mrs Amp, whose huge wen, like Saint-Evremond's, made her look more than ever like some heavily wattled turkey, a chicken gumbo; for the rest Risi-bisi Mabel Dodge, *bêche de mer*, beer steak, and Capri pie.'

They all meet in a room 'with a few Longhis round the walls, a Lupanar by Guido Guidi, and over the bed an outsize Stuprum Sabinarum by Rubens – civilised people the hosts, evidently.' A few mistakes are carefully planted to catch the uncivilised. ' "But how can you, how can you?" It was Ursula Groyne. "How *can* you when there are two million unemployed, when Russia has re-introduced anti-abortionary legislation, when Iceland has banned *Time and Tide* [the Lesbian weekly of the Thirties], when the Sedition Bill hangs over us all like a rubber truncheon?" ' It is a heavenly caricature of the fatuities we used to have to put up with from progressive women, dedicated do-gooders, in the Thirties.

Even the sainted Orwell, yet another fellow Etonian, gets an irreverent bucketful splashed over him in 'Year Nine'. 'Having some minutes to spare before the Commonmeal and because it was raining slightly, we took shelter in the glorious Artshouse. There were the ineffable misterpasses of our glorious culture, the pastermieces of titalitorian tra, the magnificent Leadersequence, the superstatues of Comradeship, Blatherhood, and Botherly Love, the Leader as a simple special constable. . . . Mr Abject looked at me with profound commiseration till he received a nudge from the other commissar, and said in a loud voice: "This is your man." I was marched out between them while serried ranks of my old beltmates sang the Leaderchorus and cried: "Show mercy to us by showing no mercy to him, the dog and the traitor." Outside the newsboys were screaming, "Long live the Censor. Gumlicking wrecker discovered." ' '

I fear this is more or less what would have happened to Connolly at the hands of the Writers' Union in the brave new world of USSR, the incarnation of human freedom to Left intellectuals like the asinine Sartre or the criminal Brecht. An intelligentsia, being rootless and without practical responsi-

bility – as Ernest Bevin diagnosed – tends to be Leftist. Didn't
Lenin, *after* he had got into power, write a tract on *The Infantile
Disease of Left-Wing Communism*? There was Connolly, trap-
ped among his fellow intellectuals of the Left, when I suspect
his real feelings were more exactly expressed by his quotation,
in *The Unquiet Grave,* from Norman Douglas's *Siren Land*:
'Has any good ever come out of that foul-clustering town-
proletariat, beloved of humanitarians? Nothing – never; they
are only waiting for a Leader, some "inspired idiot" to rend to
pieces our poor civilisation.'

That was written as early as 1911 – it points directly to
Hitler, *der Führer*, the Leader years after. Norman Douglas
knew his Germans: he was half an Austrian himself.

In the Thirties, when there was some question of returning
their former Colonies to Germany, the joke used to go round
our circle that we might return the Connollys. And jokes
against Connolly recur here and there in the novels of Evelyn
Waugh, with whom Cyril's relations were rather ambivalent.
I don't think that Evelyn, who was Lancing and Hertford –
and a terrible snob about such things – much cared for Cyril's
being Eton and Balliol. Of *The Unquiet Grave* – which made
Cyril's literary fame and fortune – Evelyn wrote: 'Half commonplace book of French maxims, half a lament for his life. It
is badly written in places, with painful psychological jargon
which he attempts to fit into services of teleological problems.'
Evelyn of course, as a Catholic *dévot*, knew the answer to
those. I thought at the time that the book's *réclame* was
excessive, partly due to its appearing when it did, in 1944
when the war was nearing its end and we were culture-
starved; and for the rest it was stuffed with, mainly written by,
Baudelaire, Horace, Pascal, Petronius, Sainte-Beuve, Apol-
linaire, Virgil, Epicurus and, of course. Flaubert. It was a
fascinating example of book-making.

How then do the two dubious friends compare?

Cyril was much the better educated, with far wider range of
reading, and altogether fairer judgment. Evelyn's judgment
was, to an extreme degree, at the mercy of his prejudices, no
notion of justice of mind. Stylistically, though Evelyn may
have been a more exact writer, Cyril was the more poetic one,
with greater brilliance of colour and phrase – even if his was a

poet's eye turned to journalism. On the other hand, Evelyn was inspired by the demon of creative genius, and that is everything.

I fancy that Connolly is a better writer than people think, than perhaps he himself thought and, if not a creator, he has his own inspiration. His best work is not in *The Unquiet Grave,* which had more success, but in *The Condemned Playground* and *The Evening Colonnade,* which had little or none. It is amusing to watch him becoming towards the end an Establishment figure, which Waugh would never have become – too far out on the Right, and he detested everything about contemporary society. Today the Establishment has been taken over by the Left; the Leftists of the Thirties – those who have survived – considerably be-knighted. It is nice to think of Connolly as Sir Cyril – appropriate enough; after all, old Col. Connolly was an Anglo-Irish gent.

After a briefer time than usual lying in a trough of depreciation, the purgatory lying in wait for all writers, Connolly is re-emerging into sympathetic re-appraisal. Peter Quennell, his contemporary at Balliol – and my opposite number as Eng. Lit. scholar (he did not stay the course, any more than John Betjeman did) – has edited a Selection of Cyril's Essays with a very just appreciation of his work. Peter sums him up: 'He and Edmund Wilson, I think, were the most individual critics to appear during the last half of the twentieth century.' To that I append – Connolly was a poet in prose, Wilson was not. 'And Cyril, we must not forget, was also the finest satirist and parodist we have had since Max Beerbohm.' To that I add a third distinction: he was exceptionally gifted as a travel writer, a glutton for seeing places and things – particularly the exotic – as for eating and drinking in them. With his restlessness from childhood, travelling here, there and everywhere, he was really rather rootless – except in literature.

This goes with his Irishry, or Anglo-Irishry. It is odd that he hated being regarded as Irish, when all his characteristics went irreversibly back to the Irishman in him. He was virtually the stage-Irishman, making fun of himself to amuse the English. (It won him his place at Prep. School as well as entry into Pop at Eton: 'Connolly's being funny' attracted the crowd.) He had also the self-indulgence and the self-pity, what the English regard as weakness of character. He had generosity, and a certain seedy gentlemanliness (like Joyce), with a bit of caddishness – witness his, and the Franco-Scot Orwell's, mean disloyalty about the poor Prep. School owners who had done their best for both of them. Connolly certainly had the gift of the gab, a rare and beautiful way with words, like so many writers with the Celt in them – though he never got over the Irish misuse of 'will' and 'would', for shall and should. Did he even notice it? That other stage-Irishman, Wilde, knew that his usage was uncertain, and used to get an English friend to vet his text.

Connolly was no more a scholar than Wilde was – too superficial and impatient. Connolly never noticed that 'Mr W.H.' of Thorp's dedication of Shakespeare's Sonnets was Thorp's man, not Shakespeare's; Wilde simply invented a Willie Hughes, who never existed, under the usual misapprehension, as well as fancying that the Sonnets were homosexual, as he wanted to think, when they are not. Connolly was uncertain about Shakespeare, knowing little if anything about the Elizabethan age. He thought mistakenly that Montaigne gave Shakespeare the idea for *The Tempest*; he reviewed my biography of Shakespeare sympathetically, but couldn't get the facts right.

Nor was he much of a thinker. All things considered, it is remarkable that he was so good a critic. I think this was due to good taste, he had an instinct for quality in literature, as for places and for food and drink. The publication of his biography, with an early Journal, adds little to our knowledge of him – he was such an obsessed egoist that he has told us everything about himself. I learned only one thing of concern to me that I had not known: when we were all undergraduates together Cyril did have a crush on Richard Pares, my chief friend at All Souls. Cyril denied this in a letter to me. Perhaps he had forgotten; or, no historian, he was not very strong on facts. Never mind: he was something better than that, he had a touch of genius – more than the quantitative Edmund Wilson.

Wilson reproached him with spending himself reviewing other people's books, instead of writing his own; and Connolly regretted writing 'brightly' – 'being funny' again – about so many bad books. But what would he have written? Would he have been capable of writing otherwise than he did write? I think not. He fulfilled himself as he was, what he had in him to fulfil, in character pretty exactly.

The Infantilism of Evelyn Waugh

Because I propose to deal with Waugh intellectually with some severity, I should make clear that I am an admirer of his genius as a pure writer – of his fiction and satire, his comic gifts in stories, essays, letters, and as a stylist (as against the parsonic didacticism of a Grigson). Of his Letters, which I shall treat as a revelation of the man, I think I have never been so fascinated since reading the Letters of Horace Walpole. Waugh's offer a scintillating picture of our time and of many people whom I too knew, for we were exact contemporaries at Oxford, and of so many whose variegated personalities cross these pages: Graham Greene, Cyril Connolly, Harold Acton, John Betjeman, Peter Quennell, Lord Longford, Lord David Cecil, and others.

Waugh was a mass of crusty prejudices – and these can be amusing, if taken in the right, light spirit. They were not mostly to be taken thus by Waugh, who held to them firmly and constructed his intellectual position, such as it was, out of them. I, of course, never took him seriously as an intellectual: that was not his function or his gift. We do not have to take seriously what even the greatest writers suppose themselves to think. Consider the utter nonsense Tolstoy wrote about both Shakespeare and Beethoven. Much of what Milton thought and believed was nonsense;[1] not the least remarkable thing about William Shakespeare was that he doesn't seem to have thought any nonsense at all.

Not so Waugh. On the anniversary of the Massacre of St Bartholomew (1572) – one of the bloodiest and most dis-

[1] cf. my *Milton the Puritan: Portrait of a Mind*.

astrous experienced in French history, when thousands of
decent Protestants were killed by their fellow Christians who
were Catholics, Waugh writes to Nancy Mitford, 'Today is a
glorious anniversary in the sad history of your adopted
country. I hope you are keeping it with solemnity and
splendour.' This is all very well for a tease – well, no, it is not
well, when one considers the lives that were lost to France, a
great man like Coligny, an outstanding man like Ramus, etc.
But it was not a tease: Waugh really believed this kind of evil
nonsense.

He tells us, consistently, that 'for me Christianity begins
with the Counter-Reformation' – of which the Massacre of St
Bartholomew was an outward, and not uncharacteristic,
expression, compare the *autos-da-fe* of the Spanish Inquisition.
Imagine beginning the history of Christianity with that, and
ignoring the work of early Christianity in civilising the
barbarians of Northern Europe, the marvellous expressions of
the high-water mark of medieval Christianity in the cathedrals
of Europe, in the literature, Dante, St Thomas Aquinas, the
deeply moving Latin hymns of Saint Bernard, Abélard, and so
on!

Similarly with English history. Elizabeth I 'survived alive
because of the high Christian principles of Mary Tudor, when
in any other royal family she would have been executed. She
was jockeyed into place by a gang of party bosses and executed
the rightful heir, Mary Stuart. All the newspapers are full of
the glorification of Elizabeth Tudor, the vilest of her sex.'
Infantile, of course. It is all very well to lay down the law, if
you know the facts. Waugh didn't trouble to learn them, any
more than Belloc did. The facts are that, after Wyatt's Rebel-
lion, Mary Tudor sent Elizabeth to the Tower and wanted to
have her executed. There would have been revolution in the
country if she had done so, and even her husband, Philip of
Spain, did not want a French woman to succeed to the English
throne, when he was at the time engaged in war with France.

So, too, towards the end of Waugh's life, when reading
Churchill's Life of the great Duke of Marlborough, linch-pin
of the Grand Alliance which defeated Louis XIV's overween-
ing ascendancy in Western Europe, threatening other nations'
independence. Louis had very nearly extinguished the

independence of Holland in 1672, but for the resistance of the Dutch people under the heroic leadership of William of Orange. William's whole life was inspired by the aim of reducing Louis XIV to size, preserving the balance of Europe; to this end he booted out his stupid father-in-law, James II, to bring England into her proper place in the Grand Alliance.

Waugh on this: 'I lately read Sir Winston's *Marlborough*. How he alienates all sympathy. I found myself on every page praying, "Oh God, do defeat the Grand Alliance." ' Well, God didn't. Nor do I suppose that Waugh knew that the Pope, Innocent XI, was a supporter of Protestant William and of the Grand Alliance, having had more than enough of Louis' arrogance to put up with, even in Rome. It must have been a Protestant wind that brought William to victory in 1688, as also presumably against the Spanish Armada in 1588.

Waugh gets no better marks on American history. '*Of course* the Americans are cowards. They are almost all the descendants of wretches who deserted their legitimate monarchs for fear of military service.' Why write such rubbish? Why not get the facts right – it is apt to lead one to such wrong judgments of contemporary affairs for another thing. In 1947 it is: 'Big things will happen in Palestine, where the American Jews have made it possible for the Red Army to reach its goal in the Mediterranean.' We all know that the exact opposite was the case.

What accounts for this? Sheer perverseness was very strong in his make-up and a constant factor from schooldays to the end. A certain streak of infantilism is apt to go with genius, as psychologists should be aware: men of genius are often not well-rounded individuals, sometimes noticeably not grown-up. In Waugh's case he took up a position out of prejudice, either of taste or emotion, by an act of will, and then stuck to it contrary to all reason. Of course he called it 'reason' and said that he arrived at it by a process of reasoning, like his conversion. But it was not; he spoke more truly when he said that that was 'a step in the dark'.

He was no less perverse about religion than about history. One would have thought it a good step when Christians of various denominations ceased persecuting each other, to stand together for common purposes, especially against the challenge of Communism – or the advance of Islam – around the world. Not so with Waugh. The Jesuit Cardinal Bea had been promoting good relations with the Anglicans and the Greek Orthodox Church. However, 'I was greatly cheered to read yesterday of the rebuffs given to Cardinal Bea at Patras. That should put off Ecumenism for a millennium.'

Again, 'all this talk of ecumenism is exceedingly painful'; and, of Hans Kung, its theologian and promoter, 'in a happier age Kung would have been burned at the stake.' When even his friend Woodruff inclined to ecumenism, it was 'a senile infatuation for a very dangerous clergyman called Kung, a heresiarch who in happier days would be roasted.'

In his last years, when the new vernacular rite was adopted by the Roman Church, though much less moving than that of the Anglican Prayer Book – Waugh is off to Rome for Easter, 'to avoid the horrors of the English liturgy.' Then Rome lets him down. His last letter is pathetic: 'Easter used to mean so much to me. Before Pope John and his Council – they destroyed the beauty of the liturgy. I now cling to the Faith doggedly without joy. Church-going is a pure duty parade. I shall not live to see it restored.' Serve him right for having been so infantilely perverse.

By sheer prejudice, mere wilfulness, Evelyn had taken up an Ultramontane position, like Belloc, and then found that the Roman Church let him down. He expected the Second Vatican Council to repeat the absurdities of the First, with its declaration of Papal Infallibility, etc: 'As in 1869–70 the French and Germans are full of mischief but, as then, the truth of God will prevail', i.e. what Waugh fancies, that is Truth. 'The spirit of that wicked Père Couturier still lives on in France and must be destroyed.' This was a highly intelligent Dominican who disagreed with Waugh. He says that he simply cannot understand why everybody is not a Catholic – but this evidently means his sort of Catholic. Everybody who does not agree is a heretic (as with the equally assertive C. S. Lewis, another intellectual bully, on the other side).

All this comes out in Evelyn's bullying Penelope Betjeman out of the Anglican Church into the Roman (though she had propulsions of her own), and the attempt to bully her husband, John Betjeman. 'It is impossible for someone like

yourself, who is in formal heresy, to realise the horror which
heresy inflames in an orthodox mind. What seems to you a
harmless and amusing speculation is, to me, a denial and
perversion of God's truth', *sc.* Waugh's opinion. And then to
his friend Betjeman himself: 'Awful about your obduracy in
schism and heresy. Hell hell hell. Eternal damnation.' This
gave Betjeman's gentle nature fearful nightmares. Fancy taking Waugh's not very well-developed, not very adult, intellect
so seriously, intellectually – they were all of them, for all their
other gifts, not very strong in the head.

Evelyn persisted with his proselytising: 'I wouldn't give a
thrush's egg for your chances of *salvation* at the moment.'
What does that precisely mean, one might ask? The poor wife
was driven to protest: Betjeman 'is in a dreadful state. He
thinks you are the devil and wakes up in the middle of the
night, and raves and says he will leave me at once if I go over.'
However, it was no use bullying a jelly – it was like Paul
Claudel trying to bully André Gide: same tactics, similar
results. But Evelyn did succeed in driving a wedge between
Penelope and her husband, and creating great unhappiness.
(Was this very Christian? Evelyn was a Catholic, but was he a
Christian?)

After her brother's suicide, Penelope did go over, leaving
that 'Empty Pew' in their village church, where John continued to worship alone – of that touching poem which he
never felt able to publish. From that time the marriage came
apart and the couple began to separate. John had met with an
intellectual bully before in C. S. Lewis, who was his tutor at
Magdalen College – also of no effect, except by way of
reaction. (Lewis set Betjeman against Shakespeare, and he
subsequently went down without a degree.) C. S. Lewis was a
far more formidable proposition than Waugh intellectually,
and both Lewis and Betjeman remained in the bosom of the
Church of England.

Similar bullyings are delivered by Evelyn to others among
his friends – in the case of Lady Eden, reproaches for not
keeping up with Rome. 'Clarissa's apostasy has upset me
more than anything that had happened since Kick's [Kathleen
Kennedy's] death. I can't write about it, or think of anything
else.' To Lady Eden herself: 'I don't suppose you deliberately

chose the vigil of the Assumption for your betrayal, or deliberately arrived in a Catholic capital on the Feast. But I am sure Our Lady noticed. Anyway on your jaunt in Portugal did you never go into a church to glance at the Emanuel style? When you found yourself, then, in the presence of Our Lord, what had you to say to him?' etc. Poor Clarissa Churchill compounded her offence by marrying a Protestant, Sir Anthony Eden – and on her wedding morning received a rocket by telegram such as no friend should dream of sending to another. 'I have been thinking of her with deep compassion, but then she had herself photographed going to a Protestant church, so all my kindness was turned to despair again.'

No compassion for fellow Christians in other churches. 'Many things have puzzled me from time to time about the Christian religion, but one thing has always been self-evident – the bogosity of the Church of England.' The Pope in Canterbury Cathedral must have made him turn in his grave. Lord Longford's 'prurient interest in Protestantism disgusts me.' On a friend's son leaving Eton for a Catholic school, 'I am sure that St Henry in heaven constantly prays for the rescue of the unhappy little victims of his perverted foundation, and that he is to be thanked for this triumph of Grace.' Henry VI was indeed the founder of Eton, but he never achieved the status of a Saint – bad history again. Waugh never seems to have drawn the conclusion from the admission he makes at one point: 'God knows I don't blame the Poles for any shifts they have to resort to; but I have the undeserved privilege of living in a country where compromise is unnecessary.' That is because Britain was neither Communist nor Catholic – hence compromise was of the essence of her successful record in history. Did he never think that out?

Allowing prejudice to determine his intellectual position meant false judgments in literature as well as in history. Proust was a 'mental defective' – a mind far subtler and cleverer than his own. Rose Macaulay 'was, I think, quite devoid of the gift of faith' – she was in fact a believing Anglican. Edith Sitwell's conversion greatly pleased Evelyn – her junior, he became her godfather. Neither conjuncture seems to have done her much good – she was soon as unhappy as before. One motive had been to go one further than T. S. Eliot, in his conversion to

Anglicanism. How childish they were! One finds infantile anti-Americanism all through, not worth going into: 'There is no such thing as an American – They are all exiles uprooted, transplanted and doomed to sterility.'

Wrong too about his friend Maurice Bowra: 'I believe all his pretentions to understand foreign poetry an imposture.' Maurice had a genuine passion for poetry in all the various languages he knew: Cyril Connolly paid generous tribute to that. Nothing generous in Evelyn's judgments about other writers – unless they happened to be Catholics, fellow members of his Club. Maurice knew that trait well in Evelyn: it accounted for his over-estimation of Fr. Ronald Knox ('if he had been an atheist, he would have had the O.M.'), his campaign for the historical novels of the reformed alcoholic, Alfred Duggan, or his public acclaim for Graham Greene's work.

I well remember reproving Greene for his thoughtless statement that, if he had to choose between living in the USA and Soviet Russia, he would choose Soviet Russia. He cannot have meant it, if he had thought about it, or he wouldn't have given such a false lead. Why are these people so unaware? Waugh always presented a firm public front on behalf of his own free-masonry; but, in his Letters, we descry what he really thought of his co-religionists' work. Of Greene's *A Burnt-Out Case*: 'M. Grisjambon Vert [Mr Greene has gone to live in France, understandably for tax-reasons] has written a very sorrowful novel.' Or, 'And now Graham Greene has written a most distressing work.' To Graham on his play, *The Potting Shed*: 'It was an enthralling evening. It seemed to me that all the audience was enthralled.' To his wife Laura (who had much to put up with) he confided: 'The play is great nonsense theologically, and will puzzle people needlessly' – himself being an authority on theology. QED.

When these people make such a statement as that our whole life here is but a preparation for a life elsewhere, a hypothesis, a preparation for the non-existent, do they realise that they are making a non-sense statement? Similarly when Waugh allows that American monasticism may yet 'save' the world, it *means* nothing. To the world at large it means nothing, nine-tenths of which cannot be regarded as Christian. The Chinese alone constitute one-fifth of the human race; there are 100 million Japanese, besides the teeming millions of South-East Asia. India will have a population of a billion by the end of the century. Islam advances in vast numbers in the Middle East and across Northern Africa; then the rest of proliferating Africa, Central and Southern America, to say nothing of Soviet Russia and Communist countries, mainly atheist.

Christianity was really a European export, and Waugh would even subtract from it all that is not Roman Catholic. Methodism is the largest Protestant denomination in the USA, and Waugh would throw over all Protestant Christians.

Evelyn Waugh and Connolly came up to Oxford in the Michaelmas Term of 1922, as I did – both of them with History scholarships, though they should have taken the English School, which I was intended for as a scholar in English Literature. (My opposite number as an Eng. Lit. scholar at Balliol was Peter Quennell.) Evelyn and Cyril were not cronies as undergraduates, and I knew neither then, though I knew Richard Pares – Evelyn's 'dearest friend' – who became my closest friend at All Souls – through the Labour Club. In Waugh's 'First Volume of Autobiography', *A Little Learning*, he writes, 'There was already an active Labour Party to which Richard Pares and many clever men belonged. Indeed it comprised so many of the best brains that I advised a middle-brow socialist acquaintance, before he came up, that he would find the competition too hot and that he had better make his appearance as a Conservative. He took the advice and prospered.' Ingenuous and sincere, I did not think in such terms and did not take such a prosperous course. Moreover, priggish and rather puritanical, I disapproved of the Hypocrites Club to which they belonged, with all that drinking and smoking – Graham Pollard, John Sutro, Terence Greenidge, Evelyn and even dear Richard.

Connolly was already taken up by Maurice Bowra – Evelyn did not make that grade until he began to be known as a novelist. In my early days at All Souls Maurice tried to take me up, arriving in my rooms afternoon after afternoon for a walk; I did not encourage this attention – too frivolous. Evelyn notes that in *Enemies of Promise* Cyril said little of his Oxford life, and

I have noted that he regarded it as a decline from Eton. Evelyn – ambivalent as they were about each other – says that, when Cyril should come to write about those days, 'he was suffering, I think he will tell us, from poverty. At the university he found himself on an inequality of expenditure with his old friends from Pop. This never worried a man in precisely the same position, Christopher Hollis [another contemporary, who wrote an indifferent autobiography, I thought], but Cyril was haunted by an Anglo-Irish ghost of dandyism. Balliol was ill-suited to his mood; it was not a luxurious college; next only to Keble [Evelyn's anti-Anglican feeling comes in here] it was the least luxurious. The architecture is dismal. Cyril would have been happy in Peckwater [the aristocratic quarter of Christ Church; I lived in the Latin Quarter of Meadows] with an allowance of £750 a year.'

Knowing so many of Evelyn's friends, I felt that I knew him quite well enough. I had several periscopes trained on him, even from his schooldays, where Max Mallowan told me how unpopular he was, and Hugh Molson how badly he treated his sentimental old father, whose ninetyish sentimentality the difficult son could not stand. However, what an advantage Evelyn and Alec Waugh started with, with a father already high up in the publishing world.

The fact was that, like many men of genius, Evelyn had a divided, almost a split, personality. We must allow that, on one side, he had great charm and, when he behaved himself, could be irresistible. (I had nothing to complain of from him – better not!) He was fearless and lion-hearted, and always amusing, sometimes even when naughty. Hugh Molson told me that, when young together, those gifted boys, Richard and Evelyn, were like brilliant children with their prattle. I recognise them both as such. Evelyn himself recognised that, on the other side, he had a nasty character and sometimes wondered why. (He was resentful of his appearance, at being so short, and made himself up as an Angry Old Man.) One thing to be said for Protestantism is that it encourages moral effort: Evelyn never tried, but said that, without his Catholicism, he would have been worse. A Catholic, but not a Christian – unlike Pope John, of whom he did not approve. (Randolph Churchill to the Pope: 'Do you know Evelyn

Waugh? He's a Catholic too.')

Waugh had a complex about his tutor at Hertford, C. R. M. F. Cruttwell, whom I knew intimately as an All Souls man. Evelyn's portrait of him in *A Little Learning* is authentic enough, a recognisable description, but only one side of the human being. 'Cruttwell's appearance was not prepossessing. He was tall, almost loutish, with the face of a petulant baby. He smoked a pipe which was usually attached to his blubber-lips by a thread of slime. As he removed the stem, waving it to emphasise his indistinct speech, this glittering connection extended until finally it broke leaving a dribble on his chin. When he spoke to me I found myself so distracted by the speculation of how far this line could be attenuated that I was often inattentive to his words.'

The rest of Evelyn's account of Cruttwell is caricature. It is true that he offered a target for caricature, and Richard and I used to study him from this point of view. Richard described him as 'the Dong with the luminous Nose', which was more accurate than Evelyn's 'petulant baby'. Cruttwell had a comic vocabulary for colleagues, which made us laugh: dons were 'hacks', women-dons were 'hags' or 'breast-heavers'. It was highly inventive – I wish I could remember it all. Once, walking in the Meadows, we passed 'Nippy' Williams, an oleaginous Canon of Christ Church, strutting beside his large wife: 'There go Mr Spiritual Pride with his wife, Mistress Carnality', said Cruttwell – Evelyn himself could not have done better. Or Maurice Bowra, on my friend David Mathew, an enormously fat Roman ecclesiastic: 'A perfect specimen of the Word made Flesh.'

It is true that Cruttwell's table manners were bad; I never can understand why hearty masculine types can't eat their food neatly and not plaster crumbs over their faces, let alone pipe-spittle. I detest smoking – and Evelyn himself was a filthy cigar-smoker. However, I did understand the whole man in Cruttwell. He had had an appalling war in the trenches on the Western Front, and emerged a wounded man, physically and psychologically. Before the war he had been a good athlete, a fine heavy-weight footballer; after it he was lamed, and crippled with rheumatism. He was a believing Christian, who gave surreptitious financial help to many an undergraduate, though barking at them if they fell down on their work – as he did not, in spite of his physical disabilities.

The most impatient of men, he was extraordinarily patient with me and my Leftism. I had been brought up under the influence of the Russell and Brailsford nonsense that the British were as responsible as the Germans for the war in 1914, and was maddeningly persistent in arguing this line when I first arrived at All Souls. Cruttwell, himself a victim of the Germans, scarred by his ordeal, was astonishingly patient with me; all he said in reply to me about the Armistice of 1918 (it proved to be no more than an armistice in the long career of German aggression) was: 'It was an almighty deliverance.'

Mentally, he was a victim of sex-repression. As I became more and more ill, we became companions on our afternoon walks for exercise. He had a gruff tenderness towards me. I confess that I had begun by being afraid of his whiplash of a tongue, but once I stood up to him all that vanished. He showed more forbearance towards Evelyn as his tutor than I should have done. After all, he had given Waugh his scholarship, a good one, and expected him to work; Evelyn was a slacker and a drunkard. He tells us how he behaved. 'It was Terence who imaginatively imputed to Cruttwell sexual connection with dogs and purchased a stuffed one, which we set in the quad as an allurement from his return from dining in All Souls. For the same reason we used rather often to bark under Cruttwell's windows at night.'

On Evelyn's last night as an undergraduate he says that he climbed into Hertford from the garden of All Souls. I don't know how that was possible, he may have been let in by Richard Pares, or he may have been mixed up. I remember him dining with Richard only once, and then drunk. He seems to have realised that Cruttwell scored with his valedictory notes: 'I cannot say that your Third does you anything but discredit: especially as it was not even a good one; and it is always at least foolish to allow oneself to be given an inappropriate intellectual label. I hope you will soon settle in some sphere where you will give your intellect a better chance than in the History School.'

Fair enough: that shows that Cruttwell realised that Evelyn was capable of better things; but for the time it meant a series of undignified jobs in disreputable Prep. schools, from whence he emerged with *Decline and Fall*, and after that found himself. In subsequent novels Waugh worked off his grudge by using Cruttwell's name for various shady characters, male or female. I suppose Cruttwell could have had him up for libel: he never bothered, and all he said to me about his unsatisfactory pupil was, peaceably, 'I could have sent him down.'

I do not know if Cruttwell knew about Evelyn's love-affair with Richard Pares; though Richard was my greatest friend, he never spoke of it to me. Nor would I mention it, if it were not now in print in Evelyn's Letters. In 1954 'I went to Oxford and visited my first homosexual love, Richard Pares. At 50 he is quite paralysed except his mind and voice, and waiting deterioration and death. . . . He would have been Master of Balliol if he had not been struck down. A very harrowing visit.' Unaware as usual, little did he realise that he sickened poor Richard – patient, resigned, heroic, never a word of complaint – by puffing cigar-smoke over him.

It marks a sad contrast with the old gay days just after going down. In November 1925 it is: 'I went to Oxford and contrary to my intentions stayed the night. John's [Sutro] party consisted of Harold Acton, Mark Ogilvie-Grant, Hugh Lygon, Robert Byron, Arden Hilliard and Richard Pares. After luncheon which was hot lobster, partridges and plum pudding, sherry, mulled-claret and a strange rum-like liqueur, I left Hugh and John drinking . . . and then to the New Reform where I found Terence and Elmley drinking beer. I drank with them, and went to dinner with Robert Byron in Merton Hall. I found Billy (Clonmore) and after dinner went to the rooms of a hunting man and drank beer. . . . Next morning I drank beer with Hugh and port with Preters [Molson] and gin with Gyles Isham, lunched with Hugh and Desmond Harmsworth. Harold and Billy saw me off at the station feeling woefully tired.' It is the world – and some of the characters – of *Brideshead Revisited*.

Evelyn writes of Richard, 'the first friend to whom I gave my full devotion did not enjoy drinking and as a result we drifted apart. He was Richard Pares, a Balliol Wykhamist [*sc.* Wykehamist], with an appealing pale face and a mop of fair hair, blank blue eyes and the Lear-Carroll-like fantasies of many [?] Balliol Wykhamists [sic]. I loved him dearly, but an excess of wine nauseated him, and this made an insurmountable barrier between us . . . He withdrew, or was withdrawn, from our company' – and into mine, I may say. John Sutro, a rich dilettante, regarded it as 'a defection to All Souls' – where I occasionally met him, with his remarkable talent for mimicry, dining with Richard. 'Once, before his withdrawal, he had a dream in which one of us was convicted of the unknown vice of "vanoxism". . . . We founded a club named the Vanoxists who met for breakfast now and then at the Trout at Godstow, all of us united in nothing but affection for Richard.'

Evelyn goes on to an account of his next affair under a pseudonym. Not until twenty-one did he graduate, as Connolly did too – to the girls. As an undergraduate Evelyn had three satisfying homo affairs. Then why the later vicious attacks on homosexuals? I find this yet another strain of unawareness – odd in one who had been one himself. My old friend Cecil Roberts, the novelist, complained to me of Evelyn's appalling behaviour to him in the *foyer* of the Grand Hotel in Rome. Evelyn came up to him and said, 'You old bugger, I thought you were in prison years ago.' I told Cecil, 'You must forgive him. Don't you realise he was mad?' – as he was: he had gone off his head with drink and drugs. That passage in his life he characteristically turned to good account with *The Ordeal of Gilbert Pinfold*. On board ship he was persecuted by voices accusing him of being a homosexual – as he had been. Why should that be a subject for paranoia, when it is normal enough, common enough surely?[2]

It was just after the publication of this remarkable book that I met Evelyn, when I was staying at Dunster Castle with hospitable Alys Luttrell, its *châtelaine*. At the end of September 1959 he writes to his daughter, 'Did I tell you we went to luncheon at Dunster on Sunday? It was to meet a reformed socialist Fellow of All Souls named Rowse.' Evelyn was on his best behaviour – he had better be – ear-trumpet and all. He was still animadverting against Trevor-Roper, with whom he had had a controversy, at the end of which Evelyn advised him to

---

[2] cf. my *Homosexuals in History*.

change his name and go to Cambridge. Trevor-Roper followed the advice on both counts, with results that were yet to be seen. We did not speak of the controversy, though I had followed it closely and thought of intervening on Trevor-Roper's side.

Evelyn and Laura had come over from Combe Florey, which I did not visit until after his death. The place was touchingly full of his presence, the possessions he had gathered around him, the atmosphere he created. The spacious Georgian house was full of the Victoriana he affected: in the rather shabby drawing-room the big carpet he had bought from the proceeds of a libel-action he had won, and a large Burgess bureau. Upstairs was a yet more complicated piece of Burgess furniture, which I think Betjeman had given him: combined dressing table and washstand with metal apparatus (I think now in a Museum). In the hall a bust of himself, his Captain's cap of *Officers and Gentlemen* stuck on at a jaunty angle. In the dining room a picture of travel in the Victorian age – the interior of a railway compartment; with a companion piece he had had painted of air-travel, the space-age.

Then into the beautiful library, with painted shelves, which he had created: the heart of the house. Here one had one's finger on the pulse of the dead man yet alive in his work. On the shelves inscribed copies of the books of his friends: from Harold Acton, 'To gallant Evelyn, away at the war', from Maurice Bowra, Edith Sitwell, Graham Greene, fellow campaigner. (Curious how all that anguished concern about religion has vanished. No-one thinks about it in the social revolution that has overwhelmed us.) And at last the writing-desk, pens, ink and paper; the Diary open in that academic-artistic handwriting – he wrote everything longhand – for me to see. The firm squat figure might be seated there at the desk, puckered, angry expression, hand poised ready to throw his dart.

The Personality of C. S. Lewis

C. S. Lewis was an odd and gifted man, much odder than his numerous disciples knew. Those who observed him from close at hand, like an historian friend of mine who was for years a colleague of his at Magdalen College, Oxford, and observed him closely, knew how odd. It is the business of historians to watch and observe – not dogmatise, like Lewis – and the first thing that my friend observed was that Lewis's Academy-prized book, *The Allegory of Love*, was not in keeping with the facts of medieval life. K. B. McFarlane was a medievalist, the leading authority on the fifteenth century: he knew that Lewis was theorising as usual and not getting it right. Lewis had an idealised view of chivalric and courtly love which was not in keeping with the *facts*, which have prime authority with historians. As an historian I clashed with Lewis, the theorist, at Oxford on similar grounds.

I am reminded of this by Lewis's autobiography, *Surprised by Joy*, a rather noble book, for Lewis was a good man with the highest standards. Then I knew from my friend's intimate information what Lewis was referring to in a crucial gap in the autobiography, an omission of 'one huge and complex episode.' This refers to the domestic circumstances of his life away from college in the cottage he inhabited with two women at Headington. He did not live in college as Fellows who were bachelors almost all did at that time.

One day a couple of the Fellows walking on Shotover were caught in a downpour of rain, and sought shelter in Lewis's cottage nearby. No-one was at home, but they were surprised to see women's clothes lying about, and drew the obvious conclusion. So this was Lewis's secret! They were wrong in their conventional assumption: the truth was much more odd.

Lewis lived there with *two* women – the mother and daughter of his closest friend, who had been killed in the war of 1914–18 and wished the care of them upon him. He took on what he regarded as a duty, a burden which bore more and more heavily upon him as the years went on. For he had nothing in common with these commonplace people. Bearing it must have appealed to the masochistic element in his make-up.

McFarlane noticed another, rather analogous, element. Lewis was full of *fear*: he had something wrong internally, but was afraid of an operation. His autobiography confesses to the fears and terrors of his childhood, his 'terror' of his father, though that may have been a rhetorical exaggeration.

The rhetoric and the exaggeration he got from his Welsh-Irish father – 'that fatal bent towards dramatisation and rhetoric: I speak of it the more freely since I inherited it.' Another trait which he inherited was an inability to listen to other people – his father never listened and always answered at cross purposes, showing that he had not understood what was being said to him. 'He could never empty, or silence, his own mind to make room for an alien thought.' Neither could the son; he never tried; he was a dogmatist, equally cocksure both when he was an atheist, and when he became a kind of fundamentalist Christian. I had a couple of instances with him when he simply didn't, or wouldn't, take in the point. 'Words came to him and intoxicated him', he says of his father; something of this was true of the son. A little more scepticism, a little less cocksure, both of his atheism and of his Christian belief, would have been salutary and more cogent.

To return to the point of Fear. McFarlane was convinced that it was the terror of war approaching once more that unnerved Lewis and brought him to the Christian faith. This was understandable, especially for the men who had been not much more than boys in the First German War and had known the horrors of the trenches on the Western Front. It was so with Maurice Bowra, who could not bear to think of it, it had been such a cruel experience. I don't see why Eliot should have made such a cult of 'The horror! The horror!', when he wasn't caught in that.

★

For all Lewis's fulminations against the 'Personal Heresy' – it would be 'heresy' if he didn't agree with it (like his dogmatic father) – he is very much to the fore personally in all his writings. Naturally in an autobiography; but there he reveals himself in lights he wouldn't suspect, for though an able man intellectually, he was not a subtle or perceptive one.

There is the constant trick of writing himself down. This is very popular with readers who do not realise that it is a way of writing oneself *up*. Self-depreciation is inverted pride. I prefer taking oneself plain, simply and directly, with a proper opinion of oneself (which, of course, should be justified in work).

'Whatever I know – it is not much – of courtesy and *savoir faire*' . . . he does not need to write himself down: Lewis was always, and in every relation of life, a gentleman. 'I was, no doubt, and was blamed for being, a conceited boy.' He always had a good conceit of himself, and rightly. He immediately justifies himself with, 'but the blame was usually attached to something in which no conceit was present.'

'Up till now I had committed nearly every other sin and folly within my power, but I had not yet been flashy.' Here is the parental tendency to exaggerate – how absurd to write like that of a boy of sixteen, a Public School boy too: what else? It is hardly sinful for a boy to be flashy. He goes on about all his 'slips from virtue', which he would not impute to a young schoolmaster, who 'made sad work of certain humble and childlike and self-forgetful qualities which (I think) had remained with me.' There is a note of smugness in that, which became characteristic of him – one saw it in the expression on his face. 'I began to labour very hard to make myself into a fop, a cad, and a snob.' Exaggeration again, to condemn a mere schoolboy in this fashion – but it is a way of recommending himself to an imperceptive reader.

Speaking of the two sins he was never tempted to commit, 'impure love' of his own sex at school, and gambling – 'This means then,' the reader (of whom he is very conscious) is supposed to object, 'that all the other vices you have so largely written about . . . Well, yes, it does, and more's the pity.' I just don't believe it: Lewis was a naturally good man, and evidently an exceptionally innocent boy at school. Exaggeration again – to impress the reader.

He condemns himself for not worrying about the war, putting off thinking about it: 'No doubt, even if the attitude was right, the quality in me which made it so easy to adopt is somewhat repellent' . . . I find this moralising about oneself distasteful. 'In the depth of my disgraces, in the then invincible ignorance of my intellect, all this was given me without asking' . . . I do not detect any disgraces. 'There was a humility in me, as a reader, which I shall never recapture.' I knew him well enough, but I never detected any humility – not that that is a count against him, for I regard humility as an exaggerated virtue, if a virtue.

What everyone could see was his father's dogmatism – that did not take much detecting. He always thought Bacon, for example, 'a solemn, pretentious ass.' An absurd judgment to anyone who can appreciate that tolerant, all-comprehending, ecumenical intellect. Lewis, always too ready to condemn what he has no fancy to, thinks keeping a diary 'a time-wasting and foolish practice.' Absurd again, especially to an historian who reflects how much we should be impoverished without the diaries of Pepys and Evelyn; or to a person of literary sensibility, who can appreciate Dorothy Wordsworth or Kilvert. But, then, Lewis – who disapproved too readily what he did not like – seemed to think that English poetry had reached its term with Chesterton (!) and, like his older colleagues in the English School at Oxford, conventional academics, depreciated Eliot.

'The moment good taste knows itself some of its goodness is lost.' One should ask, why? The reason for his laying down the law about this is that he was anti-aesthete. To anyone who thinks that the apprehension and experience of beauty offer the redemption of man from the slime, this *is* a sin – in my sense of the word, not Lewis's, which would be merely theological. He goes on further about 'good taste', 'Even then, however, it is not necessary to take the further downward step of despising "the Philistines" who do not share it.' Why 'downward'? It is a duty for anyone who knows the redeeming quality of aesthetic values – for all people, not only the elect, in so far as they can apprehend them – to disapprove of Philistinism in any form.

Actually, there was an element of Philistinism in Lewis – hence his word of defence: all that beer-swilling, pipe-smoking, pub-crawling heartiness of the Inklings, C. S.'s cronies at Oxford. I thought it vulgar.

'Hymns are extremely disagreeable to me' – that is no recommendation, simply a defect; and an aesthetic defect when one considers the haunting beauty of the Latin hymns of the medieval Church, by some of its greatest spirits too – St Thomas Aquinas, Abélard, St Bernard or Adam of St Victor: the nostalgic evening hymn, shutting the shutters upon daylight and the day's work, 'Te lucis ante terminum.' Or,

O quanta qualia sunt ista sabbata.

Lewis, by way of self-promotion, to show that he is 'with it' will condemn 'the wicked institution of Church Parades.' What is there wicked about Church Parades? They may very well do some people some good. It was just that he didn't like them, either at school or in the Officers' Training Corps. Once again, what he didn't like is generalised into a proposition if not a rule. This becomes important intellectually, when it is carried over into the fields of literature, philosophy or theology.

He was unhappy at his Public School, which his brother, a year or two older, simply loved. Why couldn't C.S. take it in his stride? The Public Schools were geared to ordinary fellows, *l'homme moyen sensuel*; he was odd man out, a misfit.

He makes an important point when he says: 'For the last thirty years or so England has been filled with a bitter, truculent, sceptical, debunking and cynical intelligentsia.' This is true – and it is even worse today, with the lowering and vulgarisation of standards. Lewis rightly pin-points the fact that 'a great many of them were at Public Schools and I believe very few liked it.' I never had this difficulty to contend with, since I went as a dayboy to a grammar-school and loved every moment of it: for me it was a liberation from, and an enrichment of, the cultural waste-land of working-class life (as with D. H. Lawrence). The grammar-schools, of which the great Education Act of 1902 created a nation-wide system, have been dealt a destructive blow in the interest of monochrome egalitarianism, no matter about education or educational standards. Lewis and I would agree about that.

What I did not like was his perpetual disputatiousness, seeing everything in terms of argument. Whatever his success with readers – who, for the most part, I suspect, ignore the arguments – not all his pupils and colleagues at Oxford would stand for it, any more than I would. John Betjeman, a gentle soul on his way to being a good poet, could not bear it, wilted before the intellectual bullying, did no work and was sent down. Ironic flecks of Betjeman's experience appear in his early work:

> 'Objectively, our Common Room
>   Is like a small Athenian state –
> Except for Lewis: he's all right
>   But do you think he's *quite* first rate?' –

inquires one don of another. While in the Preface to *Ghastly Good Taste* Betjeman pays tribute to his old tutor, 'whose jolly personality and encouragement to the author in his youth have remained an unfading memory for the author's declining years.'

John Cooper, a tougher spirit, refused to go to Lewis for political theory tutorials. Magdalen College asked me to take him on; he was the best pupil intellectually that I ever had, a very difficult, cross-grained individual of great promise. He had had a bad time in the Second German War, and lost the one person he loved in it, his only brother. He became a distinguished historian before he died, still young. But he wasn't taking C. S. Lewis, any more than I was.

My disagreement with Lewis, and his with me, was an intellectual one: we were at opposite poles in war-time and post-war Oxford. Lewis was essentially un-historical, in one sense anti-historical. His mind was philosophical, in the old-fashioned way in which he had been trained. The old Greats School at Oxford believed in the primacy of metaphysics – the situation is different today, in the wake of Wittgenstein, with the philosophers busily engaged in sawing off the bough upon which they formerly sat, showing up metaphysical problems

as largely due to confusions in the meaning of words, superfluous if not positively bogus. Even while Lewis was at
Magdalen the College had an original philosopher in J. L.
Austin, devoted precisely to this business of analysis, a solvent
of so much metaphysics. If anything is 'a waste of time' I
regard metaphysics as more so than keeping a diary is.

Lewis misunderstood the issue between us, just as his father
would have done. He insists, quite rightly, that a view or a
theory may be out of date, but that 'tells us nothing about its
truth or falsehood.' This is obvious. He tilted against the
'chronological' heresy, mistakenly equating it with historical
relativism, as if that were all there was to it!

I was the proponent of historical relativism, and Lewis pin-
pointed it as the enemy (one of them). He gave it a special
name, which no one knows now – 'bulverism'. I cannot here
expound what historical relativism means: I did so at the time
in the central chapter of *The Use of History*. This attitude of
mind is a solvent of the claims of most abstractions – in
politics, economics, philosophy, theology – to absolute truth.
That is not to say that the abstract propositions of mathematics
do not possess self-certifying truths; but abstractions in most
fields are apt to be determined by extraneous considerations,
historical, sociological, etc and have no absolute validity.

This was anathema to Lewis, for it undercut the ground
upon which he pontificated – and pontificate he did, laying
down the law all round. It was the disputatiousness that I
disliked, and the cocksureness it led to even more. (All
historians are impelled towards scepticism, and apt to become
moral indifferentists, like Gibbon, another Magdalen man.)
Lewis got this disputatiousness – as if this led one to knowledge! – from both his father and Kirk, the tutor who so much
shaped his adolescence. 'The most casual remark was taken as
a summons to disputation.' When the propositions referred to
mathematics, 'I grasped the principles but my answers were
always wrong.' We may apply this to some of his conclusions
in other fields, and ask then to what point the principles?

Not all of them were wrong. When Lewis went to Cambridge and wrote his *Experiment in Criticism* he dislodged
Leavis from his position with singularly little fuss. Nothing
surprising in this, for Lewis *was* a first-rate mind, where Leavis

was a second-rate one. Lewis was an excellent scholar, Latin and Greek, French, German, Italian, Anglo-Saxon and Middle English. Leavis knew hardly any other language but English, and that badly.

It was, however, possible to catch out Lewis on a point of scholarship. When he wrote his volume in the *Oxford History of English Literature* on the sixteenth century, I gave the book a warm welcome in a review. I had some reservations to make – Lewis wrote of Cardinal Allen as one of the best of Elizabethan prose-writers. Now he hardly wrote anything of any significance at all. But the famous Jesuit, Robert Parsons, was a prolific and important writer, whom Jonathan Swift considered one of the best masters of English prose.

Lewis came up to my railway compartment, on my way to Cambridge, to thank me for my review – always polite and gentlemanly. I asked him why he had so over-estimated Cardinal Allen, who wrote hardly anything, and ignored Father Parsons who wrote so well and so much. Lewis astonished me by saying that he didn't think Parsons important! He simply didn't know. The significant thing is that he wouldn't take telling by someone who did – his father's trait coming out again.

I think I have read most of his books: I doubt if he had read a single book of mine. We once were invited to debate on the issue between us, in an upper room in St Mary's, the University church.[1] Lewis spoke first, and after my speech he had to go, leaving me in possession of the field, if not of the argument. In any case, nothing would have persuaded him: he was impermeable, at bottom insensitive.

Take his attitude to Renaissance humanism. He was prejudiced on the subject, because Renaissance humanism undermined the transcendental authority of religion. Not that the greatest of scholars, Erasmus, was irreligious: he was deeply, but undoctrinally, religious. He cut away all the superfluous accretions of late medieval Catholicism, especially scholastic logic-chopping, to concentrate on single-minded devotion to God.

That was not good enough for Lewis: he insisted on the

[1] I have described this in *A Man of the Thirties*.

doctrine, the more unbelievable the more he insisted, in his Ulsterman's bullying way. The chaplain at All Souls went to hear a sermon in which Lewis insisted on belief in every little circumstance of Jesus' 'resurrection' – as our chaplain protested, 'nails and all.' I hardly think it did the chaplain's faith much good – Lewis's absurd book on *Miracles* is enough to undermine anyone's faith.

In his autobiography he says dismissively, 'I do not much believe in the Renaissance as generally described by historians.' No, because he did not like it, and did not hold with historians. Humanist scholars like Erasmus presented the texts in themselves, not overlaid by theological argy-bargy. But the latter was precisely what Lewis liked. No matter – the significant point is that his theological preconceptions warped his literary judgment. He preferred medieval obscurantists.

There were besides specific judgments on Elizabethan writers and poems I did not much care for, on Marlowe or on 'Venus and Adonis'. I do not think Lewis was at his best on Shakespeare: he had a heavy preference for the epic and the allegorical, which I do not share, but where I am content to learn from him. (Would he learn from me? No, but he was eager to commend such a second-rate work as Chesterton's *The Everlasting Man,* because it fitted in with his prejudices.) In any case, I am chary of summary critical *judgments*: I prefer critics to interpret rather than to judge. And too much literary criticism strangles the appreciation of literature.

The importation of so much heavy theological speculation leads to sometimes ludicrous results. In his *Preface to Paradise Lost* there is a passage about an erection (sexual) – can blame be attached to the object, if involuntary, etc? This led one innocent girl in a class at Oxford to ask what an erection was. A passage nearby discusses what the sexual relations of Adam and Eve were before the Fall: Lewis, is for once, uncertain but thinks that they were something ineffably beautiful!

He is always very certain about Hell, and the Enemy – the Devil. 'Divine punishments are also mercies.' Are they? Even if, assuming them to be divine, they might sometimes be to others observing them, are they to the persons afflicted? To a little child dying already of cancer, for instance? Flannery O'Connor, another religious, thought so in the case of a young girl she knew, dying of cancer in the face. Not so brave myself, I cannot think so.

The problem of pain is insoluble to anyone who believes in a personal God, who knows us personally, loves and cares for us – and afflicts his creatures with incurable suffering. Not a hair of your head but God knows; the 'fall of a sparrow' gave me a spasm of unbelief, when quite young. The belief in an impersonal God, soul of the universe, involves no such strain; while to those of no belief the problem does not exist.

Lewis was always ready to attack an extreme position with an even more extreme assertion, or with paradox, or to mount an unconvincing argument which his fellow-philosophers would not accept, riding his high horse in *The Problem of Pain*. At All Souls we possessed the copy that had been owned by another Magdalen man, a young R.A.F. officer who was killed in the Second German War. It was fascinating to read his marginal comments, affronted by the perverse ingenuity of the arguments, as I am by those of the book on *Miracles*, where Lewis insists on the literal fact of Jesus' Walking on the Water, the Feeding of the Five Thousand with a few loaves and fishes, the Raising of Lazarus from the dead, etc. Common sense and historical sense alike tell one that Jesus was a healer, a not unnatural phenomenon; it also tells one that ordinary humans will believe anything. Lecky, the historian of European Morals, tells us that humans will believe against the evidence, or in spite of the evidence; but hardly ever what is in accordance with the evidence.

Lewis, no historian, really anti-historian, was not bothered by that. Because he wanted to believe he accepted the infantile beliefs of primitive fishermen, and then used his logic-chopping propensity to put them across the public. Of course, they too want to believe, want re-assurance or consolation or whatever their *guru* gives them. In all the suffering of wartime thousands needed such solace and comforting. Stoicism, the real creed of most of the men fighting, was no creed for their dependents at home or their women. That time was the apogee of Lewis's *réclame*.

We come to the core of Lewis's religious position with his statement: 'Theology says to you in effect "Admit God and with Him the risk of a few miracles, and I in return will ratify your faith in uniformity as regards the overwhelming majority of events." ' Give us this ha'porth of tar and we will save the ship. 'Theology offers you a working arrangement, which leaves the scientist free to continue his experiments and the Christian to continue his prayers.'

I do not object to this bargain, which is the central demand of all Lewis's religious books. There may well be a spirit of the universe, working in and through it; or why not take the cosmos itself for base? But there is no evidence of Its being personal to us – It is far and away beyond us and our petty concerns. There is no evidence that It cares for our pain and suffering. And the mystery of it all is beyond human comprehension.

In his autobiography Lewis makes a case, step by step, for such a belief, a God-inspired universe. But what led him to go further and accept the Christian myth? He unaccountably skips over that leap he made, apparently in a bus going up to Headington – like Paul Claudel's by his pillar in the nave of Nôtre Dame. The fact is that he *wanted* to believe, he was '*intérieurement préparé*', to accept.

Having submitted his reason, Lewis – like the Welsh-Ulsterman he was – went the whole hog, to swallow illusions that are unnecessary to reasonable belief. His dogmatism actually diminishes his credibility, the sensible part of his argument.

We can go some way to meet him by agreeing that there are phenomena as yet unexplained. But the area of rational explanation of such is being constantly extended. That is the rational way to further knowledge, not subjecting the reason to the illusions of primitive minds, apt to take things literally, when it is quite unnecessary, even for believers, to do so.

Since this book is intended as one of personal memories and associations, rather than rebarbative arguments, perhaps I may conclude with an Oxford story revealing of both Lewis and Eliot. Both were Christian believers, defenders of the faith before the public, but had not met each other – and Lewis, who would have liked most of all to be a poet (he wrote verse), did not think well of Eliot's poetry. Charles Williams, whose work Lewis preached up because he was a fellow believer, knew both and invited Eliot down to meet Lewis at lunch, appropriately, at the Mitre.

Eliot was a sensitive man, apt to fumble a move on the board from shyness; Lewis was neither sensitive nor shy. Eliot, who had prepared his opening move on the way down in the train, began nervously:

> You are a younger man than I thought – judging from your photographs.

Lewis did not encourage this approach, though both absurdly condemned 'the personal heresy', the biographical approach. Lewis remained silent, so Eliot tried again:

> I have been reading your book about Milton . . . The passages about *Virgil* are very good.

This was not well received: Eliot was heretical about Milton. Eventually Eliot gave up, before the waters closed over his head, with the modest

> Well, speaking as a publisher . . .

Lewis did not help him out. It is often a mistake to bring two luminaries together: their lights are apt to put each other out.

12

The Real Betjeman

Betjeman has been so much written about by people who did not really know him, or thought they knew him, or did not know him at all, that it is as well that someone who knew him on the intimate side for forty years, more than half a lifetime, should have a go at delineating his elusive personality. For – naturally, with a man of genius – all was not as meets the eye. There was much ambivalence about him, much that was paradoxical, ironical, not easily penetrable, given to guying things that he really held seriously – and this took simpletons in.

It didn't at any time take me – and I don't think that John supposed for a moment that it did: essential basis for friendship. I have paid tribute elsewhere to his poetry, which I love.[1] (And loved him for writing it. When I said this at a joint Christie Minstrels turn we did at Port Eliot, to raise money for Historic Cornish Churches, I added that I hoped that at our age that was all right; only one clergyman in the audience appreciated the joke.) Here I shall confine myself to the personal, as elsewhere in this book, remember associations that were idiosyncratic, like no other – an enrichment of life.

John Betjeman was from his schooldays an 'original', and always recognised as such: there was, and never has been, anybody quite like him. Where on earth he came from, that personality utterly *sui generis*, heaven only knows. There is ambivalence at once in the very name. It was never mentioned, obviously the source of a deep complex, going right back to Prep. school days in the first of our German wars,

[1] 'The Poetry of John Betjeman', in *Portraits and Views*.

when he was persecuted by the other boys with shouts of 'Betjeman's a German spy/Shoot him down and let him die.' I was led to believe, in the usual manner after the impression the Germans made in this century, that his ancestry was Dutch. His biographer tells me that the family was not Dutch, but German from the Bremen area: 'The Dutch smoke-screen must have been put up in the First World War . . . I think, however, that J.B. sincerely believed he was of Dutch ancestry to the end.'

So he was not all that English, the persona he so successfully – and genuinely – projected upon the public through his writing, prose as well as poetry, and latterly most effectively through television. He loved England with the self-conscious passion of one who does not inwardly belong, when the purely English take that kind of thing for granted.

Similarly with the assumption of Cornishry. Some public prints would refer to him as Cornish – fancy the idiocy of anybody supposing that a name like Betjeman could possibly be Cornish! Betjeman was passionately devoted to that bit of the north coast of Cornwall around Padstow, Trebetherick and Rock, which was bound up with his happiest childhood memories, on which he had a life-long fixation and about which he wrote some of his best and most moving poems.

That is not the same thing as being Cornish, though we are grateful to him for his love of Cornwall. In writing to me – and I have a wad of his letters from the 1940s – he would often sign himself 'Jan Trebetjeman', once 'Jan Killigrew Trebetjeman', and draw a shield of the fifteen bezants (arms of the Duchy) with our motto 'One and All'.

More important, he was projected upon the people as one of them. What a joke! There was hardly anyone who was less like the ordinary boring human being. He was put across them as a cult folk-figure, a kind of sugar-daddy whom everybody recognised and thought they knew. That was one side, genuine enough, the kindly, sentimental family man, with kiddies and their interests at heart (also genuine enough, for like many men of genius he never grew up, remained a child at heart). Inside, he was much odder and queerer: religious, but given to doubt and depression; in company cheerful and gay, full of jokes, but when alone given to melancholy, needing solace and support.

There were other ambivalances. The more sensitive of those who have had the advantage of sex-education at a Public School are apt to know about bisexuality, and the doubled perception, intuition and receptivity it gives – as against the limitations of the unisexual. One can see the understanding and the sympathy in a number of the later poems, though there exist adolescent poems as a surprise for the imperceptive. (Henry James: 'Nobody ever understands *anything*.') John, with an Oriel crony of his with whom he used to go church-crawling, took me up to the Trout Inn at Godstow to peer in at a beautiful, blue-eyed kitchen boy whom they called 'Chick-abiddy.' Anything for a lark, or larks! Not having their sense of humour, I didn't see much fun in *that*.

Actually, I didn't know John as an undergraduate and, rather prim (not having been to a Public School – wish I had!), I would have disapproved of him wasting his time, careering around in a motor-car his grandmother had given him, dining at the George, neglecting his tutorials, and getting sent down for failing Divvers (Divinity, of all things). People hardly realise what a gulf there is between one brief undergraduate generation and the next: only two or three years, and there is all the difference – one has a completely different lot of friends. My contemporaries were Harold Acton, Graham Greene, Cyril Connolly, Richard Pares; as already a young Fellow of All Souls I didn't know John's, Hugh Gaitskell, John Sparrow, Douglas Jay, Frank Pakenham – I came to know them later, and sooner if they came to All Souls. I knew Maurice Bowra quite well, who took up John and to whom John owes so much: Maurice gave him his start on an architectural review, base for a career. But my later friendship with Maurice (I wouldn't be taken up or become a member of his circle) was a private, not a public one.

Significantly enough my first contacts with John were architectural. Any good historian should have an interest in architecture – 'frozen history', in which periods of time so eloquently reveal their spirit. John took me to see things in Oxford I had never seen before. I had never penetrated into the splendid eighteenth-century interior of Oriel Library, with its grand scagliola columns; we trespassed into the Senior Common Room below to see the drawings of Tractarians like Newman, delicate feminine features, and the admirable historian Froude, who learned how to write from him. John took me into the beautiful chapel of the Cowley Sisters, not open to the public, pointing out the Scottish-Gothic inflexion of his friend, Sir Ninian Comper: 'dear Sir Niminy-Piminy', finest church decorator of the century.

Then to pretty little Stockcross church near Newbury, which Comper had entirely re-decorated, with his unerring and eclectic sense of beauty – Jacobean-style rood screen, stained glass window with its modern touch of a handsome young sailor we did not fail to appreciate. Quite lost on the heavy Teutonic Pevsner, of course, with his dogmatism and fixation on the toneless expressionism of the modern German school. He never missed an opportunity to depreciate Comper. All that he has to say about this beautiful work is – 'almost entirely re-fitted by Sir Ninian Comper. Comper's anaemic E. window replaces that which is now blind and hard to see.'

John brought Comper to lunch with me in Hawksmoor's oval buttery at All Souls. I recall Sir Niminy-Piminy telling me that he had been asked to design vestments for the Cardinal Archbishop of Paris, and 'I absolutely powdered them with fleur-de-lys.' He at any rate had a sense of humour to add to his lively sense of beauty; and I remember still his rich Scottish pronunciation of 'churrch'.

Upon occasion John and I went church-crawling in Cornwall. I can see him now, the schoolboy excitement with which he fitted the key into the south door, bending down with 'What *will* it be like inside?' Or, again, his popping down quite un-selfconsciously on his knees to say a prayer, leaving me standing. His attitude was really nearer than people think to Hardy's 'hoping it might be true'. Alas, if only it were! A North Coast man, he didn't know the Victorian churches around St Austell, so when he came over from Trebetherick I took him to the little barn-like church of Biscovey, with its Street spire, and the 'Good Shepherd' at Par; also the pretty church of my poem, 'Passion Sunday in Charlestown Church', which he specially liked, for in addition to Oxford, Cornwall, and architecture, we had poetry in common – though I was rather cagey about that, he a full-time professional, not averse to baring his soul in public.

His visual memory was extraordinary. He knew every one of the Wren churches of the City, before so many of them were damaged or destroyed by the barbarian Blitz on London. He could remember individually a dozen or fifteen churches seen in one day, when I could visualise only five or six. He would come over to lunch, sometimes with Penelope, both at Polmear Mine above Charlestown and later at Trenarren. At one such occasion he was fascinated by the very unfascinating character of a failed painter with a raging inferiority-complex – he was no good and a great bore – whom an early girl-friend of mine had incomprehensibly married. This was not mere politeness: John was fascinated by dimness – partly genuinely, though it was also, like so much with him, a comic turn. At Oxford he had a line in dim peers, especially if they were Irish, like Lord Wicklow. He introduced me to the Earl of Hunting-don whom he had taken up, a very rare bird for he was also a Labour man: 'Meet the dimmest peer in Britain.' (John, luckily, had no politics and no comprehension of them.) Similar remarks about Kolkhorst, the eccentric Anglo-Portuguese don at Oxford, whom John had a cult of: he always called him 'the Colonel' – I never acclimatised myself to the derogatory remarks to him. I suppose John himself could be called an eccentric – another of those ambivalences the great heart of the public was not alerted to.

It was John who introduced me to the beauties of Victorian Cheltenham. We jogged across the Cotswolds in his tumble-down ramshackle, grimy old car, painted and patched but totally unwashed – like John himself in those days, until Elizabeth Cavendish kindly took him in hand and tidied him up. ('We have ruled sex out.') I dare say Penelope got tired of keeping him in order – a full-time job – and rather fancied a career for herself. In those days John had an objection to taking a bath. Ordered upstairs by Penelope to take one, he went up, filled the bath with water, went on talking, swishing the water with his hand, 'Ooh! lovely bath', etc, and after a decent interval came down again never having got in.

His appearance was no less *sui generis*. Someone wrote of his green complexion; carious teeth, full lips, dribbling a little with enthusiasm; large and beautiful brown eyes, full of varying expression, puzzled, swivelling, sympathetic, kind, amused; rich, plummy clerical voice, like an archdeacon, which later turned out such an asset on TV; then giggles, gales of laughter, always finding or creating something funny. Never serious for long – at any rate with others: he thought it good manners to be light in conversation. He was a card.

Eccentricity was the order of the day. He and Penelope, neighbours of Gerald Berners at Faringdon, would often come over, Penelope bringing her white horse into the drawing-room to tea. There is a charming photograph of that hospitable tea-table, the horse quite at home, muzzle hovering over the sugar basin. Then there was Archie, John's teddy bear whom he had always slept with from childhood and continued to do into his married days. One day, when there were 'words', Penelope threw Archie out of the bedroom window – then there nearly was a Divorce! Archie was either a Strict Baptist or a Paedo-Baptist, I forget which – John has written a book about him.

Where ordinary people's children grew up saying 'dear doggie', or 'my pussy cat', or whatever, their children were brought up to say 'Sarum Use' or 'Immaculate Contheption'. No wonder that, when John and Penelope went inside to view a church, the children remained firmly entrenched in the car reading their Penny Dreadfuls. Everything was in inverted commas, turned to fun, guyed, but with poker face – you could easily be taken in. I remember John saying solemnly to me, of a high-brow don at Balliol, John Bryson who collected pictures: '*He*'s cultivated', then a giggle. Penelope cultivated a Cockney accent (John genuinely was Cockney, witness the Cockney rhymes in his poems), and this rather flummoxed people in a Field-Marshal's daughter. (Socially, John always knew which side his bread was buttered.) He had some talent for drawing. I remember one of a grand luncheon at Longleat, with Penelope in schoolgirl pig-tails electrifying the table with ''ow, Lord Bath [the old Marquis], 'ow do you do these stoofed eggs?' She was a very good cook.

Anything for a lark – larks all the time. When David Cecil became Professor of English Literature at Oxford, he announced an Inaugural Lecture on 'Reading'. On the morning of the lecture there arrived by post a little book labelled

Reading: it turned out be a specially bound book on the topography of the town. An envelope would be addressed to one 'First Class Male.' I don't think he called me by any other than my name in family and College, Leslie – unattractive in itself and wrong for a Cornishman. But, then, I dislike all three of my names: I should like something recognisably Cornish, 'by Tre, Pol, or Pen.' Not that I want to go too far and be called Penaluna or even Penhaligon.

I always loved John's topographical poems about North Oxford, territory which he made especially his, and hardly ever go there without thinking of his laburnum and red-may flowering gardens and 'St C. S. Lewis's church' – the dogmatic Lewis had been John's tutor at Magdalen, whom he could not abide – and 'Goldylocks' Myfanwy Piper bicycling around those dear suburban pavements. Very early in our friendship John bought for me Piper's beautiful *gouache* of the derelict fifteenth-century chapel at Hall, above Bodinnick Ferry – I'll bet it is a complete ruin now, original wagon-roof, bell-cote and all. It was through John that I came to know 'Mr' Piper, as he always was – John had names for everybody. At All Souls his old friend John Angus Hanbury Sparrow was 'Spansbury', my friend Geoffrey Hudson was 'Chinese Hudson', after 'Chinese Gordon'.

Cornwall and poetry were far more intimate bonds between us than architecture or people, and most of his letters to me are about the first two. Very early on he took the trouble to copy out two passages from Robert Ross's *The Georgian Revolt*, which represented what he himself thought and felt about poetry. 'At some times there are more great poets than at others. But there are always poets . . . and they will go quietly on their way, saying nothing where they have nothing to say and, when they cannot help saying something, saying it in a form they cannot help.'

This was by Gerald Gould, who in Lansbury's days was literary editor of the *Daily Herald*, when the paper had some quality and of course a small circulation. John reviewed novels for it – in dozens, wasting his time on trash, though he used to get some of the reading done for him by girl-friends. He told me at the time, 'my energy is terrific'.

From Ross John quoted for me: 'For most poets [in the 20s] it was simply a case of fight or die, coterie warfare or poetic oblivion. The slow, often halting development of the individual poetic genius along lines determined by its own uniqueness, which had been the priceless jewel of English poetry for generations, seemed likely by 1920 to become a thing of the past, a sacrifice to the collectivist urge and the relativist spirit of the onrushing twentieth century.'

These two statements must have spoken for John, who stuck to his last, his own original inspiration all the way along, without caring tuppence for what literary critics thought, or what ephemeral poets wrote to keep in with temporary fashions. John was wise never to write 'criticism' of poetry: it is dangerous to be self-conscious about, and tamper with, the seed-bed from which real poetry is created. That is why so much of the 'poetry' patronised by the media and the literary modes today is bogus – as John and I knew, no less than Philip Larkin or Kingsley Amis who has dismissed it as not being poetry 'in any sense of the word sense.'

John was writing to me on the day of 'St Loy, Cornish Calendar, 1944, that great agnostic Saint the Rev. J. M. Thompson, the only nice man in Magdalen, tells me you have his topographical poem. If you can find it – and I know how one loses mss and also what hell it is putting things into envelopes, hence this post card – I wd. be v. glad to see it.' This was a rarity. Thompson had been 'inhibited', or whatever, by the minatory Bishop Gore – who was very censorious about his clergy – and Thompson became, more usefully, a good history tutor at Magdalen and wrote a book on Robespierre for my series, 'Men and their Times'.

In August 1945 came a characteristic coloured post card written in antique capital letters from 'Skimmery, Oxford' – was that St Mary Hall, part of Oriel? This must have been the time of his illness recorded in the poem, 'Before the Anaesthetic, or A Real Fright.' 'N°T AT ALL Al. I C°VLDNT M°VE F°R A L°NG WHILE & THEN WENT TO BEAULIEV. [That would be when he wrote 'Youth and Age on Beaulieu River, Hants.'] W°VLD LIKE T° SEE Y°VR NEW PO°EM. G°ING T° ABERYSTWYTH °N XIVTH F°R A F°RTNIGHT (D.V.) AT°MIC B°MB A BIG

ADVANCE IN CIVILISATI°N. J°HN B.'

That was how he thought about the horror of the age we
live in, as all pereceptive people do – compare my poems of the
Thirties, clearly realising the approach of war, when the blind
and stupid wouldn't or couldn't see. John, no politician, saw
well enough and was terrified by what he saw: no cosy
comfortable illusions such as ordinary people – his later
addicts – cherished: 'Come, friendly bombs and rain on
Slough', etc. I wrote to the same effect in '1937':

> A day will come when there shall descend on them
> From the skies they do not observe, some stratagem
> Of fate to search and sear their flesh with fire . . .
> Liquid fire will rain down from the air,
> Will suddenly arrive upon them there
> And lick their bodies up and burn their bones . . .
> For these are they who, warned of what's to come,
> Walk blindly on to their appointed doom.

They would not take warning: they went on supporting
Chamberlain in thinking that he could appease Hitler.

Next thing, a missive framed like a picture, 'To A.L.R.
Called in to say how much I enjoyed THE USE OF HISTORY & that
I have cracked it up in this week's *Daily Herald*. A little friend
of mine – his mother is the Emily of my poem on Ireland –
Peter Patrick Hunphill, son of a drunk Irish baron of that name
is coming up from Downside to BNC [Brasenose College]
today for an entrance examination. I am taking him out to
luncheon at George. Do come if you can, 2 o'clock.' What a
time! I rarely went out to lunch anyway; he gave me his new
home telephone number, but I never ring up either, if I can
help it.

Another invitation to lunch came on a post card of beautiful
Farnborough Old Rectory under snow, high up in the Downs
above Wantage. I never went up there, but Gerald Berners
told me what an exquisite Queen Anne red-brick house with
cupola it was; and how inconvenient, no water laid on and no
electric light, John coming to the door with a lighted candle in
hand.

I find a number of letters thence from 1948–9. 'I have taken to drink and am much better. Brandy-&-Soda. It all came about through reading one of the GREATEST ENGLISH NOVELISTS – G. J. Whyte-Melville whose Hussars and hunting men always have a B-&-S. when discussing their chops. Read Whyte-Melville (not old Herman-Whyte) [*sic*] – a most upper-class writer & *Kate Coventry* & *The Brookes of Bridlemere* are the two I've liked best so far. Read Whyte-Melville & take to drink.'[2]

I followed neither piece of advice. There followed more helpful advice I wanted for projects of my own, an illustrator for some Oxford book in mind. Sharp's Plan for post-war development of the city was not yet out, but he 'has taken offices under Ye Olde Payntedde Roommie so I'll see the plan before anyone. Dom Julian Stonor has identified the beehive between Brown Willy and Rowtor as St Petroc's hermitage and written a delightful account of it and my beloved St. P. in the Downside Review. What on earth is all this about Herefordshire? Is it to be bombed out of existence?'

Evidently I had been ill again, and thinking of a Cornish slate slab with good lettering, like that which John had put up to his father in St Enodoc church. 'Monuments are better done by someone you can trust – leave it to me to look after in your will, and in the event of my pre-deceasing you, I can give you a few good reliable names of younger men.' Dear John, alas!

Next was from Trebetherick, August 1948. 'Here I am on the eve of my 42nd birthday amid the tamarisks, slate, mesembryanthemum, hunting wasps, tennis, golf, shorts, baked bald heads of my contemporaries, greying hair of my seniors, sherries, churchbells, cliffs, cars, hard wet sand of the only place I ever want to be in.' I had put up a proposal for a book of his essays to Odhams, which I was then advising.

[2] This Victorian author, who was killed in the hunting field, had 'considerable literary powers, which he himself was inclined to underrate, and would have brought him greater fame', according to the *D.N.B.* Locker Lampson says that 'Whyte-Melville never sought literary society, preferring the companionship of soldiers, sportsmen and country gentlemen. Had he been more assiduous in cultivating literary men, his reputation might have stood higher with the general public, though he could scarcely have been a greater favourite with readers of his own class.' No doubt. An interesting case, and a suitable subject for John's admiration; while myself I have never played the literary game.

'YES. I can collect the essays and they fall into the headings you enumerate, i Lit. ii Arch. iii Top . . . Lit. might be made to include sentimental-pious, e.g. Christmas Nostalgia of last year. Please put the matter to Odhams. Terms suit me fine. They will lose on it. But they can afford to do so . . . No petrol. We could get over.'

It then transpired that, while I was away, he made 'this sad discovery that I was committed to Murray's about the book of essays, and since then a contract which I signed ten years ago and forgot all about has turned up. Murray's and I are now engaged in trying to find periodicals in which I have written articles. I am always so disgusted with what I write after it is printed that I keep very few specimens of past work. I think the best thing to do is to wait and see what is left over that is worth printing. Murray's want a volume that is entirely topographical; that should leave an immense amount of material over which is not, and which is about poetry and literature. Ah! to see you again would be nice. Would you ever come out here for a meal, if I came and fetched you. You have never been here.' In fact there *is* an immense amount of John's dispersed prose, some of which is worth bringing to light: not the novel-reviews, but material from *Time and Tide*, and I used to like his miscellaneous bits and pieces in the *Spectator*.

May, 1949: 'I shall, I fear, be in Newcastle-on-Tyne (D.V.) on Saturday next when I should, if I followed my own inclinations, be having luncheon with you and your distinguished guests. Blast. I should have loved it. I have *never* been to Launcells. It is an ambition I have never had the petrol to realise. Is it as good as the photographers say? [Better: quite unspoiled.] I have put in Parson Hawker's account of Shipwrecks in 1858 into my readings for Victorian Provincial Life in the West of England. I am nervous of not living up to the fine and flattering description you gave of me in that stimulating and excellent opening broadcast for the series.[3] I go to HAYLING ISLAND tomorrow. Ever been there? Nor have I. That poem of yours "Alfoxden" haunts me. Do propose yourself here for a meal. I will come and fetch you.' Alas, I never went.

---

[3] This was a BBC series I had arranged, published as *The West in English History*, to which John contributed 'Victorian Provincial Life'.

By 1951 the Betjemans had descended from the hills to the pleasant 'The Mead', Wantage – nearer to Wantage church-bells – and I had dedicated *The English Past* to the two admirable Johns, Betjeman and Piper, 'whose genius re-creates something of the English past.' I had realised earlier than most that the great days of England were over, had come to an end in the flames and glory of the heroic years 1940–1945, and that the past of this country was far more interesting than its future was likely to be.

'How can I enough thank you for the unexpected and generous dedication and present of your book, for? You cheer and encourage me at the very moment when I most need cheering, for I feel that the Pevsners who kill every object they classify, are in the ascendant. "First class", "important", "fully documented" are the only adjectives which they use in commendation. They see things only in terms of things not of people. Your essay on All Souls is a glorious condemnation of Pevsnerism and the crashing specialists. What people don't recognise about you is how good you are as a prose-writer, how imaginative and <u>melodious</u> a writer. That is because you are a poet.

'I am really honoured, old top, by sharing with Mr Piper (whom I saw this morning) this dedication. Ta ever so. And I really mean it. We are allies against the professionalising of what is art. You are an artist. Proud to know you, old top. Notice my new address THE MEAD (an ugly small Victorian villa in a nice site), WANTAGE. Come and see us. Will telephone. Yours till death.'

Actually 'The Mead' was quite a pleasant house: I include John's remark merely to show that he was not uncritically fixed on everything Victorian. He knew well enough that Georgian architecture was better. There was an element of the comic in his cult of Victorian extravaganzas like the piece of Burgess furniture he gave to Evelyn Waugh, who also pre-ferred Victorian to much that is modern. John had a great influence in opening our eyes to what was good in Victorian architecture and art – we may discount the jokes about 'dear Sir Gilbert' [Scott, of course] that took in solemn asses. Ian Fleming made a collection of first editions of books that exerted an historic influence; alongside of John Locke and

Darwin, John Ruskin and Karl Marx were two or three books of Betjeman's.

Penelope set up her rest, in the Elizabethan phrase, in the birthplace of King Alfred, and opened a little cake shop, 'King Alfred's Kitchen'; but refrained from advertising 'Burnt Cakes a Speciality.'

In September 1952 he was at Bodare, Trebetherick 'but, ALAS, only till next Monday.' I had been away in Dublin lecturing: 'v. pleased to have your Oirish post card. I'm glad you like I.C. churches, as Church of Ireland churches are called by the Irish Churchmen. But I was particularly delighted to have your Presidential Address to the English Association. It is most stirring. What a dim organisation to take such a deal of trouble for. . . . I am honoured to be mentioned. Who wrote that splendid bit of blank verse about asphalt roads and golf balls? I ought to know, but don't.'

It was of course a line from Eliot's Church-pageant, 'The Rock' – dear John's education at Marlborough and Magdalen was oddly patchy. 'See you next term. Joe Lynam and Philip Landon are here': the one an old schoolmaster from the Dragon School at Oxford, the other a rather dim don such as John adored to cultivate – like the unknown Pembroke don of whom he wrote a virtuoso poem when he died. John had a cult of Pembroke, not the most scintillating of Oxford colleges – Balliol wouldn't have been in it, not a word about that institution of 'plain living and high thinking'. Besides, little Pembroke had the best cellar in Oxford.

His next letter came on *Time and Tide* notepaper, where he had a job as literary editor, under the supposedly liberal but really autocratic Lady Rhondda, the owner. Its printed heading described it as a strictly 'Non-Party Weekly Review', but John had inked this out to read, 'A jolly Party Weekly'. 'I am horrified by what happened to your review. We are printing your letter in full.' Some fool of a girl had cut several sentences, omitting a 'not', which made me say the exact opposite of what I had written – the kind of thing that often happens when the third-rate think they can improve on the first-rate. What one has to put up with as a reviewer, from cuts and inserts and silly captions missing the point!

'I have had written up in huge letters in the book room "NO

REVIEWER, HOWSOEVER MILD, MUST BE CUT OR ALTERED IN ANY
WAY WITHOUT CONSULTING THE REVIEWER FIRST." I was away
the last fortnight at the death-bed and then funeral of my old
mum. Had I been up here, this tragedy could never have
happened – the altering of your review I mean, not my
mother's death. Buried at St Enodoc, sea mist lifting over
Stepper, waving tamarisks, granite—: very moving. [With all
my experience of Elizabethan handwriting, I often find it
difficult to read John's: he would apologise for it as illegible.]
Happy Christmas. Come and see us at Vintagia if you are in
Oxford. Love.' – Alas, I have never been at Oxford for
Christmas.

John's job with *Time and Tide* did not last long, for all that he
enlivened that dim periodical with his jokes and bright ideas
for competitions, etc. There was a certain liberal-minded,
broad-bottomed fatuity about Lady Rhondda – and one day
she took him out to a good lunch and suddenly sacked him. A
poem on the manner of it takes her off to the life:

> 'I'm making some changes next week in the organisation,
>   And though I admire
> Your work for me, John, yet the need to increase
>   circulation

[It never did: circulation went down and under her
administration]

>   Means you must retire:
> An outlook more *global* than yours is the qualification
>   I really require.'

True enough, John's outlook was anything but *global*, silly
woman. Fancy losing him, just like that!

> I stood on the pavement and wondered which loss was
>   the greater –
> The cash or the pride.
> Explanations to make to subordinates, bills to pay later
>   Churned up my inside.

In the end, I think that that Lesbian millionairess got her comeuppance.

I must have had a lunch-party at All Souls, for next, 'We all enjoyed ourselves *immensely* and Philip Landon, so silent usually, has been full of it all today – especially the bit about the last of the Trevannions (Trevanyons? Trevanion?) of Caerhays.' Third time lucky – he got it right. I must have told them the extraordinary story of the end of the family there, in a riot of extravagance, and their incestuous fixation on the Byrons, which I did not write up until years later in *The Byrons and Trevanions*. Not until I had retired from heavy historical research at All Souls had I time to do the more literary books I had had in mind to do all along. John ended, 'Penelope and Aunt Elsie were full of it all too. Ta muchly, as we say on the North Coast.' There followed a bit of Old Irish I cannot translate: 'Jan Treb:'

In 1953 he was giving me the name of a sculptress in Berkshire 'who would fill the bill nicely for St Mabyn's statue.' That fine church had had its interior completely scalped by an aristocratic Rector, bloody fool, in the early nineteenth century; rood-screen, bench-ends, monuments, everything. I could scalp him for the destruction he wrought. John wanted me over for a lunch party, holding out enticingly a 'Mrs Villiers-Stuart, Greta Hellström of one of my poems, a girl from Oxford (Trebetherick)', somebody from Boar's Hill and a nice young man who is given the mysterious label Q. (which always means Quiller-Couch to me). The mystery is resolved by a P.S.: 'Have you read *The Heart in Exile* by Rodney Garland. It goes farther than any novel heretofore *on a certain subject.*'

Not much of a modern novel reader, I had not heard of the book. In those days people were absurdly more cagey about that subject, one of the simple facts of life about which people have become more sensible since. Subsequently, I was to write a straightforward book, *Homosexuals in History*, to say how natural it all was and how silly to make such a fuss about it – historians had known the facts all along. The book was to be attacked by the Gay Lib. people in America as being unsympathetic, [!] and because I laughed, was insufficiently solemn – when so much about sex is comic and makes fools of us all.

With his ambivalent nature, his doubled sensibility, John was always sensible on that subject – anybody who belonged to Maurice Bowra's circle would be more than sympathetic. (I kept out of it, and Maurice too thought that I was unsympathetic. How imperceptive people are!) John's sympathies are quite clear in his poems, as in mine: I realised all along that one can express everything in verse, for people are so obtuse they don't know what you are saying. Very early on John had written 'The Arrest of Oscar Wilde at the Cadogan Hotel' – *there* was a fool, flaunting his vulgar exhibitionism, bringing trouble and suffering down upon hundreds of poor innocents, instead of going abroad for a breath of fresh air as Bernard Shaw advised.

Towards the end there is a moving poem:

> . . . and that you did with said intent procure
> the aforesaid Sidney Alexander Green
> being at the time a minor . . . [etc.]

John understood all about the subject and its literary ramifications. His son Paul, for instance, was always called Pauli – after the good-looking young lawyer with whom Samuel Butler was hopelessly in love. One day John said to me of another couple, who got into trouble with conventional types, that at least they loved each other. John was a Christian, and had charity.

October 1954: 'I am very happy indeed to have *A Cornish Waif's Story*.' This was an astonishing story of a poor child who had been *sold* to a sailor: they made a living by travelling the roads with a barrel-organ and a monkey. I think the book may have been sparked off by my *Cornish Childhood*, for it came to me out of the blue a mass of semi-literate manuscript. I made a book of it, cutting it down, shaping it up into chapters and paragraphs: it was simply the story that was so extraordinary, and *Nihil Cornubiense alienum a me puto*. But the sequel gave any amount of trouble with the (perhaps understandably) psychotic character of the authoress. 'I suppose the convent she went to was St Faith's at Lostwithiel. The nuns are obviously Anglo and I should think they are Wantage Sisters. I

wish you would let me know if this is true. [I think not.] I wish
you'd come out and have a meal with us, old top. Give us a
tinkle on the telephone and I'll come along and fetch you.
How often do you see Philip Landon? He loves Cornwall like
you and I do. Yours Jan Trebetjeman.'

I hardly knew Philip Landon – he had no allure for me,
though Trinity was Q.'s old college; I didn't go out much to
other colleges – none had the interest of All Souls, not even my
undergraduate college, Christ Church, which thought itself so
grand and with which I had broken: mistakenly, no doubt.
After so much illness and wasting time on politics I had little
time for anything but work. And, alas, though John was
always urging me to come out to see him – as Eliot had urged
me earlier to come up to London – I hardly ever did. I once
took Gervase Mathew out to Wantage, a close friend for years:
a totally unwashed Dominican from Blackfriars, a regular
consumer of my sherry, a conjurer with my match-boxes and
a great converter of souls, to whom both Graham Greene and
Frank Pakenham owe their salvation. Gervase was my *protégé*,
whom I was for ever feeding and sherrying; only in that
respect was I his victim. In any other he would have had no
more luck that Father D'Arcy – who did for Evelyn Waugh –
had had earlier. I was impressed equally by Penelope's deli-
cious cooking and John's collection of Victorian illustrated
and architectural volumes.

From Wantage 'I have sent a sub for 1 copy of the *lovly*
book' – this was a joke, because I had said that one could
always tell homos by their constant use of the word 'lovely'
(and heteros by their halitosis). 'The Historic Churches
Preservation Trust have made a large loan to Par for the Street
job to be repaired' – I had been largely concerned in founding
the Cornish branch. His next p.c. from Trebetherick, on his
return from Sicily in 1966: 'Bright sun here, green Atlantic and
sailors in blue shirts on the cliffs . . . I am vastly flattered by
your kind, generous and perceptive remarks about me . . . on
my work for an Arsse at BBC programme.'

Next year, 'Have written you a three-page (both sides)
letter of praise and thanks for *Cornish Stories*. They are magnificent – much better than my poems. [Rubbish, dear John.
My stories are the kind I like to read, but I *love* your poems.]

"Death of a Principal", though not necessarily Cornish, is agony and deeply moving.' It was, in fact, based on the agony of George Gordon, President of John's own college, Magdalen, which I had heard all about from Bruce McFarlane. 'Your descriptions of Tamar and other valleys and of the china clay district are so good I feel myself there *and* you have narrative power and can sketch character. Love. Jan Treb:'

If my stories were good enough for Betjeman, they are good enough for other people and to be reprinted. . . . He was sufficiently moved to write again next day, a long letter. 'The *Cornish Stories* are marvellous. Never mind my verse, these stories of yours *are* Cornwall and flecked all through with description that makes me inly stirred.' He then gives chapter and verse, taking trouble to go into detail. 'Do you think Lambethow could be Laneast? or Launcells?' No: 'The Advowson of Lambethow' is based on the authentic parish story of Blisland, and today the Rector tells me that old folk there recognise it as such. Blisland on the edge of Bodmin Moor was a favourite church of John's, about which he wrote a beautiful piece, with its dedication to St Protus and St Hyacinth. (Who on earth were they?)[4] 'What I also enjoy about them is their warmth and humanity and your beautiful ear for Cornish dialogue. The curse Mrs Slade gives is terrific.' It meant more to me that it was authentic.

'I started the book this morning, resumed it waiting for the dentist – Mr Graham of Beaumont Street – and now can't get on with a mountain of letters for joy of reading it. I read a story between each letter and have reached "The Squire of Reluggas". I very much enjoy the subtlety of the difference between Higher Quarter and down there by the sea. I fancy "All Souls Night" was an early one.' It was: nothing to do with All Souls College – where it was a favourite with Halifax, a connoisseur of ghost-stories – it was based on authentic experiences at Wardour Castle, staying with John Arundell,

---

[4] Apparently they were third century martyrs in Rome, two brothers, one of them executed, the other burned, in the kindly human way. But how on earth did Blisland church come to be dedicated to these obscure Saints? – the only church in Britain to be so. That is the problem. I can only suggest that some medieval patron was responsible, perhaps a bishop of Exeter who had been to Rome and seen their tombs or whatever.

who died after years of prison camp with the bestial Germans at Colditz.

'It has a Doidge-like quality about its plot – do you remember Doidge's Western Counties Annual?' I did not: it never penetrated my illiterate working-class home. 'Some of the Doidge stories are Hardyesque melodrama and Hardy might well have contributed to it, as did his secretary Lois Deacon who is still alive. But *the* story in your book so far is the "Death of a Principal." It couldn't be old Murray, but how right was that dying man's advice and how moving your picture of his death.' George Gordon dying had urged McFarlane, then Vice-President, *not* to become President: he himself had been 'meant for literature', but had wasted his life on college chores. Happily Bruce missed this unhappy consummation, largely by the efforts of A. J. P. Taylor whom I had urged upon him as a colleague. Nevertheless, Bruce left all his written work to be produced by his pupils, unable to produce it himself. (Hence his psychotic attitude to my work – hard to take from a close friend; but that is what academics are like, John not, himself creative.)

' "Trespittigue's Vote" is a very subtle piece and oh how sad.' It is based on a true Cambridge story, as John Sparrow recognised. 'Is Lansillian Luxulyan?' Indeed it is: 'The Wicked Vicar of Lansillian' is the authentic eighteenth-century parish folklore; it was not much appreciated by my friend, the Vicar at the time, who had seen the apparition in the haunted drive. He lived in that granite vicarage alone: I shouldn't have much cared for that.

'*Indeed* I went to Trewithen and have since been down your way with Sir John Tremayne, looking at the filthy scum of china clay on Pentewan beach, and how many more streams than the St Austell White River are white.' We came to call it the White River, but its old name was the Cober, which simply means stream, represented still by the place-name Gover at the head of it. I did my best to be an honest broker between Air-Marshal Tremayne and Sir Alan Dalton of English China Clays, both my friends. In the end the militant Air-Marshal won; English China Clays are very public-spirited and conservation-minded, and the streams are now flowing clearer. 'On the moor, they're pumping the stuff away artificially and not polluting.' China clay detritus is completely harmless anyway, merely white granitty sand; and English China Clays, under Lord Aberconway and Alan Dalton, both gardeners, have planted trees galore and covered sand-burrows with rhododendrons and lupins, purple and gold, bless them.

'All the same I prefer polluted streams to streams of visitors. I suppose you're safe in Trenarren but I don't go down in Summer at all. I'm going to Spain with the C. of E. Ramblers next month but hope to look in between lets at Daymer Bay in May. You and I love the same places, Oxford and Cornwall, and really for me there are no other places so good. It is good to read a book like yours. I must now go on and read some more. God bless you dear and great Cornish writer for these stories and your remembering your old chum.'

'St George's day 1967, *Cornish Poems* have now arrived. I have read them all with pleasure. Of course the American ones mean less to me as I don't know the places they are about, but they are vivid enough for me to *imagine* the places. You have a piercing eye for significant detail. I have read out aloud the Cornish ones several times to 2 different lots of friends. That last poem in the book is v. good simplicity – but *the* poem, yes *the* poem is the Charlestown Mass. I didn't realise you have been brought up "High".' I wasn't: I brought myself up High Church – I couldn't bear Low or Broad, let alone Nonc. There follows more I can't quite make out, except that by now John was 'v. busy on Telly in London.'

This was followed by a p.c. of the White Horse at Uffington, not wholly legible, with characteristic news: 'All noisy on the Wanton front. Trees going. Villas increasing. Martin Bell is a good poet. So are you.' Was John being too generous? Even so, it was clear that, apart from Cornishry and Oxford, he liked my poetry – he especially liked the poem about my mother's death-bed, which I could never read to anyone. Here again, it is the general point that is important, not the particular one. If my poetry was good enough for him and Eliot, who published it and wrote the blurbs, for Edith Sitwell and Kathleen Raine, Edmund Blunden or Philip Larkin who chose one poem (not the best) for the *Oxford Book of Modern Verse,* then it is certainly good enough for the hack reviewers.

I know as well as the next man that one is not supposed to say such things. John had the Public School technique, like Connolly, of deflecting criticism by writing himself down: he would say to me 'I'm an emmet, a worm.' It is only too obvious a game to write oneself down – Larochefoucauld and the French epigrammatists knew two to that one. Not a Public School man, I think it beneath me, and am always willing to tell the inferior their rating. It is a duty to do so in an egalitarian society where they think they know as well as their betters – how otherwise are they to learn (if at all)? So when I hear nonsense about Shakespeare or the Elizabethans, Marlowe, Bacon or Richard III, or about England's record in history, or Germany's, or Appeasement, etc, I have no compunction in telling them that they do not qualify to hold an opinion – any more than I would on nuclear strategy or science in general. Anyway, I never waste time on ordinary people's opinions – almost always nonsense, whether about religion or sex, politics or economics; with *them* I exchange only facts. There are very few people in all the world with whom one can discuss the things that matter: there is so little to discuss *with*.

A historian knows that there is a sociological point involved. All expert knowledge is by definition élitist, and only the elect know it. In a properly organised society, hierarchically, this is obvious and accepted. In a squalid society like today's, run by egalitarian humbug – though more humbug than any real equality – the truth about these things is evaded, slobbered over by smoothies. It is the historian's duty always to tell people the truth, whether they like it or not (contrast a Churchill with a Baldwin). John knew these things well enough, though too smooth to say anything about it – so he got away with it, and became a folk-figure to the great heart of the people, to whom he did not at all belong. Unlike D. H. Lawrence and me – and see what we think! No one was more élitist really than John. Like all the creative spirits of our time: they hate its guts and the society that engulfs us, whether Akhmatova or Shostakovich, Pasternak or Solzhenitsyn; whether Yeats or Eliot, Lawrence or Evelyn Waugh, Joyce or Connolly. Myself, I have found an answer: withdrawal into solipsism. Contemporary society? – They can get on with it.

John's next letter was from 'Roscarrock Manor Farm, Port Isaac: Look where I am writing from. I return to horrible London on Sunday.' His hosts who ran the place were Cornish, 'but brought up by the Revd Sabine Gould at Lew Trenchard.' John told them of a paper I had written on Nicholas Roscarrock: had I a copy for them? It was published in a *Festschrift* for G. M. Trevelyan, now out of print.[5] Roscarrock was an Elizabethan Catholic antiquarian who left an immense manuscript Lives of the Saints, into which he had collected information about the Cornish Saints and the old rites and usages. The Cambridge University Library had kindly deposited the vast folio in the Bodleian for me to work at, conveniently across the street from All Souls.

In capital letters across the top: 'YOUR ANTHOLOGY IS SUPERB [of Cornwall] NEVER CAN BE BETTERED.' It proved a favourite bedside book of John Sparrow at All Souls, since it had not been written by me, merely compiled. Oddly enough, it gave me a great deal of trouble. I had thought of it nearly forty years before, and wrote to Q. suggesting that he do it. He passed the buck back, and suggested that I do it. For years I simply couldn't; in the end I discovered that the only way to do it was to think out a logical scheme, partly by subject and time, and partly geographical by place, working naturally from east to west, as one would exploring Cornwall.

John sometimes took the trouble to write me by airmail to America. In 1968 he was writing from his hide-out in the City – a very open one, though I never visited him there – 43 Cloth Fair, E.C.1. 'My sec. has flu. Penelope is in New York and hating it.' She loved India, where her father had been Commander-in-Chief – and what a marvellous job the British did for India, and how many of them were in love with it! Kipling is a far better guide than E. M. Forster, as Indians know – Left intellectuals, as usual, not.

'I am well and thankful not to be P.L. [Poet Laureate], and

[5] *Studies in Social History*. Edited by J. H. Plumb.

writing hymns à la D-Day Lewis, as Osbert Lancaster calls him.' Perhaps it was his Leftist sympathies of the Thirties, expressed in demotic adjurations, that promoted him. It is fair to say that his later poetry is better than his poems of the Thirties. The letter is mostly concerned with some question of conservation at St Austell, which I had raised, I forget what – some piece of destruction. John had now become a public figure, when I had ceased to be one, since I dropped my long and excruciating candidature for Penryn and Falmouth. (After a decade of hard work, it went Labour in 1945 – an almighty deliverance that I was out of it: I should have been killed by it.) Television made John a public man, and nobly he took up causes of preservation, continually trying to save relics of better days from destruction – and how hard he worked at it! He should have been made an earl for his pains. He couldn't pronounce 'without going down to the site – of course I agree with you about it – which I am proposing to do in mid-Feb.' I was chagrined by what the County Council was doing at his Wadebridge: destroying the finest medieval bridge, fifteen arches, in the West Country and building a new one. They might have kept the fine old one for one-way traffic, and built a new one for the other way. But I had given up hope, John not, more credit to him. 'What about the pollution of river and sea by the China Clay Co.? I feel for Sir John Tremayne.' As I said, he won, with the agreement of the excellent Company. Oddly enough, sometimes the right course even prevails – but I no longer care; I grieve privately, not publicly; I live in the Elizabethan Age, not this. John concludes, 'Oh it's a joy to hear from you and to know that you are back with the Elizabethans.'

I next sent him, for his interest in Ireland, my abridged version of Froude's remarkable novel, *The Two Chiefs of Dunboy*. Froude was an historian of genius, who fell into no conventional categories and so has been overlooked, when people have gone on and on writing about Macaulay and Carlyle. Froude was a better stylist than either – he got that from Newman – where I find Carlyle's intolerable. He is the last great Victorian awaiting revival, when so many inferior to him have been regurgitated. As a young Fellow of All Souls I hoped to produce a Life and Letters of Froude follow-

ing in the wake of G. O. Trevelyan's Life and Letters of
Macaulay, a delightful book. I was frustrated – a curious
story.[6] Nor did my more readable version of Froude's novel
– the original was too long and discursive – have the least
effect in reviving him. (How unimaginative can you be?)
'I've asked Batsford to send you a bit of bookmaking of
mine, of old photographs of London, a poor return for your
kindness.'

During my absence in America I had been taken advantage
of and framed as Patron of the Appeal to finish the spire and
furnish the bells for Charlestown Church, where my poor
parents were married way back in the early 1890s. Folklore
said that the Victorian vicar had drunk up the funds – and
certainly when he died a large consignment of bottles surfaced
from the vicarage. 'Penelope is in India. Wantage is let to
Americans. My house here [Cloth Fair] is to be pulled down
and rebuilt next summer. I am in a bad way financially, so all I
have been able to do is to order from Jock Murray two copies
of Summoned by Bells [he had told me that he was coming down
to Trebetherick for peace and quiet to concentrate on it],
which I'll inscribe especially for the Appeal and send to the
Honorary Treasurer, so that he may be able to get rid of them
at some sale. I think it is marvellous of you to give a thousand
pounds to the Bells, and I pray that before you die they will be
ringing across the water to Trenarren.'

Thereupon Noël Coward wrote me fan-mail to say how
much he admired A Cornish Childhood, and that it brought
back vividly the summer holidays he used to spend as a boy at
Charlestown. I took my opportunity to tell him that he could
then give a bell – I was giving three. He sent me £350 for one
by return of post, generous fellow. So we called the top bell
Noel, for he was born in Christmas week; when he died, the
ringers rang a muffled peal for him out to sea. They make a
beautiful light peal of six, but, alas, I cannot hear them from
Trenarren: perhaps they will ring a muffled peal for me out
across the bay.

In December 1971, 'I've just come back from Australia,

[6] I have told it in my Introduction to the novel.

where Cornwall meets one at every turn in place names[7] and in mining, and it is lovely to find all this about Trecarrel. How beautifully your Commemoration address is worded. How sad its concluding paragraphs. I have just heard from Arthur Bryant that he is willing to come to St Albans for some discussion you and he and and I are to have there. . . . I shall be delighted to do so. It will be a meeting of old friends. I am now dotty about Australia and now find the green of England rather strident and vulgar after all those glorious olive silvery light-fretting gum trees and those huge skies and suns on copper-coloured earth. Penelope is back from Injer and I may see her tonight. I am glad we are all still alive.'

We three duly turned up for our goggling turn for the St Albans Festival. We were tied up and gagged for recording in huge black dentists' chairs, blinded by fierce TV lights, to face a vast dark pit where one could see nothing. For once I felt distinctly nervous; John was completely at home with this sort of thing, and I felt relieved when he led off with a piece about St Albans. He had done his homework and broken the ice: that was the way to do it, I registered, impressed. After that he had little to contribute and left the running to Arthur, suave and smooth, and me. One ass there regarded my forthrightness as 'controversial', the usual conventional cliché nowadays; but that it was appreciated by the audience – as it always is – is clear from the fact that I was the one invited for the next year and again a third. Never pay any attention to what the critics say! In this a contrast with John, a gentle, sweet nature, a prey to constant depression; criticism wounded him and got him down, made him grieve and undermined his confidence. Not so this Cornishman: fortified by contempt, I get stimulated

---

[7] For years I had been trying to incite Australian professors to follow up my *The Cornish in America*, with which I had blazed the trail for the remarkable story of the Cornish in Australia. For all that it made a significant subject, with plenty of research material, for a book – where there can not be very much – I could not get any of them to move. People are so slow in the uptake. At last, a couple of decades later – with a pure Cornishman, Bob Hawke, as Prime Minister – they are beginning to wake up and take notice. There should be similar studies of the Cornish in New Zealand, South Africa and Canada – so far no response, as usual – to complete the picture; for most of the Cornish people are overseas.

and take the offensive. My substitute for drink?

'Monday after Trinity Sunday [which I always keep: St Austell parish feast], Hill Farm, Oaksey, Malmesbury: Penelope and I are staying here with the famous jockey John Lawrence, now Lord Oaksey, and coming through in the train I saw "lanterned Uffington" – exactly the right adjective for the tower and the position of the village below the White Horse. I had not realised how very good a topographical poet you are, not just of Cornwall – where you are unbeatable, and all the Cornish ones in this book are the best you have done. But I also can appreciate the American ones without having been to the places you describe. Tell the Warden to read "Ardevora Veor" and "Distant Surf".' I did not waste time doing so: precious little appreciation of my poetry in that academic quarter.

'I absolutely understand about an unbelieving "Anglo-Catholic". So am I. I *hope*, that is all. Faith, Hope and Charity – and the greatest of these is Hope.' There is a difference between the two old friends: I am without hope, I despair. 'Thank you and Thank you for *Strange Encounter*. Let us have another.'

Ambassador Walter Annenberg inspired a grand *livre-de-luxe* about Westminster Abbey, and public-spiritedly financed it. Architecture, monuments, works of art all specially photographed; sculpture, frescoes, mosaics written up by experts; Prologue by John, Epilogue by Kenneth Clark; the main body of the book, the story of the Abbey, I was called on to do. Once more John wrote with enthusiasm: 'I always knew you were a great historian, but your essay on Westminster Abbey is SUPERB – Learning so lightly worn – Every period alive – Such insight – such humour – such *poetry*. I am proud to be near you in that funny, American-inspired book. I had thought there were enough books on the Abbey what with Dean Stanley's, but your essay adds a new dimension and inspired your old chum. . . . Once more thanks and thanks and thanks for your genius.'

Why quote these tributes to one's work all through a hard-working life, starting with nothing? After all, John did not need to write a fellow-contributor at all, unless he felt an urge to do so. I quote them, from a fellow man of genius, to teach the unimaginative, the mean and ungenerous, a lesson. After all, if they are not told, how can they tell?

Next year, 1973, 'Batsford's and I have made a selection of old photographs of Cornwall, trying to cover all aspects of life in the Duchy. We *may* have failed. I feel sure that something important has been left out. You will know.' So John wanted me to come in on this, as his knowledge of Cornwall, considerable as it was, was mainly North Coast and there are at least – people may not realise – half-a-dozen different landscapes in the small but elongated county (not Duchy, by the way: that is something different). Thus came about the illustrated book, *Victorian and Edwardian Cornwall*, which goes on selling through the magic of the Betjeman name.

We have had Daphne du Maurier's *Vanishing Cornwall*, Winston Graham's *Poldark's Cornwall*, and eventually *Betjeman's Cornwall* – none of them Cornish, all of them having adopted Cornwall. I am the real thing, 100 per cent Cornish: when is someone going to see that a 'Rowse's Cornwall' would be a rather different matter – history, antiquities, villages, crevices, holes and corners, relics, what is beneath: the *real* Cornwall?

Next, generous as ever, a word from Tonbridge. 'Staying here with the very rich and well-appointed – with the garden of England all round changing to deep blues in the gloaming, gratitude rises in my breast. Chiefly it rises to you for your really doing the CORNWALL book and giving me the credit. I wish they hadn't said I was a Cornishman in the blurb. I am and always have been a furiner. But I am proud to be linked with you.' The selection of photographs was entirely John's, but I rather think that I did all the letter-press.

There follows another tribute, largely illegible and unidentifiable, to a poem about a character who 'grasped once in his full cruelty is TERRIFIC. Who was he? I know what he was like and have met such. But I don't know this one's name. I loved Encaenia but missed C. S. Lewis. Ta ever so and love yours Jan Trebetj', accompanied by a drawing of the shield with fifteen bezants, derived from the arms of Richard, Earl of Cornwall and King of the Romans. (He thought to buy the crown of the Empire with the wealth extracted from poor little Cornwall, an exploited people: hence Cornish Nationalism, a forlorn cause.)

Encaenia is the honorary-degree ceremony at Oxford, when All Souls gives a grand luncheon in the Codrington Library – all the College plate out, flowers, scarlet gowns, ladies in their best: a splendid scene. John, now a famous public figure, had been awarded a D.Litt.: there he was in all his glory, spruced-up and arrayed in scarlet, the old look of nervous anxiety gone from the bland, clerical features, beaming on us all. He said to me that he had seen the heavens open and C. S. Lewis, his old tutor whom he could not abide, looking down: it must have been a shock for Clive Staples, undoubtedly in Heaven.

Maytime 1975: 'When I got back here from Cornwall I found your magnificent book on Oxford. It could not be better for balance and wise selection of pictures. All my favourite things are in it and all my unfavourite are not in it. You are quite right about your poetry being overlooked. I am going to take your *Poems of Cornwall and America* to Derbyshire tomorrow [i.e. with Elizabeth Cavendish to Chatsworth], and to Penelope in the Black Mountains, when I'm back from Canada. Poetry reads differently in different places. Really it's best where it was born; but Wordsworth brings the Lakes to us and I am certain you are going to bring Cornwall to Derby and Hereford. There are no things more enjoyable than discovering a good poet in an old friend. I thought that the American poems in the book you gave me in Cornwall deliciously effective and depressing' (in some of them I cast a cold eye upon demotic civilisation).

A pretty coloured photograph shows little St Enodoc church in its hollow, bent spire, churchyard with graves, blue Daymer Bay and Stepper Point beyond. 'Expect *Summoned by Bells*, a Cockney Childhood, next week. I *loved* the poem, particularly the 6th verse. Would I were worthier.' This was the poem 'Easter at St Enodoc', with its little tribute:

> Up the lane the poet lives,
> Flowering currant at his door:
> Inspiration receives, and gives,
> From hill and valley, stream and shore.

That spring, 1975, 'I much like the idea of seeing you, even if it has to be the BBC.' We did a joint reading of poems, mainly Cornish, from Plymouth. 'I like your poems. I like Charles Causley's and him and Ted Hughes's and him. Poets are more than pen counters (?). Poor Griggers. Not good enough, but he does know about good and bad.' (Not always: he could not recognise that John and Dylan Thomas and Edith Sitwell were good poets, himself not so good. Nor can one stand the parsonic didacticism.) 'Penelope's garden in the Black Mountains is full of hippies under canvas. She is their Queen and loves them.'

After the recording, 'I thought your poems came over splendidly the night before last. Beautiful, haunting, and very Cornish. Elizabeth Cavendish and I are here [Trebetherick] till Tuesday week. Give us a "tingle" (Australian for "tinkle") if you are free to come over. You are wisely not in the directory, but then nor is your devoted old fellow poet.' Not content, he followed this up with another St Enodoc post card: 'And, of course, "Distant Surf" is *a great poem*.' It is a sad, nostalgic, but authentic one – unlike most contemporary verse, simply not authentic.

Next year, 'My sight gets worse and worse. I think that Patrick Garland, who did the Kilvert programme, would make a lovely Hawker programme with you.' (Parson Hawker of Morwenstow's centenary was coming up.) 'In fact he ought to make several programmes with you. He is a brilliant producer. Literate and loving his subjects . . . He did that production of Aubrey's *Brief Lives* in London some years ago. His father was sent by my father to Paris with me to teach me about sex with ladies, but it failed because I fell ill.' (Not only, I should say.) Nothing came of the programmes either. Marooned on my headland in Cornwall I had never heard of the great BBC producer. As another TV star, A. J. P. Taylor, says of his experience, you need to be 'in' with these people, and I lacked the Public School technique of 'sucking up'. So I turned my back to them and my face to America – more responsive in every way.

There followed a series of John's coloured Underground post cards, his writing hardly legible. There was Elizabeth now to help with his typing – and what a chore: TV had made him so popular that he would get some thirty letters a day. I wouldn't answer them, sheer waste of time, but I suppose a public figure has to. A typed p.c. says, 'Would you be free to have Evelyn Duchess's grand-daughter and the adventurer to luncheon at Trenarren? . . . It would be lovely to see you and have a laugh.' Elizabeth's grandmother, whom I knew as Dowager Duchess of Devonshire, had been a good friend to me: had me to stay several summers at historic Hardwick, most exciting of Elizabethan houses, got over original mss from Chatsworth, for me ᴛᴏ work on, of Bess of Hardwick, a comparably formidable personality, her predecessor.[9]

We did have several laughs, exchanging reminders of the Duchess's ducal – or should it be, duquessal – dicta: 'I always say, when in doubt plant an avenue', for one. If only one could! We also had some serious talk about poetry. I quoted Paul Valéry's saying that one was given a line, and from that one went on – a donné: it might be one or two lines, one doesn't know where they come from, from on high or from the depths, rather, of the subconscious. I don't think John read much in any foreign language, and earlier his line was that he hated 'Abroad'. But he agreed: a line or lines came into one's head involuntarily, and 'the rest is hard work', an act of will. Verses can be made by the will, an intellectual process; poetry comes from something deeper, welling up from the depths of one's being. I cannot write a poem unless moved emotionally; I can hardly ever write just verses. Nevil Coghill told me that he had written thousands of lines of verse – his modernisation of Chaucer, for example – but not one line of poetry. John was most excited by this: 'Did he really say that?' I said that John had the right qualification for Poet Laureate in that he could write both poetry and verse. He then said the most serious thing he ever said to me, emphasising it quite solemnly: '*I have never compromised.*' The only claim he ever made for himself.

It meant that he had never fallen in with any of the prevailing poetic fashions at any time, Yeats or Eliot in the 1920s, or his contemporaries Auden and the Boys of the Thirties: he simply held on his way, being his own unique and original self, true to his own inspiration and intuition, taking

[9] v. 'Bess of Hardwick' in *Eminent Elizabethans*.

no notice of what anyone else might say. That is the right way. And he certainly reaped his reward: for long a poet of only a few, an esoteric taste, he eventually came across to thousands, the most popular Poet Laureate since Tennyson – though Kipling also was a poet with the widest public.

Tennyson was John's great love. I remember, when first taking part in a broadcast programme with him, being slightly shocked at his not caring for Shakespeare: he had been put off the Elizabethans by C. S. Lewis for good (or bad) and all. When he gave a reading at Port Eliot – the candle-lit house crowded with his fans – he began with a long piece from Tennyson. Eyesight was failing, I had to find the places for him in his own poems; the enthusiasm was no less. John wanted me to read my poems, but I had only the poem I had written for his seventieth birthday with me, 'Marytavy'. Some farming gent came up to compliment me on the clever 'pastiche' of Betjeman he thought it: I am incapable of pastiche, but for once let the well-meaning ass get away with it. We made over £1000 that night for the Cornish Churches Trust.

'The pale but strong white fingers of Elizabeth are typing this because I cannot write legibly. Our journey back after the paradise of Trenarren was another paradise through Rowseland.[10] We came a mysterious way through St Austell and then suddenly on the horizon, like an illustration in a Walter Scott novel, rose Roche Rock. After that the more familiar lanes and shacks to Wadebridge and those thin elms that "tug at the heart" [quoting me]. We read out to each other seven of your poems, the Cornish ones, on our return. They go right home, and you must never lose your poetic fire. You must be the only historian who has written truly topographical poetry. Macaulay's is geographical, but not such haunting poetry. Hawker may have tried history but I don't think of him as an historian.' Nor was he: a good folklorist, rather.

'Elizabeth continues to speak of the wonder of your house and view, and I of that Paul Sandby, the Gainsborough and Tilly Kettle, and poor Elizabeth liked the Kit Wood best of all. Your Piper is one of his best. You buy on eye not names; so does your grateful old friend, Jan Trebetjeman, pp Passmore

---

[10] Pun on Roseland, of course.

Edwards. P.S. Tregonetha is a dream village on our route.'

Passmore Edwards was a Victorian-Edwardian philanthropist who gave libraries to Cornwall early this century. Tregonetha is indeed a queer, haunted place: a tiny ring of tumbledown, derelict cottages round a green, one little Bible Christian chapel, the road virtually shouldering its way between two houses. Atmosphere of the last century, sad and forgotten.

In *Blackwood's* 1978 I wrote an essay about John's poetry, about which he wrote to the editor: 'I am delighted with the trouble dear Leslie Rowse has taken over it, and the discernment it shows. . . . I was glad to see *Blackwood's* keeps its tidy and traditional typography: just as I remember it from when my father subscribed to it.' Of course, this historic literary journal, going right back to the Edinburgh of Sir Walter Scott and all the famous contributors throughout the nineteenth century, has had to close down.

To me John wrote: 'I cannot thank you enough . . . It makes me feel less of a fraud than usual, and quite encouraged to try and write about my Irish friend, the least known peer in the world, Lord Clonmore (Wicklow) who has just died. Kindly keep alive yourself.' Billy Clonmore was one of the Bright Boys of the Twenties at Oxford, whom one reads about now in Evelyn Waugh's Diaries and Letters, and in John's poems: Basil Dufferin and Ava (killed in Burma), Patrick Balfour, later Lord Kinross, Hugh Lygon (of *Brideshead Revisited*), Robert Byron (drowned in the Mediterranean); members of the Bullingdon set, regulars of the George, Fothergill dinners at the Spread Eagle out at Thame. What a time they had while the going was good!

March 1978: 'I re-read your poems all yesterday.' Then, 'I am fascinated by the autobiographical honesty of your poems and the love of landscape they display.' Well, my poetry contains all my inner life and secrets, where the prose books, history, literature, politics, deal mainly, not wholly, with the outer. 'And now I must top writing to you, and write about them for *Books and Bookmen*.' Another Underground post card followed: 'When I saw it in *B. and B.* I thought it too short and not generous enough. I should have added "all your Cornish poems" should be put into one book, and a record made of you reading your favourites of them.' This has yet to occur to someone!

'I was much intrigued by John Edwards. I suppose he is the — Edwards of Colvin's *Biographical Dictionary of English Architects*.' I couldn't find out anything about him, and I don't think John knew either. But he was the builder of one of the most beautiful late Georgian houses in Cornwall – Carclew, consumed by fire in the 1930s, and the grander mansion of the Bassets – Tehidy, burned down in the 1920s. Two casualties of the hideous, destructive age we live in.

In August, 'I am so pleased to have "Withiel Church". I suppose the Rector must be the grandfather of Nancy Trethewey, a real breath of the Twenties and the toast of the Bodmin tennis tournament when I was a boy. Of course Withiel and its rectory were the remotest Cornwall I ever found in my bicycling days, and that lichen-crusted area of steep hills and little farms and deep woods seemed full of witches. I wonder why Griggers can't do it. He has the feelings and the eye, but something gets in between.' It is easy to see what – self-consciousness and didacticism. 'I am off to Derbyshire, the home of witches and Keltic survival. I have left you a shell-model of St Mary's, Penzance, in my will, if you survive me – which I hope you do.'

February next year: 'It was very nice seeing you in that Wren church by Bodley yesterday. It was good of you to talk to me as I was wearing the wrong tie, which Frank Pakenham noticed – I could feel it – but his wife kindly ignored. Frank is no longer red. The craze among vicars for pulling down screens is all part of the kitchen table which is being substituted for the altar, and making things simple for the kiddiz, which is getting rid of mystery. It is Pevsnerism as opposed to Tractarian. It is out of date, which the C. of E. is so afraid of becoming. . . . Pray God for a bit of mystery. It was kind of Bodley to have left that City church for us to eat in. . . . Penelope is in India conducting a cruise. I am in Chelsea misconducting myself, or would that I were.'

On a visit to lecture in Dorset I entered a church with a very fine tower, and noticed a decorative chancel screen, late Victorian and of considerable beauty, flowing lines and tracery. Thereupon I learned that an ignorant and tasteless vicar was intending to remove it to the back of the church to make way for a nave altar. Actually it would make a very good background for his nave altar; all he need do would be to remove the front pew to make room for it. So I wrote to the Bishop, who proved to be more interested in ski-ing. I alerted John, who forwarded my protest to the Council for the Places of Worship. 'Pevsner of course does not mention the screen, which means that it must look very well as he has no eye or feeling for mystery. As there is glass by Kempe in the church, the screen is possibly Bodley. How good it would be if you went into this matter.'

How good it was of John to take it up – he had scores of calls like this on his time, in the never-ending struggle to prevent clerics and vandals from destroying things of beauty. He was a public figure, and never spared himself in what he regarded as a duty. I do not know what transpired. I gathered the advisory committee on churches in that diocese was neither well informed nor instructed. A scholarly cleric of the older gener-ation tells me that the younger have little knowledge of or interest in architecture or history. I'll bet that, if I go back to that church, I shall find that fine screen shoved away at the back where it can't be seen, or possibly got rid of altogether.

A letter, of September 1980 from Derbyshire, reads, 'A lovely poem on Endellion. We must save it from being amalgamated with Port Isaac. It is a holy kingdom on its hilltop. Your *Road to Oxford* poems are a constant pleasure to me – so are your vigour and Cornishness.' A last letter to me commented on the final poem in my *A Life: Collected Poems*, 'Intimations of Mortality'. This poem summed up my own belief with which I had lived my life: from one moment of vision to another, holding on to a secret trail from a source unknown, whatever it may mean:

What to make of it? I cannot say.
Here and now we cannot know. I know
Only that these moments have sustained me,
Given food to the spirit, nourished mind
And imagination in the forlorn spaces,
Shafts of light into the heart of things
Though the mystery remain immutable.

John wrote back that he had often felt just that.

Providentially he died at his beloved Trebetherick, when they were thinking of taking him back in an ambulance to London. He was buried in the churchyard of his poem, 'Sunday Afternoon Service in St Enodoc Church, Cornwall', on a day of raging Atlantic rain and wind. The parson said that the huddled figures crossing the sand-dunes looked like a lot of Cornish wreckers coming up with their findings.

On a Sunday afternoon not long after I went to visit his grave: a day that somehow seemed more in keeping. Sun-drenched dunes, people picnicking, figures further off on the sands, boats bobbing white on the blue of Daymer Bay, the loved vision of Stepper Point across the estuary opening out to sea. There was the little bent spire, the church itself hidden, crouching in the hollow sheltered by Bray Hill. As I went down the slope, keeping the grey spire in view, phrases from the poem floated hazily in mind:

> Sand in the sandwiches, wasps in the tea,
> Sun on our bathing dresses heavy with the wet . . .
> Blessèd be St Enodoc . . .
> Blessèd be the springy turf, we pray, pray to thee . . .

In at the gate, the enclosure surrounded by tamarisks, the newly made grave dug out of sand and rock on the right, flowers wilting in the hot sun, a plain wooden cross: JOHN BETJEMAN. Across the path to the church-porch, on the western verge of the little place is his mother, not far off. Into the church, Sunday afternoon service just over, there on the right is the Cornish slate tablet to his father, beneath which John sat or knelt in church: 'Ernest Edward Betjemann of Underdown in this parish.' There is the ambivalence: the two German nns, one of which the family dropped when the father died.

From what curious ancestry did John come, where on earth did his spirit come from? I think in the end of the image from the early Anglo-Saxon Bede, of the bird flying from the dark in-to the lighted hall and out again into the night.